Understanding WPA Readiness and Renewal

Studies in Composition and Rhetoric

Alice S. Horning
General Editor

Vol. 22

Understanding WPA Readiness and Renewal

Edited by
Joseph Janangelo and Mark Blaauw-Hara

PETER LANG
Lausanne • Berlin • Bruxelles • Chennai • New York • Oxford

Library of Congress Cataloging-in-Publication Control Number: 2022053883

Bibliographic information published by the **Deutsche Nationalbibliothek.**
The German National Library lists this publication in the German
National Bibliography; detailed bibliographic data is available
on the Internet http://dnb.d-nb.de.

Cover design by Peter Lang Group AG

ISSN 1080-5397
ISBN 978-1-4331-9316-3 (hardback)
ISBN 978-1-4331-9440-5 (paperback)
ISBN 978-1-4331-9441-2 (ebook)
ISBN 978-1-4331-9442-9 (epub)
DOI 10.3726/b19260

Published by Peter Lang Publishing Inc., New York, USA
info@peterlang.com - www.peterlang.com

This publication has been peer reviewed.

Dedications

Joe: For Yolanda C. Janangelo, Peter Janangelo Sr.,
Farrell J. Webb, and Carmella Fiorelli.

Mark: For my family, my supportive colleagues, and my students.

Table of Contents

List of Illustrations and Tables

Acknowledgments

We begin by thanking Alice Horning, who reached out to us early in the process of conceiving of this book with encouragement and the suggestion that we work together. Throughout the book's journey, Alice provided clear and direct feedback to both us and our chapter authors with the goal of helping the book reach its potential. Along with Alice, we extend our thanks to the rest of Peter Lang International Academic Publishers, especially Anthony Mason, who also provided support and feedback. We thank Charmitha Ashok and the production team for their careful editing, Jaganathan Rajapandi for indexing, and Thiyagu Kumaraselvam for help designing our book's cover. We also thank the two manuscript reviewers for their careful reading and generative advice.

Our chapter authors were consummate professionals and scholars. Thank you for lending your expertise and experience to this project. We know that future and current WPAs will be educated and inspired by your words.

Joe thanks Mark for generously sharing his intellect and enthusiasm with him and the authors. You will always be Emperor Mark Blaauw-Hara, HRH.

Mark thanks Joe for inviting him to be a part of this project, and for showing him the ropes of putting together an edited collection. One could not ask for a wiser or more patient co-editor.

Understanding WPA Readiness and Renewal: Of Preparation, Pipe Dreams, and Possibilities

JOSEPH JANANGELO, LOYOLA UNIVERSITY CHICAGO

We begin by thanking you for reading our book and sharing two questions that inspire our work:

- How do people develop readiness to serve as WPAs?
- How do experienced WPAs find or create renewal opportunities that help them move forward throughout their lives and careers?

"Throughout" is an important concept to us because *Understanding WPA Readiness and Renewal* examines WPA journeys and journeying. In our book, we seek to offer readers nuanced understandings of how aspiring, early career and seasoned WPAs plan, lead, build, and re-build their careers and working lives. We also hope to help graduate students and early career WPAs better understand the enticements and entanglements of their intended career's complex, daunting, rewarding, and important work. Moreover, we seek to offer mid- and later-career WPAs ideas for rekindling interest in work that has become stagnant, unchallenging, and even discouraging. We contend that understanding WPA "readiness" and "renewal" involves questioning inherited definitions of those patented, patinated terms. It also involves engaging in candid and self-aware scholarly conversations that reflect, and reflect on, WPAs' plans, desires, trepidations and fears for and about their work.

We view renewal as a vital part of long-haul WPA work. As WPA work has evolved, more WPAs are mid-career at a wide range of institutions than in the past and need work that speaks to their experience and existence. More importantly, we see mid- and later-career WPAs are valuable and uniquely vulnerable members of the WPA community and are eager to pay attention to their ideas and needs. We say "vulnerable" because these individuals are underrepresented and understudied in WPA scholarship. Perhaps understandably, Writing Studies graduate programs and the Council of Writing Program Administrators (CWPA) pay close attention to pre-service and early-career WPAs who are beginning their journeys, especially in terms of preparation and onboarding WPAs and mentoring them through "the early years." Yet, there is so much more journeying to notice and to try to understand.

Our goal in including WPA readiness and renewal in the same volume is to bring those concepts and colleagues into conversation with one another. We experience and regard WPA workplaces and working lives as continuums. WPAs, aspiring and experienced, are there for a while at various moments in their lives and careers and strive to do good and rewarding work during that time. We hope our book contributes to intergenerational understandings among pre-service, early-career, and mid- and later-career WPAs.

In composing our book's title, we don't strive to be gratuitously alliterative. Moreover, while this book has two sections, we don't think of readiness and renewal as discrete experiences, but as permeable, porous ones. In these pages, we and our authors portray WPA readiness and renewal as existing in complicated twinship with each other and engaged with animating and competing logics and priorities. For example, WPA readiness and renewal are in close communication with one's personal life and career trajectories, one's institutional mission and identity, colleagues, and students, world events (e.g., pandemics), and evolutions in higher education.

We choose "understanding" as our guiding verb, even though *Merriam-Webster* defines it primarily as a noun, as *an* understanding. Consider that dictionary's top two definitions: 1: a mental grasp: COMPREHENSION 2: a. the power of comprehending *especially*: the capacity to apprehend general relations of particulars b: the power to make experience intelligible by applying concepts and categories. For readers' further edification, *Merriam-Webster* offers three "Example Sentences" replete with sexist, gender-based characterizations:

> He has a thorough *understanding of* the subject.
> She has a basic *understanding* of the process.
> I hope to get a clearer *understanding of* the issues involved. See More.

In search of complex understandings of WPA readiness and renewal, we do see more. We suspect more as well. Our suspicions are fourfold.

READINESS SUSPICIONS

Suspicion #1: We believe that WPA readiness is more than a matter of graduate preparation. Coursework and other graduate experiences, however intensive and valuable they may be, don't fully guarantee WPA readiness. We question the idea that people can fully "suit up" for WPA work in advance. We also suspect that the project of making WPA experience "intelligible," as *Merriam-Webster* puts it, obtainable, and even transferable, is something graduate programs do in order to make a compelling case for their work and existence. We see WPA readiness as part of a functional equation that goes like this: graduate programs implicitly promise to produce and deliver capable and ready WPAs; hiring committees take such programs at their word. Put plainly, writing programs need WPAs who are ready to lead, advise, and mentor others. Institutional and programmatic stakeholders, many of them impactful and vulnerable themselves, take serious interest in what the "new WPA" will do on campus as the new hire works to serve their school and build their ethos and career. It is thus in everyone's functional interest for that equation to be said to work and work out well. Thus, imagining WPA readiness as possible via rigorous graduate preparation is in everyone's practical interest and belies collective stakeholder investment.

Suspicion #2: WPA readiness is neither linear nor expedient. Nor is it all of a piece. As a WPA, being ready for some of the work and experience (the interactions, disappointments, and successes) does not mean being ready for all of it. On campus, WPAs have unforeseen content-based and relational work to do for others and themselves. Whatever training one brings to the job, the WPA workplace is where preparation and advice (scholarship, shadowing, simulations) meet tests of readiness. On campus, important challenges welcome new WPAs, often with high expectations and strict timelines. New WPAs often have unforeseen and familiar work to do for others and themselves. Moreover, if things don't work out, perceived WPA underperformance is attributed to individual or small-group failure, rather than the flawed assumptions surrounding WPA readiness.

RENEWAL SUSPICIONS

Suspicion #3: The talents and needs of mid- and later-career WPAs are too often minimized or effaced in scholarly discussions of WPA work. Seasoned WPAs' concerns can get lost in scholarly and programmatic / institutional conversations, especially when those WPAs are officially performing at high levels. Writing Studies has focused its attention, perhaps understandably, on preparing graduate students to become WPAs and to have a successful launch. As then CWPA President, Joe recognized the talents and hungers of those valuable, and understudied and under-recognized members of the WPA community, what Joe calls "WPA World." To help serve those colleagues, Joe sponsored a "Renewal Workshop" at the annual CWPA conference and co-founded The WPA Mentoring Project. It soon became clear that, beyond spot shot workshops and individual mentoring, experienced WPAs need something more, and often something new, to help sustain them throughout their working lives.

Suspicion #4: We doubt that, once WPAs meet traditional career benchmarks such as promotion or tenure, they remain intellectually renewed throughout their careers. For seasoned WPAs, excelling at your work, and even loving what you do, don't guarantee eternal or even episodic WPA renewal. There is a tacit assumption that once WPAs are deemed "successful," and earn the familiar accolades, they remain steadily interested and engaged in their work throughout their careers. That pipe dream ignores the reality that, while ongoing WPA experience can offer enjoyment and satisfaction, experienced WPAs also contend with new, lingering, and unsuspected aspirations and challenges. We hope that the accounts of ongoing renewal struggles found in this book can show us all something new and valuable about long-term WPA work.

Beyond the aforementioned suspicions, we contend that tacit understandings of WPA readiness and renewal are tethered to at least two limiting and pernicious assumptions:

1. The idea that preparation for WPA work at four-year comprehensive universities transfers unproblematically to successful program administration at liberal-arts colleges, community colleges, and more.
2. The practice of discussing, teaching, and theorizing WPA apart, or only being minimally conversant with, experience and scholarship of diversity, equity, and inclusion (DEI).

To address these assumptions and oversights, we include authors who teach at a range of two- and four-year institutions. They represent aspiring, early career, and seasoned WPAs holding ranks including pre-career, NTT, and assistant through full professor. Thus, you will hear from several generations of WPA scholars. You will also hear from several Scholars of Color and members of LGBTQ+ communities. By including the voices of mid- and later-career WPAs, we hope to give readers (especially graduate students) a "long view" of WPA working lives crucial to envisioning possible career trajectories and their complex peregrinations.

Discussing their career learning curves inclusive of pressure points, lessons, complications, satisfactions, and evolving insights, authors pursue WPA work from preparation as graduate students, to planned departures including intentional rotation and envisioning retirement. Please note that we don't entertain the fantasy of achieving complete "coverage." Our intended contribution is modes; we hope our book work offers you thinking and talking points for more inclusive and capacious understandings of WPA work, both by pointing out oversights and slights and amplifying discussions of topics that are addressed here.

WPA Scholarship That Inspires This Book

Before discussing our book's chapters, we pause to pay tribute to work that means a great deal to us. In conceptualizing this book, we are influenced by several in particular. Here are some of the many virtues we see in these stellar texts:

- Sheila Carter-Tod and Jennifer Sano-Franchini's Special Issue: Black Lives Matter and Anti-Racist Projects in Writing Program Administration in *WPA: Writing Program Administration* 44.3 (Summer 2021) holds the WPA world and Writing Studies accountable for its injustices.
- Aja Y. Martinez's *Counterstory: The Rhetoric and Writing of Critical Race Theory* (2020) shows how unjust practices could and can change. This book offers important structural, theoretical, pedagogical, and philosophical frameworks and examples for reckoning with injustice, challenging it, and moving forward.
- Courtney Adams Wooten, Jacob Babb, Kristi Murray Costello & Kate Navickas's *The Things We Carry: Strategies for Recognizing and Negotiating Emotional Labor in Writing Program Administration* (2020) details the dedication, toll, humiliation, shame, and persistence that undermines and animates WPA work. The book offers vivid lessons for living and reflecting on one's working life.
- Staci M. Perryman-Clark and Collin Lamont Craig's *Black Perspectives in Writing Program Administration: From the Margins to the Center* (2019) shows that there is so much more to WPA work than what was traditionally thought of as "WPA work." The editors and authors show the enduring damage of abuse and inattention. Chapter authors also theorize and describe the culpability of writing programs, individuals, and institutions that prosper by (even tacitly) endorsing racism.
- Rita Malenczyk's *A Rhetoric for Writing Program Administrators* (2016, second edition) is a model of stellar content and clarity. Malenczyk and her authors persuasively explain just how capacious and involved WPA work

is, with so many areas and constituencies meriting WPAs' attention and expertise. What a great tome for recognizing the complexity of WPA work.

- Ryan Skinnell, Judy Holiday, and Christine Vassett's *What We Wish We'd Known: Negotiating Graduate School* (2015) shows the importance, victories, and complications of strategizing and planning one's career. Authors also show the enduring importance of learning from experience, reconsidering one's options, and developing an ability to make new plans.
- Debra Frank Dew and Alice Horning's *Untenured Faculty as Writing Program Administrators: Institutional Practices and Politics* (2007) discusses the co-existence of strength, vulnerability, and creativity that guides untenured faculty who work and serve as WPAs. Authors underscore the role and value of persistence and tenacity when facing daunting challenges and working conditions.

Our Book's Structure

As we mentioned, this book has two sections. Section One, "Readiness," focuses on graduate students and early-career WPAs. Section Two, "Renewal," discusses issues pertinent to mid- and later-career WPAs. Readers will notice that authors do not present recipes for success or advice *per se*. Instead, authors offer theorized reflections of WPA work for your edification and cogitation. We hope you will regard these authors as your colleagues. That is why we advised them to say "you" and "I," and to address you as people they care about and wish to mentor. Together, in conversation with your and their working life plans and fears, you and our authors might engage in creative problem-strategizing vs. traditional problem-solving. In other words, we invite you to read these chapters in ways that we invited our writers to compose them – as thoughtful human beings who are interested in becoming or remaining WPAs – to look up, back, around, inward, and forward to make and compose your own WPA trajectories.

You will likely notice that all chapters include discussion questions. Our hope is that the questions will offer you sustenance for thought, reflection, inquiry, debate and further research, whether in the context of taking, teaching, or (re) designing your WPA graduate seminar or strategizing and (re)planning your own career alone and with colleagues, friends, and peers. All told, we invite you, as readers and human beings, to add your questions and ideas to the ideas our authors raise. Let's think of WPA readiness and renewal as an ongoing conversation, not an endgame or static, predetermined destination.

Readiness: Redefining the Idea of a "Successful" Career Launch

Section One examines WPA readiness as a nexus of desire and design. Authors discuss their preparatory and on-the-job experiences. Contributors offer insights on what fuels and complicates WPA readiness as they seek to build their careers with and beyond graduate school.

In general, WPAs are an ambitious and entrepreneurial group. Hence, it is unsurprising that some aspiring WPAs are intentional about strategizing and building their careers, seeking leadership opportunities, pursuing secure, fulfilling, and remunerative employment, and hoping to prosper by strategic career planning. Graduate students may find WPA work attractive due to its pedagogical and leadership aspects and, perhaps, the promise of job security and relative economic reward. Whatever their motivations, aspiring WPAs tend to look ahead, often eagerly, strategically, and ambitiously. That is fortuitous because effective planning is considered a primary WPA *métier*.

Aspiring WPAs plan their careers carefully by taking the right courses and seeking advantageous leadership experiences in graduate school. Certainly, graduate faculty do all they can to steward graduate students toward WPA readiness. They work hard and purposefully to apprise graduate students of the enticements and complications of WPA work, inclusive of the work's intellectual credibility, leadership possibilities, and potential career trajectories. Taking ownership of their preparation, graduate students may assume campus leadership roles, work with, and study the work of, their forebears and peers as integral parts of their preparation. They also join committees, present at conferences, and write grant applications and scholarly publications. The Council of Writing Program Administrators (CWPA) also strives to foster readiness. For aspiring and pre-service WPAs, key portals of preparation are WPA-GO, The CWPA Mentoring Project, and The CWPA Summer Workshop. These activities help pre- and in-service WPAs find colleagues with whom they can confer, commiserate, celebrate, and collaborate across their careers.

We admire that stellar work. We also suspect that the most thorough graduate preparation can neither predict nor protect against on-the-job surprises and challenges. We don't imagine that professional preparation, advice, or counsel, however sage and prescient, can be unilaterally preemptive. There are always unforeseen scenarios, and one's reactions to them, that merit (re)consideration as well as new and evolving understandings. As leaders, WPAs often have unanticipated, and even vexing, work to do for others and themselves. That might explain why new and early-career WPAs are sometimes disappointed and vexed when their graduate school preparation does not fully clothe them for their workplace experience, and why on-the-ground advice from peers and mentors becomes indispensable. The Readiness section attempts to provide this on-the-ground advice, and the chapters are inspired by two questions: What if, despite your career preparation and most impressive accomplishments, you don't feel ready to be a WPA? What if you have more learning, and perhaps some unlearning, to do? Ultimately, this section spotlights WPA on-the-job the WPA readiness intended to help graduate students, and their faculty mentors, better understand the context-specific (e.g., programmatic, campus) realities that may inform and challenge early-career WPA leadership readiness beyond preparation offered in graduate seminars.

Readiness Chapter Descriptions

In this section, authors address these questions in creative and reflective ways. They discuss WPA preparation and on-the-job WPA experience. They advise graduate students and early-career WPAs, not as experts, but as peers or experienced elders. Seeking to help readers strategize and build their careers, contributors offer insights on what fuels and complicates WPA readiness. By spotlighting WPA readiness at two- and four-year schools, this section helps graduate students understand the context-specific (e.g., programmatic, campus) realities that may inform and challenge the WPA readiness received in graduate school. While authors give some advice, they take care to offer readers formulations for diverse and capacious understandings rather than proffered "fixes" or formulas. In sharing their understandings of WPA experience, aspiration, disappointment, achievement, and ongoing intellectual and relational hunger, contributors write less about how to do WPA work than what it means to become and remain journeying, and contributory professionals.

In Chapter One, "Leadership Readiness: Becoming a Rhetorically Mindful WPA," Melvin E. Beavers and Abram Anders invite aspiring and new WPAs to understand WPA work as leadership and imagine themselves as campus leaders. The authors offer a detailed heuristic for interpreting and practicing WPA work as creative and equity-driven servant leadership.

In Chapter Two, "(Re)Visioning WPA-GO: Finding WPA Readiness as a Graduate Student Leader," Gabrielle Isabel Kelenyi helps graduate students understand the challenges, satisfactions, and learning experiences of assuming a leadership position while in graduate school. As WPA-GO's first woman of color leader, Kelenyi shares insights graduate students can use to consider how soon, and how rewarding and costly it is, to take on leadership responsibilities early in their careers.

In "How to WPA: Career Planning, Survival and NTT Power at the Convergence of My Professional and Personal Lives" (Chapter Three), Elise A. Green helps readers understand how to live, live with, and improve upon the precarity of building a career and doing WPA work on a non-tenure-track basis. Green's chapter discusses readiness in terms of sustainability, in/security, and aspiration. Green also offers ideas for making oneself intellectually valuable to one's institution.

The next two chapters take a practical, career-driven turn. In Chapter Four, "Ready to be an Equity-Focused WPA: Reforming Community College Developmental Writing," Mark Blaauw-Hara helps graduate students understand how and why they will strengthen their chances for full-time employment by becoming ready to teach and administrate at community colleges. Blaauw-Hara also discusses curricular planning and potential equity impacts of working at community-colleges.

In Chapter Five, "Rethinking WPA Work for Open-Access Contexts: Preparing for Literacy Program Responsibilities," Erin Lehman and Joanne Baird Giordano help graduate students comprehend the preparation, some of which graduate students will have to do for themselves, to make themselves viable candidates for community college work. Lehman and Giordano's chapter signals a call for significant renovations to WPA graduate programs' foci and curricula. As Blaauw-Hara, Giordano, and Lehman point out, the focus on preparing people to work only or mostly at four-year institutions is a disservice to graduate students and WPA readiness itself.

In Chapter Six, "Ready for a Career and a Family: Experiencing (In)Fertility as an Early Career WPA," Kaitlin Clinnin, Jennifer Eidum, Morgan Hanson, and Mariya Tseptsura help readers think holistically about WPA readiness and work in the context of family planning. The authors examine fault lines in WPA work and scholarship as they apply to infertility, pregnancy loss, and difficult pregnancies. They call for a new understanding of a WPA's "presence" on campus.

In Chapter Seven, "Unlearning Writing Program Administration," Amy Ferdinandt Stolley helps readers understand that WPA work, like most leadership, entails scrutinizing, critiquing, and perhaps even abandoning some things you learned in graduate school and even early on in your career. Ferdinandt Stolley describes a pliancy of thought that can benefit aspiring, new, and experienced WPAs as they learn to adapt to new experiences and institutions and re-understand things that they experienced and were told in graduate school. In this sense, WPA readiness entails simultaneous learning and unlearning.

Renewal: What Comes after Job Security and Career Success?

While the "Readiness" section spotlights preservice and early career WPAs' aspirations and fears about building successful and fulfilling careers, our "Renewal" section portrays experienced WPAs striving to examine and rebuild their ongoing working lives. This section discusses WPA work after job security, tenure, promotion, and other traditional accolades and assurances. One luxury that mid-career offers is a chance for self-scrutiny and inquiry. As a mid-career WPA, you have plenty of experiences to reflect on, and some time to understand a few things about yourself including what you can do, what you wish you had done, and what you would still like to do in your remaining WPA career and life. Mid Career thus marks that interesting difference between building and approaching.

This section addresses WPAs' enduring hungers and persistence by showing how career WPAs stay engaged in their work while playing "the long game." In these chapters, seasoned WPAs reflect on their extended working lives. They offer insights to mid- and later-career colleagues about the challenges, satisfactions and inequities of WPA longevity. We hope this section offers intriguing understandings of important and understudied realities of long haul WPA work, its effects on people, and creative, equity-driven ideas for renewal. We also hope preservice and early-career WPAs will find these chapters compelling as they offer sketches of what could lie ahead as well as an archive-in-process of early-millennial WPA experience and its continuous, and continuously vexed, journeying.

We also detect vulnerability and disparity between the institutional treatment of newer and seasoned WPAs. For example, on many campuses, new and early-career WPAs are a bit of a protected class. They tend to get what mentoring is available. Moreover, some of their perceived gaffes are attributed to learning curves, institutional unfamiliarity, leadership inexperience, and chronological youth. Such generous understandings are not generally extended to seasoned WPAs who are expected to know and do better across the board and whose (in) actions may be judged quite critically. More is expected of experienced WPAs than of new ones, and there is no "blame it on my youth" fallback. On campus, seasoned WPAs are expected to attend effectively to everyone's needs while handling and relegating their own. Due to their job security and scholarly reputation, accomplished WPAs are seen as relatively powerful, and, barring illness or bereavement, not in particular need of understanding or help. Unprotected and, to an extent, disregarded, these WPAs are neither chronologically young nor new to WPA work and have their own talents, needs, and precarities to reflect on and understand.

WPA renewal involves more than job security or one's career plans working out. Working from that premise, we contend that WPA renewal, inclusive of successes and regrets, cannot be measured by years on the job or scholarly success. Perceptions of vulnerability do not stop with job security. As editors Courtney Adams Wooten, Jacob Babb, and Brian Ray point out in *WPAs in Transition: Navigating Educational Leadership Positions* (2018), WPA transitions can occur throughout career spans. While seasoned WPAs may not regularly experience imposter syndrome or tenure-clock pressures, there are other vulnerabilities to explore, including stalled progress, feelings of embarrassment and shame, and searching for something different, else, and more to look forward to and do. Furthermore, accomplished WPAs still need to ready themselves to face experiences for which they are not prepared or by which they are undermined and fatigued. The challenges include coming to terms with failed dreams, dreaming different dreams, modifying old ones, understanding root causes of past decisions, and recognizing and enacting career turning points. That includes understanding the lessons you wished you had learned earlier and rethinking the lessons you learned too well. Other challenges include finding the strength to say no, to become more and less forgiving of your own mistakes, as well as rallying to endure, and cause, a few more programmatic and institutional storms.

To our minds, WPA renewal is necessary work because long-haul leadership work brings new trepidations, satisfactions, and dissatisfactions to face and understand, even and perhaps especially with oneself. There are also new and abiding hungers (e.g., to be "respected" by colleagues) to quell and sate. In this section chapter authors voice and examine their hungers, talents, and actions in ways we hope you will find interesting and edifying. They make connections with their earlier WPA selves, plans, and desires and sometimes show that, if the dots aren't always pleasant to countenance or connect, they remain vitally important for imagining and strategizing ways of moving forward in responsible and equitable ways. This section shows WPAs later on, but still "on" the job, in their life and career experiences. The authors analyze WPA work in ways that help seasoned WPAs better understand what could lie ahead short-term and help aspiring and new WPAs glimpse and imagine the complications, rewards, and (self) interests of WPA longevity.

RENEWAL CHAPTER DESCRIPTIONS

In Chapter Eight, "Refusal as Renewal: An Asian/American Woman Saying No While WPA-ing," Jolivette Mecenas explains how resisting oppressive, racist and heteronormative/homophobic authority is vitally important to an equitable WPA career and personal wellbeing. The message is: sometimes you owe it to yourself to say no loudly and persistently.

In Chapter Nine, Katherine Daily O'Meara describes "What Is Gained in Transition: Lessons from a WPA in Liminal Space," Daily O'Meara explains how the sometimes-troubling experience of liminality is endemic and energizing to ongoing WPA work at various institutions and under various job titles.

In "Revolving Doors: Programmatic Renewal and Regeneration Through Leadership Reorganization" (Chapter Ten), Jacob Babb and Susan Popham describe plans and strategies for planned leadership rotation which they argue supports programmatic health.

In Chapter Eleven, "Composing your WPA Career: Pleasure, Responsibility, and Wisdom," Jeffrey Klausman reflects on his long, accomplished career to examine his leadership successes and gaffes. Klausman offers readers a long view into self-insight, forgiveness, critique, and reconciliation, all in the service of understanding one's past to move forward as a person and leader.

In "Renewal through Cartography: Designing Resilience amidst Persistent Ecological Change" (Chapter Twelve), Colin Charlton and Jonikka Charlton offer WPAs ideas for mapping and re-mapping one's career. They show readers how to recognize, value, and leverage institutional resources and change, especially when you have been working at the same school for over ten years.

In Chapter Thirteen, "It's All About the Student: Advocating for Students at All Levels of Leadership," Beth Brunk offers a focused and philosophical approach to WPA work, one that prioritizes serving students in all their diverse talents and needs. Brunk writes as a WPA who has moved from the classroom to central administration. She helps readers understand how a central philosophy can fuel and sustain a long and rewarding career.

In "I'm Still Here, Goddammit: Toward Irreverent Understandings of White Nostalgia, White Irreplaceability, and WPA *In-Situ* Longevity" (Chapter Fourteen), Joseph Janangelo asks readers to understand WPA longevity from an antiracist perspective. Questioning the idea and ideal of WPA longevity as an uncomplicated good thing, Janangelo argues that WPA work has been too long understood, and taught in graduate programs, in whitely self-focused and selfish ways.

In Chapter Fifteen, "Getting Out of the Way: Antiracism and the Unbearable Whiteness of Being a WPA," Carrie S. Leverenz continues the discussion of tacit racism and considers other variables including a WPA's need for respect and a writing program's need for new leadership. Leverenz points out that one understanding of WPA renewal worth achieving is that it can be time to leave a program's WPA leadership to someone else. The book concludes with three brief "Understandings" written by Susan M. Lang, Mark Blaauw-Hara, and Patti Poblete.

In reading our book, you will likely find authors sharing their problems and vexations. Maybe we, as editors, should not have asked authors to raise questions that inspire complicated, circuitous answers? Yet we have done just that and would do it again because it reflects some truths about WPA work as we and our authors know it. We conclude by offering three thoughts:

- It is past time to understand WPA readiness and renewal beyond public-facing successful performance of the work. A conscious uncoupling of WPA need and performance is the communion we desire and recommend.

- If WPA readiness and renewal are neither trial- nor trauma-free, they are worthy, interesting, and rewarding pursuits inclusive of creativity and commitment. That's why WPA work is worth understanding again and anew.
- Writing Studies and writing programs might do well to stop wishing that WPA readiness were linear and expedient and that WPA renewal were simple and lasting. Especially for WPA readiness, a new kind of messaging may be in order. That would release and relieve some pressure all around.

We hope our authors' complicatedly optimistic understandings of readiness and renewal will help you explore worthy truths about WPA work and your contributions to it. Here goes something…something we hope merits your attention and rewards your understanding.

REFERENCES

Carter-Tod, S., & Sano-Franchini, J. (Eds.). (Summer 2021). Special issue: Black Lives Matter and Anti-Racist Projects in Writing Program Administration. In *WPA: Writing Program Administration* 44.3.

Dew, D. F., & Horning, A. (Eds.). (2007). *Untenured faculty as writing program administrators: Institutional practices and politics*. Parlor Press.

Malenczyk, R. (Ed.). (2016). *A rhetoric for Writing Program Administrators* (2nd ed.). Parlor Press.

Martinez, A. (2020). *Counterstory: The rhetoric and writing of critical race theory*. CCCC Studies in Writing & Rhetoric Series.

Merriam-Webster. (n.d.) Understanding. In *Merriam-Webster.com dictionary*. Retrieved September 29, 2022, from https://www.merriam-webster.com/dictionary/understanding#:~:text=(Entry%201%20of%202),by%20applying%20concepts%20and%20categories

Perryman-Clark, S., & Craig, C. L. (Eds.). (2019). *Black perspectives in writing program administration: From the margins to the center*. National Council of Teachers of English Press.

Skinnell, R., Holiday, J., & Vassett, C. (Eds.). (2015). *What we wish we'd known: Negotiating graduate school*. Fountainhead Press.

Wooten, C. A., Babb, J., Costello, K. M., & Navickas, K. (Eds.). (2020). *The things we carry: Strategies for recognizing and negotiating emotional labor in writing program administration*. Utah State University Press.

PART ONE

READINESS

CHAPTER ONE

Leadership Readiness: Becoming a Rhetorically Mindful WPA

MELVIN E. BEAVERS, UNIVERSITY OF ARKANSAS LITTLE ROCK
ABRAM ANDERS, IOWA STATE UNIVERSITY

Whether you are a current or aspiring writing program administrator (WPA), you likely approach the role with relevant disciplinary expertise and a strong personal connection to the mission of helping learners grow as writers and communicators. However, you may have hesitancy or uncertainty about adopting the identity of a leader. Nonetheless, if your goal is to have a larger positive impact, then leadership is essential. Previous scholarship has demonstrated that leadership skills are an essential aspect of WPA readiness and performance (Jackson, 2018; McLeod, 2007; Miller-Cochran, 2018; Phillips, Shovlin, & Titus, 2018; Ross, 2020; Strickland, 2011; Wooten & Babb, 2018). We argue that becoming a leader is a process in which WPAs should exercise rhetorical mindfulness to balance our commitments to our multiple overlapping identities and diverse communities of stakeholders.

To engage this process, it is essential for WPAs to choose to think of themselves as leaders as an intentional act. What does it mean to act or make decisions with intention? It means what Krista Ratcliffe (2005), in her landmark work *Rhetorical listening: Identification, gender, whiteness*, defines as centering openness and doing so by engaging in rhetorical listening. In the context of WPA leadership, we argue it means acting in the moment with a strong sense of purpose—it means being a rhetorically mindful administrator. For example, you can choose to listen to the concerns of part-time faculty, often the most underserved stakeholders in your programs, and allow opportunities for them to define and shape initiatives that directly impact them. Melvin Beavers (2019), one of the co-authors of this chapter, has previously framed this approach through the concept of "administrative rhetorical mindfulness." This concept describes a leadership mindset that focuses on adaptive and situated approaches to engaging stakeholders with the goal of leading writing programs to more sustainable and ethical futures. When in doubt, pause; breathe; and ask, what would a rhetorically mindful administrator do? Ultimately, intentionally choosing to become leaders means thinking about our values and actively searching for ways to align them with our practices, so that we may act with purpose to meaningfully serve our academic communities and stakeholders.

In this chapter, we first examine how the concept of administrative rhetorical mindfulness and theories of servant leadership can help you productively engage WPA leadership challenges. Next, we share reflections on how to implement administrative rhetorical mindfulness in three key domains: practicing awareness and self-assessment, developing foresight, and building communities. Finally, we share our reflections and advice as experienced WPAs to demonstrate how we each approach and think about these areas of WPA leadership. Ultimately, we hope you will find inspiration and practices to fashion your own WPA identity and prepare for leadership readiness.

ADMINISTRATIVE RHETORICAL MINDFULNESS

What does it mean to feel or enact readiness? How does one know when they are ready to lead? If we pause for a moment and think about leaders, who or what comes to mind? We reflect; we think about the role models and mentors who have shaped and guided our paths. We think about their actions and perhaps how those actions reflect a mission or vision for the program, unit, department or institution. That metacognitive lifting, the thinking about thinking that occurs as we consider individuals or groups that have helped directly and indirectly prepare us to do X, Y, and Z—what might we call it? We would argue that it is a mindfulness occurring; it's being more present and engaged. It's taking a deep dive and attempting to understand who we are in our roles as WPAs.

Preparing for leadership readiness is an investment that can be further strengthened through a commitment to administrative rhetorical mindfulness, which is one framework new and emerging WPAs can use to develop their leadership identities more fully. Servant leadership, a style of leadership articulated by Robert Greenleaf, and documented in *Robert K. Greenleaf: A life of servant-leadership*, is a complementary path we can take to further interrogate the self and develop a leadership identity (Frick, 2004). Through a deep engagement with stakeholders, servant leadership can promote a strong and inclusive sense of shared purpose and values. The reflective administrative rhetorical mindfulness framework offered in Table 1.1 is a starting point for engaging these issues. You can use it to craft your leadership approach and become more rhetorically mindful within your program and institution.

These themes of mindfulness and service to stakeholders are also apparent in studies of WPA leadership practice. Through an interview-based study of 10 WPAs, Beavers (2019) found that WPA leaders frequently described their roles as multi-layered and not easily defined by a single priority or responsibility. However, a common guiding metaphor for leadership was exhibited in the repeated phrase that many participants used: "a desire to do more" (p. 101). Hence, Beavers (2019) developed a theory of administrative rhetorical mindfulness to conceptualize this leadership approach and synthesize three essential terms: administrative or administrator, rhetorical, and mindfulness. For example, picture a Venn diagram, and for each term, we might say that what happens in the gray area, where each term overlaps, is leadership readiness (see Figure 1.1).

Furthermore, participants in Beavers' (2019) study exemplified characteristics and habits of mind associated with Greenleaf's model of servant leadership. Participant statements such as "broadening their skill set," "feel more included," "increased flexibility," and "better faculty experiences" all reveal some of the characteristic values WPAs share, as associated with offering professional development opportunities for faculty and staff (p. 118). Taken together, these examples illustrate how servant leadership can function as a bridge between our professed ideals and how our work gets accomplished. Although servant leadership may spark negative connotations for some, such as thinking of oneself as subservient or servile to others, servant leaders do not think of their work this way. Instead, servant leaders are focused on helping employees to meet their full potential and think of those employees as important pieces of the organizational structure (Heyler & Martin, 2018, pp. 230–233). Still, like authentic leadership, which often gets linked to ideas of integrity and realness, servant leadership is tethered to a commitment to one's values. As Gardner and Karam (2021) note in their discussion of authentic leadership, "persons who strive to achieve authentic leadership and followership can be seen as everyday people who attempt to navigate the pressures and temptations of organizational life by sticking to a core set of values and principles" (p. 3). Though the statement is a reflection on authentic leadership, it connects well to ideas of servant leadership because both tend to stress an alignment of values and actions. A fundamental function in WPA work is identifying values within the program and making sure those values are a central part of programmatic goals.

Servant leadership is not the only path toward readiness for WPA work. Yet, it does offer WPAs a valuable perspective for examining their practices. As

Table 1.1: Reflection Heuristic for Administrative Rhetorical Mindfulness

Reflection Heuristic for Administrative Rhetorical Mindfulness
Practice Awareness and Self-Assessment • What can you do to increase inclusive and equitable instructional practices among instructors including graduate teaching assistants and contingent faculty? • How can you promote investment in the professional development and training of instructors including graduate teaching assistants and contingent faculty? • How can you demonstrate the ways that investing in the professional development of instructors ensure success for all students? • How can programmatic assessment practices and professional development help promote better teaching practices overall?
Develop Foresight • What actions can you take to recruit, develop, and retain a diverse group of instructors? • Do professional development activities focus on better student experience? If not, how can you change and improve your approach? • How can increased attention to the needs of graduate teaching assistants and contingent faculty increase equity, collegiality, and knowledge-sharing? • How can you anticipate challenges and build on successes related to the pivot to flexible pedagogy and online writing delivery during the pandemic? How can online writing instruction or online literacy education support face-to-face courses?
Build Communities • How can you promote a sense of community and sustain a culture of inclusion and diversity through professional development and shared decision making? • How can you share program knowledge, best practices, resources, and opportunities to support and promote the professionalization of graduate teaching assistants and contingent faculty? • How can you identify and leverage the unique expertise and skills of graduate teaching assistants and contingent faculty and make their contributions integral to the program community?

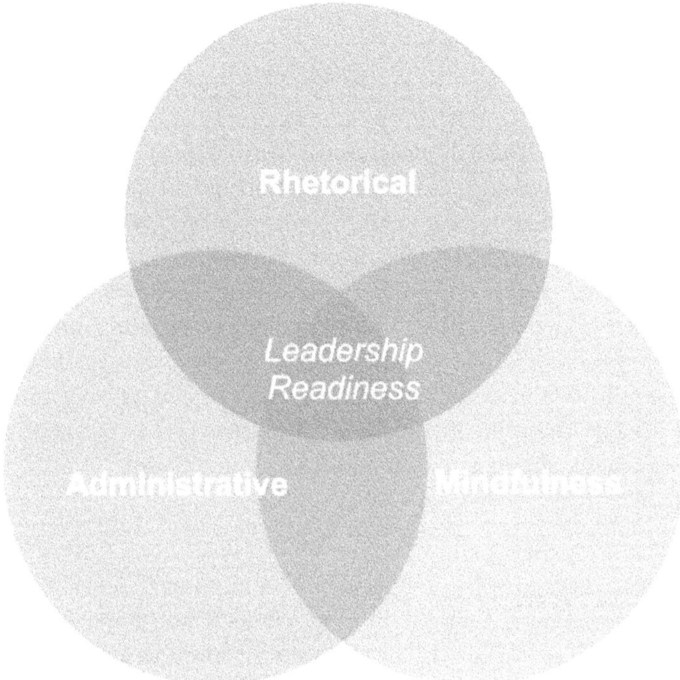

Figure 1.1: Administrative Rhetorical Mindfulness

WPAs, we often explore the many literacies our students bring into the classroom; however, how do we let our own ways of knowing inform the work we do? That's the key here: how can we mindfully leverage our unique knowledge and competencies to lead our writing programs *and* to become ready to lead those programs? Servant leadership offers some pathways toward developing models that serve (no pun intended) our local context in fruitful ways.

In the following section, we model pathways and offer reflections on the ways we have attempted to implement the values of rhetorical administrative mindfulness. Additionally, we share how we have positioned ourselves as WPA leaders who serve our academic communities, instructors, and student stakeholders. We suggest that these reflections may give you inspiration as you work to identify emerging issues within your program and plan more concrete and tangible approaches for professional development, programmatic research, or programmatic assessment. Furthermore, the heuristic can help you make reflection a central piece of the work you do to promote more mindful thinking as you develop your WPA leadership style or approach.

REFLECTING ON LEADERSHIP PRACTICES

How Can We Practice Awareness and Self-Assessment?

Mindful approaches to leadership necessarily begin with awareness, empathy, and reflection. As Beth Brunk argues in this collection, emphasizing advocacy for students can offer a foundation for humane decisions at every level of academic leadership. However, Brunk also cautions that we must guard against received notions and normalized expectations of student needs. Practicing awareness begins with searching out diverse perspectives and better understanding the situated challenges of our stakeholders. Placing the experiences of diverse stakeholders at the center of our reflective practice is an ideal way to exercise a growth mindset as a leader and develop the type of situational awareness that is essential to making positive, meaningful changes that serve the program mission.

Melvin's Reflections

There are several ways to approach developing a mindset that is about maintaining a sense of awareness. One of the first things I would encourage graduate assistants interested in WPA work or more specifically a new WPA to do is take an environmental scan of your program. Essentially, learn and come to know your environment. Learn about the institutional context and the students and staff you will be serving. Come in and ask questions about their needs as part-time and full-time contingent faculty. From there, develop an action plan that is informed by the local values and reflects those desires and interests.

Abram's Reflections

One challenge for practicing awareness is learning how to balance the often competing needs of administrators, instructors, and students in your programs. This challenge can be especially intense during periods of crisis like the ongoing pandemic. Without a clear way to prioritize and make decisions, we can easily become overwhelmed by awareness and empathy and find ourselves in states of compassion fatigue and burnout. In my experience, a powerful way to address these challenges is to start with a focus on the most vulnerable and important members of our communities, which are our students. As leaders, we can choose to *start with our students* and prioritize their needs by designing for positive impacts on student learning experiences and through assessment that emphasizes demonstrable student outcomes. This approach can help WPA leaders recognize which actions will be most beneficial and offer the greatest impact and return on investment of your program efforts.

Another benefit of centering the student experience in decision-making is that it can make creative conflict in collaboration become more productive and less personal. If you are working in a mixed team that involves diverse stakeholders—WPA leader, contingent faculty, GTAs—and addresses issues with clear institutional pressures, you may find it difficult to reconcile conflicts of opinion about decisions, especially when stakeholders have conflicting interests at stake. However, asking the question, "Which approach here will best serve students?" can help you and collaborators find common ground and shared purpose to support decision making. Furthermore, this mindset also offers a compelling way to self-assess and to set aside your personal opinions, preferences, and biases whenever they may conflict with making choices that empower others in ways that best serve your students.

How Can We Develop Foresight?

Preparing for future challenges and taking proactive actions to address problems requires strategy, planning, resources, and time. As Karen Keaton Jackson (2018) has argued, a perennial challenge for WPAs is finding ways to invest in active developmental work, even as routine operations can occupy nearly all of our time. Developing foresight builds on practicing awareness to recognize needs and opportunities, but also requires sustained investment in program and professional development activities that strengthen the collective capacities of a program as it looks to the future.

Melvin's Reflections

Set priorities. Be aspirational with the priorities but realistic; in fact, one of the easiest ways to get stagnant or become mired or siloed in the daily operations is to think in terms of parts as opposed to systems. System thinking will help you find the gaps in your understanding of your program. If you think about how the systems around you are structured, who knows what, where the information to help run your program sits and who has access to it, then you will likely find yourself talking and networking with lots of folks outside your typical sphere. Think about what the multiple stakeholders at your institution need, and plan for those diverse interests and needs by collaborating across disciplinary lines with others. If you lean into creating strong networks, then you might find new ways to solve problems, become a mentor, or advocate on someone's behalf.

Abram's Reflections

One great advantage for leaders of academic programs is the cyclical nature of our work (J. Janangelo, personal communication, August 3, 2022). Each semester presents an opportunity to innovate in the most basic sense of doing things differently to do them better. Developing foresight can directly emerge from awareness of community needs: what problems, concerns, and difficulties did instructors and students encounter last semester and how can we anticipate these issues persisting and evolving in the future? Hence, a large part of developing foresight is tracking issues and investing time and energy and resolving those issues in advance for the next iteration of your courses.

An equally important aspect of developing foresight is to make proactive investments in the future. On this point, I would argue that investing in recruiting, retaining, and developing your faculty members and their expertise is a strategically vital aspect of having foresight. For example, a faculty member who seeks your support to gain additional expertise in online learning design now, could become the leader of an online course development project in the future. We may not know exactly what will happen or what our emerging needs might be, but we can prepare our programs to become more adaptable and capable by investing in the professional development and expertise of our faculty and staff.

How Can We Build Communities?

The way that we frame our relationships to others exerts a powerful influence on both what we say and what we do. As Carrie Leverenz argues in this collection, conscientious collaboration with stakeholders who occupy different identities and positionality is essential to antiracist program leadership. Complementarily, Katherine Daily O'Meara, also in this collection, argues that an important aspect of personal development as a WPA is learning to give up control and embrace opportunities to involve the expertise and contributions of others. The mindful practice of centering the perspectives, values, and contributions of others including our instructors and students is essential to building communities and cultures that are both high-performing and ethically oriented to issues of diversity, equity, and inclusion.

Melvin's Reflections

Part of what makes servant leadership so impactful is that it relies on a collectivist mindset. It is the idea that we have to learn to speak the same language, which means understanding that communication is a key component of real change. To successfully communicate with your faculty and students, you have to understand the culture within the program and its history to some degree. If folks feel unheard, then they might be reluctant to offer advice or suggestions to help sustain goals for the program. That will ultimately create a toxic environment and one that does not build on any shared sense of programmatic identity. So it becomes really important to find ways to build bridges and connections among stakeholders. For example, find ways to bring graduate students and faculty together to collaborate on issues around curriculum and pedagogy. If you can find incentives to offer for professional development and offer it on a consistent basis, then you are heading the right toward building community.

Abram's Reflections

It has become common to acknowledge that new leaders can experience some form of "impostor syndrome" in which they may struggle with feelings of uncertainty, self-doubt, and worry about how others perceive them. To counter these feelings, some leaders can experience a strong impulse to demonstrate competence, commitment, decisiveness, and even authoritativeness to prove their fitness for the role. However, I would suggest that focusing on building community is a more productive way to gain confidence as a leader and WPA.

Building community can start with identifying and engaging collaborators and potential leaders among faculty and staff in your program. If you put your energy into empowering your faculty and staff and promoting their accomplishments, you can extend your own impact and build collective goodwill, trust, and rapport. Instead of worrying about being a "strong leader," you can focus on building a "strong program" and a "strong community." This shift in mindset can help you build a culture that demonstrates a willingness to embrace diverse ideas and perspectives and can help you achieve results that are well beyond your individual capacities.

CONCLUSION

Questions for Reflection and Discussion

We recommend that you review the *Reflection Heuristic for Administrative Rhetorical Mindfulness* above (see Table 1.1) to begin your inquiry into leadership practices, philosophies, and theories.

As you do that work, consider your own experiences in writing programs as a student, instructor, collaborator, or leader and reflect on the following questions. Also consider interviewing an experienced WPA to get their perspective on these key issues:

- How can WPAs, especially early-career ones with many other things on their plate, practice awareness and self-assessment?
- How can WPAs develop foresight, especially in the face of unforeseen and mutating circumstances such as the ongoing pandemic?

- How can we build effective and impactful communities when we are new to an institution?
- How can we ensure that those communities undertake their work in responsible, equity-driven ways?
- How is your graduate education in WPA work preparing you to become a leader?
- How might your graduate training be improved to include more and better leadership preparation?

Preparing for leadership readiness is an investment that can be strengthened through a commitment to administrative rhetorical mindfulness and by embracing the principles of servant leadership. Through a deep engagement with stakeholders, WPA leaders can promote a strong and inclusive sense of shared purpose and values. Engaging in this process can also help you build experiential knowledge and relationships that support the exercise of real leadership for meaningful change, which Valerie Ross (2020) has described as "the ability to motivate people, to get them to commit not only intellectually but actively to bringing something into being" (p. 255). Ultimately, we hope this exploration of leadership theories and our own reflections can help you develop and refine your leadership style and practices and become a more rhetorically mindful leader.

REFERENCES

Beavers, M. E. (2019). *Preparing part-time contingent faculty to teach writing online examining writing program administrator approaches* (Order No. 13859159). [Dissertation, University of Arkansas at Little Rock]. ProQuest Dissertations Publishing.

Frick. (2004). *Robert K. Greenleaf: A life of servant-leadership* (1st ed.). Berrett-Koehler.

Gardner, W. L., & Karam, E. P. (2021). Authentic leadership theory: The case for and against. *The Leadership Quarterly*. https://doi.org/10.1016/j.leaqua.2021.101495.

Heyler, S. G., & Martin, J. A. (2018). Servant leadership theory: Opportunities for additional theoretical integration. *Journal of Managerial Issues*, *30*(2), 230–243.

Jackson, K. K. (2018). A state of permanent transition: Strategies for WPA survival in the ever-present marginal space of HBCUs. In C. A. Wooten, J. Babb, & B. Ray (Eds.), *WPAs in transition: Navigating education leadership positions* (pp. 25–36). https://doi.org/10.2307/j.ctt22zmb7g

McLeod, S. H. (2007). *Writing program administration*. Parlor Press.

Miller-Cochran, S. (2018). Innovation through intentional administration: Or, how to lead a writing program without losing your soul. *WPA: Writing Program Administration*, *42*(1), 107–122.

Phillips, T., Shovlin, P., & Titus, M. L. (2018). "An exercise in cognitive dissonance": Liminal WPA transitions. In C. A. Wooten, J. Babb, & B. Ray (Eds.), *WPAs in transition: Navigating education leadership positions* (pp. 70–83). https://doi.org/10.7330/9781607326335.c004

Ratcliffe, K. (2005). *Rhetorical listening: Identification, gender, whiteness*. Southern Illinois University Press.

Ross, V. C. (2020). Chapter 11. Managing change in an IWP: Identity, leadership style and communication strategies. In J. Everett & C. Hanganu-Bresch (Eds.), *A minefield of dreams: Triumphs and travails of independent writing programs* (pp. 245–268). https://doi.org/10.37514/per-b.2016.0810.2.11

Strickland, D. (2011). *The managerial unconscious in the history of composition studies*. Southern Illinois University Press.

Wooten, C. A., & Babb, J. (2018). Introduction: Travels, transitions, and leadership. In C. A. Wooten, J. Babb, & B. Ray (Eds.), *WPAs in transition: Navigating educational leadership positions* (pp. 3–21). https://doi.org/10.7330/9781607326335.c000

CHAPTER TWO

(Re)Visioning WPA-GO: Finding WPA Readiness as a Graduate Student Leader

GABRIELLE ISABEL KELENYI, UNIVERSITY OF WISCONSIN-MADISON

"Do we even do this anymore?" I type into the Google document comment. Before I click the comment button, I hesitate. *Is this too snarky?* I ask myself. I take a deep breath and rephrase my question: "Is this still accurate?" I find myself getting frustrated at how outdated this information is, but it's likely that my colleagues are similarly incredulous. As I continue to read through the Writing Program Administrators-Graduate Organization's (WPA-GO) by-laws, I wonder about the last time someone actually read these. I mean *actually* read them and not just skimmed them or read a very specific part to answer a very specific question.

The last time I read them was when I was running for election to the Graduate Committee (GC), the governing body of WPA-GO, in 2019. It was also the first time I read them. They were confusing then, but I thought that was perhaps because I was new to the organization and to writing program administration. Looking hastily through the bylaws, WPA-GO seemed like a great way to network, make friends, and learn more about writing program administration, given both WPA-GO's and the Council of Writing Program Administrators' (CWPA) committees and opportunities to collaborate with two CWPA faculty mentors. Thus, I was eager to join. As I wrote in my GC application,

> The structural injustice that leads to a lack of diversity in CWPA members and the population of people who administer writing programs is a barrier that causes me, a woman of color, a lot of anxiety. I want to be a Writing Program Administrator; I want to contribute to meaningful WPA research and assessment. I do not want to feel as if my contributions and experiences are discounted or simply tolerated because of my identity or positionality. I want to feel confident, prepared, respected, and appreciated as a member of the (inter)national WPA community.

Bent on making the most of this opportunity, I ran for and was elected WPA-GO's Vice Chair directly afterwards.

Now, three years later, I am WPA-GO's Past Chair. Looking back on the past three years as a leader of WPA-GO, I can say that I did not feel discounted or simply tolerated because of my identity or positionality in WPA-GO and CWPA. Instead, I felt obligated to work to dismantle systemic barriers to equity, inclusion, and antiracism in these organizations. While part of that might be timing and circumstances, I can't help but wonder if it's also because of my identity and/or positionality. This autobiographical reflection (Martinez, 2020) aims to share how I went about that work as WPA-GO's first woman of color leader during the 2020–2021 academic year, a period of unprecedented turmoil and change due to the COVID-19 pandemic and rising racial unrest.

This piece is inspired by Writing Studies and critical race theory scholar Dr. Aja Y. Martinez's (2020) argument for counterstory as methodology in composition and rhetoric for its ability to help minoritized voices, subjectivities, and perspectives write their way into the academy through a "revisionist history of rhetoric and Writing Studies that includes me and people who look like me" (p. 4). In this essay, I tell my story, and I do not justify my narrative approach because, as Dr. Martinez (2020) points out, minoritized people have been unfairly asked to do so for too long. Instead, I use this space to first describe how ready I was to help WPA-GO revise its by-laws to align with the organization's antiracism goals and then how unready I was to lead GO through a boycott against its parent organization for participating in white supremacy culture.

When I ran to lead WPA-GO, I felt ready to do so—to learn about the organization and help advance its mission to support graduate student WPA (gWPA) preparation and build community between gWPAs and professional WPAs. However, when I actually led WPA-GO, I learned that readiness is a mirage: the unexpected always rears its head in some shape or form. While I thought that I needed to project resourcefulness and confidence in the face of challenges as WPA-GO's Chair, I realized the importance of finding like-minded colleagues with whom to confer and collaborate—and from whom to ask for help and perspective—as a leader. I'm grateful to WPA-GO for helping me find those colleagues.

ANTIRACIST ASPIRATIONS

My first year on the GC, when I was Vice Chair, wasn't what I expected. The GC and its committees met fairly infrequently due to having to devise and steer our own initiatives, made only more difficult by the pandemic. Sometimes those initiatives seemed to contribute to WPA-GO's overall mission to support Writing Studies graduate students, and sometimes they seemed to be merely CV material. I began to think perhaps WPA-GO was simply a CV line and not actually the incredible opportunity to meet colleagues and gain hands-on experience in an international professional organization. I showed up to meetings, contributed however I could, and planned to serve out my term according to the bylaws, which at the time were approved and ratified by CWPA's President. I let the organization's normalized policies and practices push me to the margins and deter me from realizing my goal for my position—to help my field feel more inclusive.

However, when a GC member sent the group an email about how our recently completed elections for the coming 2020–2021 academic year were decidedly *not* antiracist and actually *un*fair, my first instinct was to reread WPA-GO's bylaws. Admittedly, I had not paid much attention to its election policies and procedures. I figured the Elections Committee had it handled per the information provided in their section of the bylaws. I hit Control+F and typed in the word "election," which showed up 19 times. And while the bylaws outlined Elections Committee duties, they didn't articulate a process by which grads were elected to the GC—they simply discussed when elections were held. How could we expect the members of that committee to conduct an actively antiracist and fair election without any guidance?

The pandemic had upended everything, and there was confusion and burnout among GC members for many reasons. The Summer 2020 protests demanding racial justice in the U.S. and deepening understanding of how systems perpetuate white supremacy helped make clear how our election processes were not equitable or antiracist. And that's at least partially because we had no outlined process. As Dr. Martinez (2020) points out, no articulated process meant that latent racism under the guise of uninterrogated and normalized systems, conduct, and principles could flourish.

Antiracism requires *action* and *intention*, which would need to go beyond individuals in WPA-GO to actualize our antiracist commitments. As I transitioned from Vice Chair to Chair just after these GC elections, I realized the organization's previous commitments focused primarily on assessment, and we had no built-in policies and procedures that helped the organization as a whole enact antiracism. Thus, as one of my first initiatives as Chair, I proposed an overhaul of our bylaws, beginning with our election processes. WPA-GO didn't have to be *just* a CV line if the bylaws clarified what we did, when, how, and most importantly why.

WPA-GO's elected leadership made significant changes to our bylaws over the course of Fall 2020 to establish practices that sought to center people from nondominant communities. For example, WPA-GO held a special election open to our general membership to fill the Vice Chair, Inclusion Advisory Chair, and Treasurer executive board positions on the GC. Whereas normally these executive positions were open to current GC members only, we hoped to recruit more leaders, increasing the number of GC members from nine to twelve. Additionally, we committed to prioritizing identity-conscious representation that would amplify voices underrepresented in academia. By expanding the call and executing an actively antiracist election, we sought leaders who were committed to making lasting structural changes within our organization.

Furthermore, the GC revised and reduced our internal committees from eleven to three to be easier to manage and better represent our priorities. During the bylaws revision, and therefore our re-visioning of WPA-GO, the leadership realized many initiatives that connected WPA-GO and CWPA had fallen away. Thus, when CWPA fell behind in granting WPA-GO what was written into our bylaws but not required by theirs (at the time of this writing, WPA-GO and graduate students do not appear in CWPA's bylaws), we had to seek out mentorship, networking, and learning experiences from our "parent organization" unidirectionally. For example, our bylaws stated that graduate liaisons would serve on CWPA committees to represent the needs and interests of WPA-GO's graduate student constituency. However, no current GC member could remember the last time a WPA-GO member served in this capacity. It seemed that this was a valuable networking and learning opportunity of which neither WPA-GO nor CWPA was taking advantage. Unfortunately, CWPA didn't seem interested (or perhaps had forgotten to be interested) in the contributions WPA-GO members could make to their initiatives beyond being, in the words of then President of CWPA Dr. Mark Blaauw-Hara at a CWPA Town Hall in Spring 2021, the "conscience of CWPA." We were doing the painstaking work of re-visioning our organization, but CWPA seemed largely uninterested—mildly indulgent, perhaps—of our efforts until Dr. Asao Inoue's call for a boycott (see Inoue, 2021).

WPA-GO was never going to be just a line on my CV because I am a person who knows what it means to navigate unfair and inequitable systems every day; as an elected leader of an organization implicated in participating in white supremacist culture, I could not—would not—let my unique experiential knowledge go to waste, as Dr. Carmen Kynard (2019) refuses to do in the experiences she shares about being a Black woman WPA. Thus, my work as WPA-GO's Chair focused on who has access to WPA-GO and CWPA, prioritizing a diversity of (g)WPAs, as called for by Dr. Aja Martinez (2020, citing Harris, 2003).

In this way, I worked to help WPA-GO realize its antiracist aspirations beyond assessment practices to make it more accessible for graduate students from non-dominant backgrounds/communities in *structural* ways: through revision of our bylaws and elections.

READINESS IS A MIRAGE

As I mentioned in the introduction to this piece, when I ran to lead WPA-GO, I felt ready to do so. I knew there would be a learning curve, but I felt ready to help make WPA-GO a more welcoming and intentional organization; I felt ready to help members of the organization craft events, grants, and opportunities that aligned with graduate student needs and desires; I felt ready to put structures into place that would help build community among Writing Studies grads and open clear avenues for gWPAs to secure various kinds of support and diverse experiences.

However, I did not anticipate being WPA-GO's first woman of color leader while a boycott was being staged against GO's parent organization for participating in white supremacy culture (see Inoue, 2021). To be clear, I was not ready to lead WPA-GO through this upheaval, through moments of triage and turmoil; I was not ready to make decisions about the status of WPA-GO's affiliation with CWPA; I was not ready to feel like I needed to choose between helping our "parent organization" divest from white supremacy culture or protecting the active progress WPA-GO was making towards its antiracist aspirations. I was not ready to feel like I had to choose between honoring my lived experience as a multiracial woman in the United States and an important and powerful professional organization in a field I was just trying to be a part of. I simply was not ready.

There's no better example of how unready I was for this situation than when I woke up at 3:30am, after tossing and turning for over an hour, to write an email to WPA-GO's Graduate Committee. I was unable to expel the CWPA Executive Board (EB) meeting from the evening before from my mind, to the point where it had woken me up in the middle of the night. I wondered frantically, *What will I tell WPA-GO's GC? Can I send them an email this early in the morning? Maybe I can write it now and then fall back asleep?*

I can vividly remember how I gingerly slid out of bed, careful not to wake my partner, and tip-toed out of the room to grab my laptop from the dining-table-turned-communal-work-from-home-desk. I remember sitting down on the couch, opening my computer, and clicking "reply all" to the latest email in the GC thread. I remember trying so hard to write as objectively as I could to my colleagues about the meeting—who it was facilitated by and what the purpose of it was. I informed them of the anonymous survey that had been sent prior to the meeting and how its results were being used to guide the meeting. I described our breakout rooms and our task in them. And I wrote to my colleagues about the long silences that punctuated the meeting to the point where the EB members who were facilitating the meeting began cold calling on groups because no one would volunteer to share.

I did not write about how frustrating I found the silences of the predominantly white CWPA EB members. I did not share with members of GO's Graduate Committee about my discomfort at the thought of sharing what we talked about in my breakout room because of my *ex officio* EB member and graduate student status. I thought about trying to explain how the silences made it seem like EB members were unwilling (or perhaps afraid) to share lessons learned and identify CWPA's exclusive practices and structures, to experience discomfort and shame and "disrupt our sense of goodness and righteousness" (Condon, 2012, cited in Martinez, 2020, p. 90). But I didn't. I also did not write that the silences reflected to me how EB meetings no longer felt like safe or brave spaces for critically examining CWPA's history.

Instead, I wrote about how, at least in my analysis, the range of responses to the anonymous survey revealed a grave lack of consensus within the EB about what to focus on moving forward, what antiracism is, what an external audit is and would entail, and both recognition of and resistance to (for fear of threatening nonprofit status) a complete rewrite of the organization's bylaws. I refrained from writing anything about how the responses to the anonymous survey and the white supremacist culture baked into CWPA's bylaws (Inoue, 2021) could be seen as stalling tactics that maintain the status quo. I refrained from explaining how I believed CWPA's bylaws, if not revised with an intentionally antiracist lens, would continue to serve as gates preventing newer WPAs from being allies and co-conspirators in overcoming CWPA's challenges. I tried my best to stick to the objective facts of that meeting. But in so doing, I silenced myself out of a misguided sense of professionalism and neutrality, forgetting that my experiential knowledge "is legitimate and critical to understanding racism that is often well disguised in the rhetoric of normalized structural values and practices" (Martinez, 2020, p. 3).

It proved impossible to remain objective when I began to explain how one EB member tried to resign her position towards the end of the meeting, and in her resignation explanation, she continued to refuse to decenter herself and consider how she could still participate in white supremacy even as a multilingual immigrant. I do not regret sharing how "quick [she was] to dismiss or deny the inherited privilege associated with whiteness" (Martinez, 2020, p. 10). It was clear to me that WPA-GO could not assume "existing faculty have such issues covered and are not in need of such instruction in the same way newer, more experienced teachers (or students!) are" (Martinez, 2020, p. 27); instead, it seemed like

WPA-GO would have a lot of work to do to educate and help enact antiracism with (or even *for*) CWPA. And as Chair, I honestly wanted to (or thought I needed to) protect WPA-GO from that labor because I was afraid it would take energy away from our own initiatives and progress. Considering how CWPA's Nominating Committee had so much trouble fulfilling their commitment to assemble an all-BIPOC ballot for CWPA's general election and how much scrutiny the organization was under after this ordeal, I wondered, *Who wants to fight this fight against colleagues, peers, and mentors?* Not me. Not my colleagues. I wasn't ready to do this work under a magnifying glass. My exhausted, confused, disheartened, anxious graduate colleagues—some of whom were on the job market during this fiasco, others of whom wanted to demonstrate their allegiance to scholars and orientations they admire and respect, still others of whom were just trying to get their bearings in the field—could not risk doing this work under a magnifying glass and with faculty who seemed unsure of a path forward.

Twice—at the last two consecutive EB meetings I attended—two members of the EB offered their resignations. And twice, EB members chose to protect them and their feelings over the good of the organization, arguing that they were good for CWPA. (For more on this issue, see Janangelo's chapter in this volume.) And I understood the arguments for continuity in the organization and the impulse to not rock the boat more. However, I was wary of trying to do this work under the leadership of faculty who did not (and had not for many years, according to CWPA's shaky history with antiracism and inclusion) have these issues in hand, and I was wary of asking other grads committed to organizational-level antiracist work to join WPA-GO and be subjected to their unclear agenda for CWPA (and thereby WPA-GO). I was overwhelmed by feelings of despair, skepticism, and worry over the EB's ability to collectively move forward when there was such disagreement over what antiracism even is and the best ways to enact it as an organization.

As an *ex officio* EB member, graduate student, and woman of color watching white EB members swoop in to defend these EB members, I felt implicitly "asked to survive" a "clash between cultures" (Martinez, 2020, p. 88), to ask WPA-GO's graduate student members to continue to align themselves with an organization that seemed to refuse to recognize, let alone look for, the roots of their problems. And I was not ready to survive that clash, nor was I ready or willing to ask my colleagues to stick with CWPA, especially as many EB members seemed unwilling to start over with antiracism as the foundation; instead, they seemed to think antiracism could be used to patch CWPA's cracks through reform. So, I didn't ask them to stick with CWPA. Instead, I asked for the GC's thoughts, opinions, and questions. I asked them to help gather input from our membership so as to avoid unilateral decisions. Drs. Solórzano and Yosso (2002) note that BIPOC engaged in this work can feel out of hope, out of patience, and out of moves to suggest, and I felt the same.

Almost three hours later that morning, I pressed send. Looking back at that rough, exhausting morning, I think I'll always wonder if my email and the context of it pushed my colleagues one way or another. Either way, by the end of the email, I recognized that I didn't know how to move forward. While writing this email in the wee hours of the morning, I shed the expectation that as WPA-GO's leader I needed to be all-confident and all-resourceful and always at the ready. And in response to my unreadiness, my lack of confidence, my inability to see next steps, I asked for help from colleagues I trusted. And together we readied ourselves to press forward. (For more on caring for ourselves and others, see Mecenas's chapter in this volume.)

Shortly afterwards, WPA-GO made the difficult decision to separate temporarily from CWPA. As Chair, I was nervous I was dooming an important graduate organization to fail without a "parent organization," but I was also exhausted from sleepless nights and impatient with the unending battle to convince others to unlearn white supremacy. Even though CWPA's actions continually placed me at the margins largely due to my woman of color, graduate student, and *ex officio* positionalities, I found comfort in support from other grads, in knowing that the future of the field is actively unlearning white supremacy culture and striving to enact equitable WPA practices.

CONCLUSION

I offer the autobiographical reflection above as an illustration of the institutional racism that our disciplinary sense-making maintains in the field of Writing Studies that Dr. Carmen Kynard (2015) highlights (cited in Martinez, 2020). Even though writing this piece felt risky and I feared putting further energy into this ordeal, I wrote it anyway because I agree with Dr. Aja Martinez (2020) that narratives by folks from nondominant backgrounds, like me, are important to critical race theory and its pursuit of resistance and change. As WPA-GO's Chair, I was afforded opportunities to leave a lasting legacy of structural change by undoing some maintenance mechanisms in GO's bylaws through our large-scale revisions. We updated our bylaws to prioritize identity-conscious representation on GO's GC and outline multidirectional or mutual mentorship, networking, and learning experiences with partner organizations. However, my experience gaining a semblance of WPA readiness as an *ex officio* CWPA EB member, viewing its enactments (and protection) of whiteliness firsthand, has perhaps made me *unready*, or definitely *unsure* of my place in writing program administration.

Nonetheless, what do I hope you, as aspiring and established WPAs, learn from my story? I hope you:

- **Practice caution**: Be cautious before volunteering for leadership opportunities, and consider learning more about the organizations you join through lower-lift committee work first.
- **Ask for help**: Develop relationships with like-minded colleagues and peers whom you can trust in murky moments of *un*readiness so that you can manage the unexpected and remain open to possibilities.
- **Remain impatient with social change**: The dismantling of systemic barriers to equity, inclusion, and antiracism in professional organizations cannot come fast enough, and organizations and their leaders may never feel *ready* for it because changing everything can sound daunting; however, being open to changing everything allows us to move beyond a reform mindset and instead meet the boundless opportunities that come from a revolutionary mindset (see Kaba, 2021). You should not have to choose between feeling included and respected in your field and progress, so don't.
- **Look back just as much as you look forward**: Wondering about how my early morning email might have impacted my colleagues influences the ways I communicate my experiences in other situations now; sometimes it serves to make me braver to share, and sometimes it serves to make me hold back and listen before determining whether or not to share. Past decisions I've made, past experiences I've had, past ways I've exercised leadership by stepping up and stepping back will always shape how I see ways forward.
- **Embrace the unanticipated**: It was impossible to be ready for the context surrounding my time as WPA-GO's Chair; however, I think unprecedented times create possibilities for unexpected ways forward. For me, to embrace the unanticipated meant developing a greater appreciation for collective, nonhierarchical, more distributed leadership models (see Parker, 2020).
- **Develop your vision for leadership:** I knew I wanted to be a more inclusive leader of WPA-GO, but I didn't know this vision would take the shape of a bylaws revision and asking for help from my colleagues. I now know that inclusive leadership means interrogating and talking back to the assumptions of leadership, such as a single leader having all the answers and all the responsibility.

Dismantling the systems of oppression that operate in Writing Studies and WPA work is an ongoing effort. And to be clear, I am not recommending that we give up on this work; instead, I am advocating for intentionally prioritizing our well-being and protecting our energies while we engage in it. One way to do this is by carefully choosing who, what, where, and with whom you collaborate. And in doing so, you'll hopefully gain a network of like-minded (grad) colleagues with whom you can look forward to collaborating in the future, like I did.

REFERENCES

Blaauw-Hara, M. (2021, April 23). *CWPA Town Hall.*

CWPA. (2011, March 16). *Bylaws of Council of Writing Program Administrators* [CWPA Bylaws].

Inoue, A. B. (2021, April 18). *Why I left the CWPA (Council of Writing Program Administrators).* Asao B. Inoue's Infrequent Words. http://asaobinoue.blogspot.com/2021/04/why-i-left-cwpa-council-of-writing.html

Kaba, M. (2021). *We do this 'til we free us: Abolitionist organizing and transforming justice* (T. K. Nopper, Ed.). Haymarket Books.

Kynard, C. (2019). Administering while Black: Black women's labor in the academy and the "position of the unthought." In S. M. Perryman-Clark & C. L. Craig (Eds.), *Black perspectives in writing program administration: From the margins to the center* (pp. 28–50). CCCC Studies in Writing & Rhetoric Series.

Martinez, A. (2020). *Counterstory: The rhetoric and writing of critical race theory.* CCCC Studies in Writing & Rhetoric Series.

Parker, P. S. (2020). *Ella Baker's catalytic leadership: A primer on community engagement and communication for social justice.* University of California Press.

Solórzano, D. G., & Yosso, T. J. (2002). Critical race methodology: Counter-storytelling as an analytical framework for education research. *Qualitative Inquiry*, *8*(1), 23–44.

CHAPTER THREE

How to WPA: Career Planning, Survival and NTT Power at the Convergence of My Professional and Personal Lives

ELISE A. GREEN, LONGWOOD UNIVERSITY

We pursue lives in academia because the nature of what we study and teach pleases our souls in deep, satisfying ways. Unfortunately, that enjoyment does not always satisfy the bills. Post-graduate school, you may find yourself working as an adjunct or lecturer, earning a salary that may or may not support week-to-week living, or offer retirement options or benefits. To supplement your income, you might work more than one job, limiting the time you have to invest in the field and your institution via research, writing, and service. Or, to expand your résumé and gain upward mobility, you might accept every offer for extra work that comes your way, hoping it will lead to something bigger and better. Yet, in the midst of over-extending your professional-self, you still aspire to grow your researcher-self, and have an impact on the knowledge-making world. In this piece, I hope to use my experiences to offer you some advice as you plan your own career–maybe in a way that is entrepreneurial, where you explore, move by move, how you can chart a fulfilling career while paying the bills.

My current position as a lecturer satisfies the weekly bills, but I am also contingent, making my life full of insecurity and precarity. Yet, I have found that WPA work was (and is) the key to my survival—a priority over the ideal of happiness that Carrie Leverenz (2020), in her chapter, "Don't Worry, Be Happy: How to Flourish As a WPA," pointed out is "inevitably fraught" (p. 18). In fact, a tenure-track colleague once suggested I should be in mourning over my rank, as they called out my choice of dress, saying, "You're always so bright.

You're a lecturer—shouldn't you be wearing black?" I chuckled in response, but was dismayed on the inside. In a "publish or perish" world, I was keenly aware of my shortcomings, and the rhetoric of death used to describe my professional existence—something that, as a first-generation college student, I had worked so hard to attain—was discouraging to say the least.

In this chapter, I will share my experience on becoming and navigating the role of a WPA as an early-career, contingent faculty member. I begin by describing my path to becoming a full-time, NTT lecturer while also juggling early adulthood. This context situates the decisions I later describe on why I chose to pursue WPA work. I then extend this discussion by sharing how opportunity as a WPA has led to professional and personal conflict. This chapter concludes with some pointed advice that I hope will help in your own career planning, as well as inspire conversations with your peers and mentors.

My aim here is to be fully transparent and very specific about my experiences in the hope that pre-career WPAs can avoid some of the situations in which I found myself. Or, at a minimum, to prepare you more than I was for the struggles that lie ahead. I realize that such vulnerable writing is perhaps unconventional, but I have been emboldened to speak up as a result of the candid stories recently shared by my Writing Studies colleagues across the field. Rachel Azima (2021), Associate Professor and Writing Center Director at the University of Nebraska-Lincoln, described her experience as a professor of practice, highlighting the backwards environment in which non-tenure track faculty assume tenured-faculty responsibilities, but do not enjoy the benefits of such a position. Lacey Wootton (2021), Director of the Writing Studies Program and Department of Literature at American University, noted the risks and rewards associated with these situations and argued that the feminist ideal of "having it all" as a non-tenure-track faculty member begs exploitation and strengthens the patriarchal structure of higher education, where the people doing the most are paid the least. Liliana Nayden (2018), Associate Professor and Writing Program Coordinator at Pennsylvania State University-Abingdon, likewise explored this phenomenon, describing contingent WPAs as the working class of academia—a population of low- to mid-rank employees with supervisory responsibilities. I relate to these anecdotes well. My own readiness as a WPA was driven by my need to survive as a member of the lower faculty ranks, in spite of the power paradox in which I would find myself.

BECOMING CONTINGENT

I graduated high school in 2004, so that tells you how old I am. And when you're a female academic and hopeful mom-to-be, age matters. After working several years to support my family, I earned an associate's degree from the local community college in May of 2010. Soon thereafter, I married, and later that same year, I began a distance-learning program to earn a bachelor's degree. I was working full-time as a dental assistant to pay my tuition, and my husband was working full-time to pay the household bills. This arrangement continued through my MA program, throughout which I also worked as a graduate assistant. During this time, I gained valuable experience, and hoped someday to teach college English. I thought a career in higher education would afford me opportunities not only to advance professionally and develop academically, but also—and maybe you've considered this, as well—to raise a family. Mari Castañeda and Kirsten Isgro (2013), editors of the collection *Mothers in Academia*, acknowledge this common perception among young, female academics while also describing the tensions that exist within this ideal. Indeed, the Facebook group "Mothers in Academia" grew out of Castañeda and Isgro's project, and has provided a space where countless academic moms have shared similar ambitions, but also commiserate over the rewarding yet exhausting job of, to borrow Cheryl Matias's (2011) term, the motherscholar. (For more on this topic, please see Clinnin et al.'s chapter in this book.) Nevertheless, I was determined, and when I graduated with my MA in 2014 at almost 28 years old, I was hired as a full-time lecturer at a small, liberal arts institution.

To be honest, I was a little unclear on what a lecturer was, but the job was close to home, and with a $40,000 a year salary, the position provided a nice increase from my dental assistant wages. I also had benefits, a $1200 a year travel stipend, and no service responsibilities. My main purpose was to teach, and to satisfy this expectation, I would have a 5/5 load: five courses in the fall, and five courses in the spring. On the surface, everything seemed reasonable and manageable, so when I received my first contract, I readily signed without asking many questions.

Six weeks into my first semester, I went to lunch with a new colleague. During conversation, they mentioned that some lecturers were getting ready to "expire," and this colleague mentioned that they were glad to have me on board with a fresh "clock." I think my blank stare in response prompted them to elaborate: "Lecturers are only kept around for six years. There's the potential to be a senior lecturer after that, but not much precedent for it." They shared that I probably didn't have anything to worry about for a while, but that I did need to do well for my first review, which was approaching quickly. *Good to know*, I thought.

Certainly, I was familiar with the tenure clock; we are often taught under the assumption we will someday have the privilege of one. The academic job market does not support this notion, however, and it is quite possible you will find yourself in a contingent position, either temporarily or long-term. Natalie Dorfeld's (2022) edited collection, *The Invisible Professor*, draws attention to the shift in higher education to a disposable business model in which non-tenure track individuals are the faculty majority. In *Contingency, Exploitation, and Solidarity: Labor and Action in English Composition*, Seth Kahn, William Lalicker, and Amy Lynch-Biniek (2017) likewise examine the ongoing trend of non-tenure track labor, while contributors to the collection offer strategies for advocacy and professionalization. Gail Crimmins (2018), in "The Double Life of a Casual Academic," points out that long-term employment in contingent positions is even more likely if the individual is female. I suddenly realized I had a six-year lecturer clock: a time frame in which I had to prove myself useful and worth keeping around. Soon after, I approached my then department chair and asked, "What is a senior lecturer, and how do I become one?" They explained that to be promoted, I needed to make a significant contribution to the university. They tried to give examples of what others had done in the past, but these accounts were vague.

My first review came and went, and a letter from the Promotion and Tenure Committee arrived in my department mailbox. It offered praise and a favorable review of my teaching. But the closing paragraph ended with an uncomfortable caveat: "We are pleased to recommend your reappointment…should a position be available." Concerned about what this point meant, I went back to my department chair. "What does this line mean?" I asked. I knew I had an annual contract. What I did not know, and what the Chair explained to me that day, was that my position was need-based, or contingent. "Oh, yeah, sure, okay. Thanks!" I did my best to save face and respond as if I knew the answer to the question all along.

I felt ignorant and irresponsible for accepting a job—a job my family depended on—that left us wondering if and when I would 'no longer be needed' or if I would exhaust my professional clock before my career even began. How do you make a recognizable contribution to the university? I began by applying to PhD programs in composition and planned to focus my research on writing initiatives (e.g. first-year composition and writing-across-the-curriculum) at my home institution. I hoped doctoral training would support me in making evidence-based recommendations to the writing program, and in turn, get me the nod I needed for promotion.

I was accepted into a distance-learning program in March of 2016. Of course, I was working against a biological clock, too, and in April of that year, at almost 30 years old, I became pregnant with my first child. I began taking classes immediately in May, wanting to finish my degree as quickly as possible, as my department chair and dean offered to "pause" my lecturer clock while I was on maternity leave. The importance of this agreement cannot be understated. Rachel Connelly and Kristen Ghodsee (2011), in their book, *Professor Mommy*, recognize the aspiring parents who think like me, and advise that teaching is not all you do in an academic life. There is a great deal of invisible work behind your visible presence in the classroom, which can often create conflict with your family and personal obligations. A paused clock, something I did not even know was an option, afforded me much needed time later on to complete my degree.

BECOMING A WPA

Few, if any, PhD concentrations will prepare you for the physical and emotional labor associated with WPA work. I was fortunate to have a professor who offered a course in writing program administration because she recognized the need to train a new generation of WPAs, and also because—like it or not—she knew we would likely serve as WPAs at some point. These prospects present themselves in different forms. At times, you might be offered opportunities that will feel like a welcomed breath of life. I experienced this relief in the summer of 2017, when a colleague and mentor invited me to join in the redesign of our first-year composition course. That fall, I helped pilot and assess the course, and later in the spring, helped train the faculty cohort who would be teaching it for the first time. I continued to teach my 5/5 load, but was compensated with a modest stipend for my work on the pilot. It was through this experience I began to see what a "significant contribution" might look like.

In contrast, other opportunities will come in the form of rejection. Take care to learn from these moments. In the spring of 2018, the position for the university's Writing Center Director was posted. If I got it, my family would benefit from stability and a pay increase. I applied and had a successful first interview—a 25-minute phone chat with the 3-person search committee. As a result, I was invited to an all-day, on-campus interview. By this time, my oldest child was 1.5, and I was 12 weeks pregnant with my second. I was aware that my daycare bill, which was about $600 a month for one child, was about to double. As a result, about half of my lecturer salary was going to be absorbed by the cost required to obtain childcare. I really wanted this job.

I didn't get it. Upon asking for feedback to understand why, I learned that the selected candidate had more administrative experience and a completed PhD. In the end, the overall interview process introduced me to the grueling nature of academic job interviews, but further, this rejection also helped me realize the importance of programmatic assessment—an area in which I fumbled to answer questions and was later told I lacked knowledge.

As a result of this experience, I determined that assessment knowledge would be key in making a recognizable contribution to the university, and, in turn, could help me become indispensable. Indeed, Susan McLeod's (2007) notable work, *Writing Program Administration*, defines assessment as a measure of accountability, and Chris Gallagher's (2009) aptly titled article, "What do WPAs Need to Know about Writing Assessment? An Immodest Proposal," makes a critical argument for where WPAs should look to gain institutional knowledge. Recognizing my next step, I connected with the Office of Student Success on our campus to learn about how we determine, or assess risk factors associated with first-year students. I benefitted by gaining some helpful context about the performance demographics of our incoming students—those who I was meeting in my FYC classroom as well as those in the greater FYC program. I asked the then coordinator of first-year composition about what we did with the information we collected from annual juried assessments. They pointed me to the office of Assessment and Institutional Research, which helps coordinators set goals, collect and read data, and consider professional learning opportunities to improve future outcomes. I shadowed my colleagues in this process, and in doing so, put myself first in line for my next opportunity: to become the coordinator for first-year composition.

Of course, as a lecturer, I wasn't supposed to take on service responsibilities, but in late fall of 2019 with one-and-a-half years left on my ever-ticking-clock, I dove for this life preserver. It was exactly what I needed to earn a promotion. There was no monetary compensation, but I did receive a course release. The initial offer was either a 4/5 or a 5/4. I asked for a 4/4, and the Dean agreed. During the next year and a half, I worked closely with the office of institutional research to gain experience in organizing programmatic assessments and reading data to understand what our students were taking away from their first-year composition course. If you find yourself with a similar opportunity, you might follow my lead, as I used this information to identify topics for professional learning and facilitated workshops to strengthen our pedagogical approaches. I experienced resistance from tenured faculty who questioned their need to participate in such opportunities and met with them individually so their concerns could be heard. I began attending faculty senate meetings to learn who people were across campus, and worked to introduce myself to as many as possible. In my effort to gain exposure, I sought out the Writing Center Director, who became a great ally—a slightly ironic twist—and she began participating in our FYC faculty workshops.

In the spring of 2021, just as my lecturer clock was about to expire, I successfully defended my dissertation, and was promoted to senior lecturer. I would still be contracted to teach a 5/5 load—though it would really be a 4/4 because of my service as the FYC coordinator. I also received a $1,000 promotional raise and a two-year, contingent faculty contract. I didn't go to school to be a WPA—I became a WPA because I wanted to keep my job.

THE WPA PROMOTION

That summer, I was invited to serve as the writing coordinator for the university core curriculum. The previous coordinator—a tenured English professor in the

Professional Writing Program—had been promoted to director, and as it turned out, I had the credentials and experience to fill her former role. My duties would be similar to those I performed while coordinating first-year composition, except instead of overseeing one course that had anywhere from 12 to 20 sections a semester, I would be overseeing over 150 writing-infused courses across the university. This offer was a vote of confidence for me from the university, but I was hesitant to accept. The position would come with a much-needed $4,000 annual stipend, but I was being asked to perform tenure/tenure-track responsibilities without the promise—or validation—of a permanent position, a tenure-track base salary, or a tenure-track course load (which would be a 4/4 under normal circumstances, but a 3/3 after a release for WPA duties). I accepted anyway.

About a month into this new role, I learned there was some apprehension in appointing me as the university writing coordinator because I was not tenure-track. And further, in the event I was cut as a senior lecturer—an increasingly realistic scenario as enrollment declines—my work as a WPA would not offer any additional protection. Also troublesome was the fact that a recent vacancy for an English education professor would not be filled. As it turned out, the department was able to staff those classes without bringing in a new tenure-track hire. In effect, I was slated to teach half this schedule.

By now it was fall of 2021, and the university was doing everything it could to recover and save money from the devastating blow of the COVID-19 Pandemic. This trauma coupled with mixed messaging from the institution left me feeling fractured, as though I was living in what Karen Keaton Jackson (2018) describes as two worlds in her chapter, "A State of Permanent Transition: Strategies for WPA Survival in the Ever-Present Marginal Space of HBCUs." Her metaphor characterized both the contingent faculty and WPA lives I constantly negotiated, and it also pointed to my experience at the convergence of my professional and personal lives. Though they are separate, I functioned in both at the same time, straddling a line between the two. But ultimately, for me, the pursuit of survival was (and is) my superpower. Through all this, I've learned that though the world is literally saying you will perish, persistence can overcome precedent.

FINAL THOUGHTS FOR THE PRE-SERVICE WPA

As I write this essay, I am 35 years old. I am grateful for my job(s), and like Rachel Sanchez (2021) in the introduction to *Speaking Up, Speaking Out: Lived Experiences of Non-Tenure-Track Faculty in Writing Studies*, I recognize how fortunate I am. Sometimes, though, defeat overwhelms me because, regardless of all I've done, the occasional merit raise does not offer the validation or compensation of a tenure-track faculty job. Since earning my PhD, I have re-entered the job market, and I have assessment experience now(!), which brings me to some final, more pointed advice I wish I knew upon graduating from my MA in literature program. Perhaps you're already familiar with my points below, but nevertheless, I hope my advice will support the aspiring Writing Studies professor as they prepare for the future.

- You might be contingent. I was naive not to understand this fact about my own position. Even if you plan to accept the job regardless, it will be helpful to know how the institution defines your employment.
- You might know what contingent means and what it entails, but many of your tenured and tenured-track colleagues won't. Over time, I've experienced multiple conversations in which they share about the stress of their 4/4 or 3/3, and they respond with shock to learn about my 5/5 load. Be gentle when acknowledging their position of privilege and create alliances through these relationships. Many of these colleagues have the power and positionality to advocate for you in institutional spaces where contingent voices pack less punch.
- WPA training is primarily on-the-job, figure-it-out-as-you-go professional development that is specific to a given institution. (See Mecenas's chapter in this book for more discussion on this topic.) Looking back, I wish I'd had some of this experience at the time I took the WPA class. At the very least, I wish I'd had the opportunity to have a candid discussion, or an interview with a WPA. If you have WPA experience and are in a class with student-colleagues who do not, be sensitive to the road that lies ahead of them and offer to share your own story in a productive way.
- Don't be afraid to hear "no," and if you do, ask "why?" I was irritated when I didn't get the writing center director job, but I gained feedback on where I could improve, and carried that feedback forward. The experience taught me to market myself better, in part, because I knew what to expect the second time around.
- Brace yourself for resistance all…the…time. In many ways, we expect resistance from our students, but that resistance is often more passive. I'm talking about the resistance that occurs when two sides are pulling in two opposite directions. In a utopian university, everyone would be pulling the same way, but rope burns on your hands are more likely, as you inch closer to job security, financial stability, and professional identity.
- The rhetoric of death in the university does not have to define your existence. In my day-to-day functions, I have chosen not to adopt academia's language that is used to describe my contingent status or my publishing agenda. This issue needs deeper exploration, but in the meantime, I encourage a

heightened awareness and guard against this rhetoric that undercuts the confidence and capabilities of our working-class, which could be you.

- Resist isolation. The nature of scholarly work and teaching often positions us by ourselves. Contingent faculty work and WPA work are no different. Seek community to avoid intellectual loneliness and help establish a professional identity.
- Seek out professional mentors where you work. Decide who you want them to be, and then tell them, "You're my mentor." Naming the relationship helps identify the expectations you have for them. I recently informed a tenured friend and colleague of his new title, not because of his position of power, but because he was able to offer me a perspective about the dynamics of the institution that I struggled to gain as an otherwise isolated lecturer.
- Become one with assessment. The university thrives on data. The big "A" word sounded scary to me as an early-career academic. It still does. But I noticed that I gained opportunities around the university when I became comfortable talking about this topic and my experience with it. Go to the Institutional Research office on your campus as well as program coordinators in your department, and look for opportunities to learn the many approaches. Opt to participate, and strive to learn about what assessment looks like in not just your department, but also around the university.
- Finally, remember that WPA-ing, much like teaching, takes courage. Parker Palmer (1998), in *The Courage to Teach*, reminds me of why I aspired to become an educator in the first place: because I care. And the same heart from which I teach is the same heart from which I find the courage necessary to continue as contingent.

In sharing my personal journey to becoming a full-time, NTT lecturer as a young adult, I realize that my story is not everyone's. And yet, we will all likely experience rejection and resistance at some point. In this chapter, I mean to highlight the messy intersection at my personal and professional lives and explain the reasons behind my decisions. I hope the concluding points above will help in your own career planning, as well as inspire productive conversations with your peers and mentors.

REFERENCES

Azima, R. (2021). Practice doesn't always make permanent: Directing a writing center as a professor of practice. In J. Edwards, M. McGuire, & R. Sanchez (Eds.), *Speaking up, speaking out: Lived experiences of non-tenure-track faculty in writing studies* (pp. 15–27). Utah State UP.

Castañeda, M., & Isgro, K. (2013). *Mothers in academia*. Columbia UP.

Connelly, R., & Ghodsee, K. (2011). *Professor mommy: Finding work-life balance in academia*. Rowman & Littlefield Publishers.

Crimmins, G. (2018). The double life of a casual academic. In A. L. Black & S. Garvis (Eds.), *Lived experiences of women in academia: Metaphors, manifestos, and memoir* (pp. 181–189). Routledge.

Dorfeld, N. (Ed.). (2022). *The invisible professor: The precarious lives of the new faculty majority*. The WAC Clearinghouse.

Gallagher, C. W. (2009). What do WPAs need to know about writing assessment? An immodest proposal. *Writing Program Administration*, *33*(1–2), 29–45.

Jackson, K. K. (2018). A state of permanent transition: Strategies for WPA survival in the ever-present marginal space of HBCUs. In C. A. Wooten, J. Babb, & B. Ray (Eds.), *WPAs in transition: Navigating educational leadership positions*. (pp. 25–36). Utah State UP.

Kahn, S., Lalicker, W. B., & Lynch-Biniek, A. (2017). *Contingency, exploitation, and solidarity: Labor and action in English composition*. The WAC Clearinghouse.

Leverenz, C. (2020). "Don't worry, be happy: How to flourish as a WPA." In C. A. Wooten, J. Babb, K. M. Costello, & K. Navickas (Eds.), *The things we carry: Strategies for recognizing and negotiating emotional in writing program administration*. (pp. 17–36). UP of Colorado.

Matias, C. (2011). "Cheryl Matias, PhD and Mother of Twins": Counter storytelling to critically analyze how I navigated the academic application, negotiation, and relocation process. [Paper]. American Educational Research Association (AERA), New Orleans, LA.

McLeod, S. (2007). *Writing program administration*. Parlor Press.

Mothers in Academia. (n.d.). Home [Facebook page]. Facebook. Retrieved March 17, 2021, from https://www.facebook.com/MothersInAcademia/

Naydan, L. M. (2018). Transitioning from contingent to tenure-track faculty status as a WPA: Working toward solidarity and academic-labor justice through hybridity. In C. A. Wooten, J. Babb, & B. Ray (Eds.), *WPAs in transition: Navigating educational leadership positions*. (pp. 284–296). Utah State UP.

Palmer, P. J. (1998). *The courage to teach: Exploring the inner landscape of a teacher's life*. Jossey-Bass.

Wootton, L. (2021). Having it all: The costs and opportunities of non-tenure-track faculty's institutional progress. In J. Edwards, M. McGuire, & R. Sanchez (Eds.), *Speaking up, speaking out: Lived experiences of non-tenure-track faculty in Writing Studies*. (pp. 73–89). Utah State UP.

CHAPTER FOUR

Ready to Be an Equity-Focused WPA: Reforming Community College Developmental Writing

MARK BLAAUW-HARA, UNIVERSITY OF TORONTO, MISSISSAUGA

If you are passionate about fighting for social justice and equity, and you're frustrated by how much higher education further marginalizes students who are already at risk, please consider working at a community college. I spent two decades at a small community college, hiring in at twenty-six years old as their first-ever WPA. It was a nerve-wracking, exhilarating, frustrating, humbling, and sometimes joyful experience, and I can't recommend it enough. Like me, you may be the first WPA at your college. You will have a great many things to think about as you pull together a coherent writing program. It will be a lot of work, but I have found that the overwhelming majority of community-college writing faculty care deeply about helping students. They also care about social justice and student empowerment.

With an average student age of 28, community colleges skew towards post-traditional students; additionally, 29 % of students at community colleges are first-generation (American Association of Community Colleges, 2021). Community colleges also enroll a significant number of low-income students, with 37 % of their student populations coming from families that make less than $20,000 per year (Community College Research Center, 2021). Finally, 56 % of all Native American, 53 % of all Latinx, 43 % of all Black, and 38 % of all Asian undergraduates attended community colleges in 2021 (American Association of Community Colleges, 2021).

These students could really use a writing program that's designed to help them succeed, and you could build that program. It's true that working at a community college generally doesn't confer the kind of status and admiration of your peers that a R1 or funky, cool liberal-arts college does. However, you will be able to make a tangible difference to a great many students, and you will be able to work in an environment where exciting, cutting-edge scholarship is happening. (For more on that, take a look at Giordano and Lehman's piece, as well as Klausman's, in this book.) For WPAs who are committed to fighting for equity in higher education, community colleges are Ground Zero.

Here's something you might not know: *At the community college, developmental writing is more important than first-year writing.* Between 60–68 % of all community-college students take some sort of developmental course (Community College Research Center, 2021; Jaggars & Stacey, 2014), and among minoritized groups, those numbers are even higher: for example, 78 % of Black students, 75 % of Latinx students, and 76 % of low-income students (Community College Research Center, 2021). The outcomes for students who place into traditional multi-course developmental writing sequences tend to be abysmal: Not only do far too few students complete the developmental sequence, but even fewer ever complete the FYW sequence (Adams, 2020; Community College Research Center, 2021; Jaggars & Stacey, 2014; Valentine, Konstantopoulos, & Goldrick-Rab, 2017). If you want to make a real difference, focus on developmental writing. In this chapter, I will try to give you a sense of four main aspects of developmental writing you should consider: placement, course structure, curriculum design, and faculty development/staffing. Throughout, I'll provide statistics and data to contextualize my opinions and to give you some good sources to consider as you chart your own readiness journey.

PLACEMENT

The first area to explore is placement. Traditional forms of writing placement do a poor job and, as I noted above, they tend to put too many students in developmental writing, including a disproportionate number of students from historically marginalized groups. (For more on placement at community colleges, see Nastal, Poe, & Toth, 2022; Klausman et al., 2016; and the *Journal of Writing Assessment*'s 2019 Special Issue on Two-Year College Writing Placement). Multiple-measure placement methods are much more effective (Community College Research Center, 2021), and a number of scholars advocate directed self-placement (Barhoum, 2017; Toth, 2019). For these reasons, even before tackling curriculum, you should gather data on your college's placement methods and advocate for ones that are based on current scholarship.

The draw of standardized testing is strong at community colleges for two main reasons: first, because such tests are presumed to be externally validated, giving colleges a bulwark against student complaints; and second, because they can easily be administered on a rolling basis. This second point is particularly important to understand. As open-access institutions, community colleges need to be able to accommodate not only traditional college-aged students, but also post-traditional working students, dual-enrolled high-school students, military veterans, single parents, and more. Many of these groups have very limited time in which they could attend a more traditional placement-and-orientation session; instead, they must be able to walk into a learning center or make an appointment with an advisor at a wide range of times (including evenings and weekends), figure out what courses they need to take, and enroll in those courses. It is tempting to discount these considerations as being external to the writing program, but I would urge you to recognize their importance. This kind of flexibility is at the heart of community colleges' open-access mission: to provide quality educational opportunities for all in a community, not just those who can attend, say, a three-hour placement-and-orientation session during business hours. In other words, you need to develop a placement system that is not only effective, but relatively easy to administer quickly.

Start with external data—this is the language most administrators and student-services personnel speak. Look for quantitative studies that address issues of retention and completion, again because you are shaping your argument for placement reform around the concerns of your audience. An excellent source is *Writing placement in two-year colleges: The pursuit of equity in post-secondary education* (Nastal et al., 2022). This edited collection contains chapters that describe placement methods at a wide variety of community colleges, and most chapters present empirical data that you can use to make your case. Use the external data to justify a pilot study at your own college, and then use the resulting local data to tweak your placement system and justify scaling it up. During this process, listen to the concerns of your colleagues outside of the writing program (or if you don't have a formal program, listen to the faculty who teach courses other than first-year and developmental writing) and gather data to address those concerns.

At my former school, we found a study describing a multiple-measure placement that combined high-school GPA and ACT/SAT scores (Belfield & Crosta, 2012), and we used it to justify a small pilot. Working with our college's institutional researcher, we generated local data that showed that this change decreased the numbers of students placing into developmental writing without any negative effects on student performance. This placement system worked well for most students who had graduated from high school in the past five years or so, but it was more difficult for non-traditional students who had been out of school for some time—military veterans, and students who were coming back to school after years in the workplace. Such students tended to have a more difficult time locating their GPA and test scores, and even when they did, they frequently said that it was unjust to place them based on data that was, in some cases, a decade or more in the past. We asked those students to write a sample essay that was read by a full-time faculty member, but this method also had its flaws.

During my final year at my former institution, I worked with the incoming WPA and others to research and develop a directed self-placement instrument. This work was informed by scholarship on DSP (Toth, 2019; Wang, 2020), as well as consultation with other CC WPAs who were developing similar programs. It will be piloted with the group I referred to above—those students who have been out of school for five years or more—with the intent of refining it and eventually phasing it in across all incoming students. In addition to addressing the concerns I outlined above, we also hope it will support student equity by empowering incoming students to make their own informed choices about the writing courses that will best help them achieve their educational goals.

In summary, placement reform represents a manageable and defined goal for new CC WPAs, and I think it is where you should begin. As noted above, a key concern is over-placing students into developmental writing who don't really need to be there—especially students from traditionally marginalized groups—and many standardized placement instruments are culturally and linguistically biased. I think that DSP has the best chance of getting students into the courses that will most benefit them, and its individualized, dialogic nature helps us avoid the cultural biases that are baked into standardized instruments. That said, you and your team might decide on something else, and that's OK. Just remember that as the WPA, it is your responsibility to ground your program's placement methods in current scholarship. Once you have a placement system in which you are fairly confident, you can move on to refining your program's course structure.

COURSE STRUCTURE

As you think about how to structure your developmental writing courses, I'd like you to consider co-curricular or STRETCH models that place all students into college-level courses while providing extra help to the students who need it. At my former school, we had great success adapting the Accelerated Learning Program (ALP) developed by Peter Adams and colleagues at the Community College of Baltimore County (Adams, Gearhart, Miller, & Roberts, 2009). In ALP, all students take college-level writing in a standard-sized class; then, students who placed below a given cut score receive extra help in a much smaller section. The model has been validated and expanded upon at many community colleges across the country (Adams, 2020; Jaggars, Edgecombe, & Stacey, 2014).

ALP has several components that set it aside from more traditional models of developmental writing. Most importantly, in ALP the developmental classes give students opportunities to preview, review, and practice skills and concepts they learn in the college-level section. ALP also focuses heavily on teaching reading skills and addressing "studenting" skills like time management, developing a growth mindset, accessing college support systems, and more. In addition to reading scholarship on ALP, I recommend looking at Adams's (2019) textbook for a clearer picture of what he recommends.

Similarly to our efforts at placement reform, at my previous school we used external data to justify an ALP pilot with a small number of students, gathered internal data, and used that internal data to support bringing ALP to scale. We did double-blind readings of randomized samples of student essays that had been produced in both ALP and non-ALP developmental writing sections, finding that the ALP essays consistently scored higher on our departmental rubrics. We also worked with the college's institutional researcher to track and compare student performance between the two models, finding that ALP students not only passed the first semester of FYW in higher numbers, but they also enrolled in the second semester of FYW at double the rate and passed that course in higher numbers as well. Additionally, ALP students took more credits in *other* courses than non-ALP students. This internal data was enormously important in making the equity-based argument to phase out our more traditional sections of developmental writing (including the lowest level) and bring ALP to full scale.

Always remember that you are part of a larger institutional ecology and that significant changes within the writing program will require significant changes outside of it as well. For example, our course enrollment system did not handle co-requisite courses smoothly, necessitating each ALP student to be manually enrolled by Student Services. Student advisors had to have difficult conversations, telling incoming students who did not particularly like writing or feel comfortable with it that they would have to take six credits of writing instead of the three that they were hoping for. Additionally, the ten-student support classes cost the college money when full-time faculty taught them, which was of concern for some in the administration.

Our internal data allowed us to address each of these concerns. Being able to prove that students wrote better as a result of ALP, progressed through FYW in higher numbers, and that their tendency to take more credits more than paid for the losses incurred by giving full-time faculty smaller student-to-faculty ratios enabled us to support an equity-based argument that we needed to move entirely to the ALP system. It was better for our most vulnerable writing students, it did not cost the college money, and it was worth the advisors' extra work.

In addition to ALP, there are other ways to address developmental writing that show promise (see Barhoum, 2017, for an overview). No matter what you choose, you will need to listen to the concerns of people outside the writing program and figure out how to gather data to inform decisions that will address those concerns. When an administrator brings up money, or Student Services talks about how their software or processes will be disrupted, please don't roll your eyes. If the money doesn't work out, you will be out of a job. If your changes make other people's jobs harder, you will be out of allies.

All that said, as you consider how to approach your developmental writing courses, I encourage you to face up to the well-established fact that there are more equitable ways to support underprepared students than a multi-level developmental sequence where they have to pass course after course before they get to college-level writing. Part of your job will be to educate your colleagues—both inside the writing program and beyond—on research-based solutions, and to work as part of a team to develop the best system for your own students and your college.

CURRICULUM DESIGN

Unfortunately, developmental writing has long been the site of some of the most regressive curriculum design in writing programs. Many courses overemphasize grammar instruction. It makes sense that developmental writing courses should address Standardized American English (SAE)—a term I draw from Inoue's (2021) autobiography, which productively critiques the concept. SAE is valued in academia and the working world; however, developmental writing courses that heavily focus on SAE do students a great disservice. I think that teaching students a rhetorical approach to SAE has value in supporting their academic and professional goals, a point that has been made by others as well (Delpit, 2006; Smith, 2019; Stachnik, 2021). This rhetorical approach should include discussion of code-meshing (Young, 2014), and SAE should not be presented as superior in any way to other dialects, but rather as a communication pattern within one discourse community (Pattanayak, 2017). There should be frank discussions about the relationships between language usage, socioeconomic status, and power, with attention paid to ways the English language has been weaponized to exclude non-dominant groups. For an examination of how SAE excludes minoritized populations and an argument for antiracist language pedagogy, see April Baker-Bell (2020).

All of that said, developmental writers need to focus on more than just grammar. Just as college-level writing courses must address many aspects of writing, so should developmental ones. I admire ALP's emphasis on "backward curriculum design," which focuses on the skills and knowledge students need to succeed in college-level writing (Adams & McKusick, 2014, p. 21). The curriculum of developmental writing should not be constructed as though it stands on its own—its purpose should be to support student achievement in college-level writing.

Each institution should explore its college-level writing courses to figure out what types of skills and knowledge will help students succeed in those courses, and answers will differ. However, some trends are likely to appear across institutions. Good college writing tends to be well developed and cohesive, with a strong sense of structure. Students are expected to contribute something new to the discourse, and they are asked to support their ideas with evidence and analysis. Frequently, students need to read challenging material and respond to it. Students will also be expected to demonstrate conscious control of linguistic features within their writing.

All of these elements should also be present in developmental writing classes. This is not to say that developmental courses should be exactly the same as college-level ones—it is fair to expect that the students in developmental courses might need more time and support, and that they may have less experience with advanced writing and reading tasks. It is also likely that students may need support with non-cognitive issues such as time management, study strategies, mental-health practices, and more (Di Tommaso, 2011; Di Tommaso, 2016). The COVID-19 pandemic has exacerbated many of these needs, especially surrounding mental health.

However, developmental writing courses should not be "dumbed down" in ways that infantilize students; rather, such courses should feature challenging work and provide extensive support. Succeeding at difficult coursework is not only possible for developmental writers, but that success can lead to an increased sense of self-efficacy and confidence (Blaauw-Hara, Tebeau, Borowiak, & Blaauw-Hara, 2020), both of which are associated with student retention and persistence (Brewer & Yucedag-Ozcan, 2013; Travis & Bunde, 2020; Zajacova, Lynch, & Espenshade, 2005). If we care about equity, we need to implement curricula that not only teach writing, but also incorporate elements that help marginalized students build the skills and mindsets that are tied to college success (Jones, 2007).

This is a lot to do in developmental writing! Take heart, though: The students are ready for it. They made a huge decision to go to college, and they want to succeed. Don't strand them in courses that focus on grammatically "perfect" paragraphs; rather, teach them a deeper understanding of how the form of writing can vary depending on purpose and audience, and help them understand how grammar connects with power. Build challenging courses that ask students to do meaningful work. A rich curriculum will not only help students improve their writing skills, but will also help them build a sense of self-efficacy and teach them learning strategies that will give them more control over their own college success.

FACULTY DEVELOPMENT/STAFFING

Many community colleges have separate groups of faculty members who teach developmental and college-level writing. While on the surface it may seem as though it makes sense to have only "specialists" teaching developmental writing, in practice such specialization weakens connections between college-level and developmental writing courses.

Instead, I would advocate for a highly collaborative approach to curriculum design across all levels of writing, and I also think it is a better practice for all writing faculty members to teach both developmental and college-level writing courses. At my former college, the advent of ALP served as the impetus to break down barriers between college-level and developmental writing—certainly because of the curriculum design, but also because the prospect of teaching a course with only ten students was immensely attractive to college-level faculty members. As WPA, I recognized this and worked with my administration to put a requirement in place that anyone who wanted to teach an ALP section needed to be formally trained in the course pedagogy, which we accomplished through a combination of internal and external workshops. In the end, the overwhelming majority of faculty members not only taught both college-level and developmental writing, but were invested in the pedagogy and curriculum of both levels, which made an immense improvement in the curricular cohesion of our writing program.

Equity in a writing program cannot be achieved by one faculty member or one WPA (Craig, 2021; Branson & Sanchez, 2021). In order to be successful, equity needs to become a shared pillar of the whole program—and really, the entire college. Especially at the community college, where writing faculty hail from highly varied scholarly backgrounds and the power dynamics are frequently more complex than in university programs, inclusive collaborative structures are crucial for significant, lasting change (Del Principe, 2020; Holmsten, 2002; Tinoco, 2018). Breaking down the barriers between developmental and college-level faculty is a key part of the process. Don't let people claim ownership over college-level or developmental courses. Instead, build a writing program where faculty work together.

CONCLUSION

I hope I've convinced you that being a community-college WPA provides interesting challenges and can give you the opportunity to make a significant difference to a great many students, including those who have been historically marginalized by our educational system. It is hard work, but it matters. So to finish this chapter off, let me pull together a short list of what you should think about:

- **Start with placement reform:** A multiple-measures instrument is a good place to begin, and it will be a relatively easy sell to other stakeholders at most schools—there is lots of good, large-scale data that's been published. But see if you can push for some sort of directed self-placement, even for a pilot. To learn more, check out the *TYCA White Paper on Placement Reform* (Klausman et al., 2016) and *Writing Placement in Two-Year Colleges* (Nastal et al., 2022).
- **Collapse the developmental pipeline and push for co-requisites:** If you can, put all incoming students into a college-level writing course, and then use your placement system to identify who will need the most help passing that course. Build support mechanisms—ALP courses, STRETCH or studio models, tutoring systems, etc.—to help students pass the college-level course. Take a look at the Community College Research Center's scholarship on different models for developmental education for ideas.
- **Support faculty collaboration:** If your college-level and developmental courses are connected, it just makes sense that your faculty members would be as well. Build the curriculum together, and at least consider having your faculty teach both developmental and college-level writing. Annie Del Principe has several good articles about building faculty connections within a writing program.

Of course, developmental writing reform isn't the only thing you should focus on in order to support equity. Hiring practices and pedagogical training should play a part (Coleman, DeLong, DeVore, Gibney, & Kuhne, 2016), and developing targeted interventions for specific marginalized populations is also important (Baber, Fletcher, & Graham, 2015; Felix & Castro, 2018). Ideally, equity efforts in writing programs should integrate with college-wide initiatives as well (Del Col et al., 2021; O'Brien & Pengilly, 2021). However, developmental writing reform represents a manageable and highly impactful starting point for equity-focused community-college WPAs to make meaningful changes in the academic lives of marginalized students. As Suh, Sullivan, McGee, and Owens (2022) argue, even "little actions" make a difference, so pick a place to begin and start there.

REFERENCES

Adams, P. (2020). Giving hope to the American dream: Implementing a corequisite model of developmental writing. *Composition Studies, 48*(2), 19–34.

Adams, P., Gearhart, S., Miller, R., & Roberts, A. (2009). The accelerated learning program: Throwing open the gates. *Journal of Basic Writing, 28*(2), 50–69.
Adams, P., & McKusick, D. (2014). Steps and missteps: Redesigning, piloting, and scaling a developmental writing program. *New Directions for Community Colleges, 2014*(167), 15–25.
American Association of Community Colleges. (2021). *Fast Facts 2021.* https://www.aacc.nche.edu/wp-content/uploads/2021/03/AACC_2021_FastFacts-1.jpg
Baber, L., Fletcher, R., & Graham, E. (2015). Black men attending community colleges: Examining an institutional approach toward equity. *New Directions for Community Colleges, 172,* 97–107.
Baker-Bell, A. (2020). *Linguistic justice: Black language, literacy, identity, and pedagogy.* Routledge.
Barhoum, S. (2017). Community college developmental writing programs' most promising practices: What the research tells educators. *Community College Journal of Research and Practice, 41*(12), 791–808.
Belfield, C. R., & Crosta, P. M. (2012). Predicting success in college: The importance of placement tests and high school transcripts. *Community College Research Center.* https://ccrc.tc.columbia.edu/media/k2/attachments/predicting-success-placement-tests-transcripts.pdf
Blaauw-Hara, M, Tebeau, C. S., Borowiak, D., & Blaauw-Hara, J. (2020). Is a writing-about-writing approach appropriate for community college developmental writers in a corequisite class? *Composition Studies, 48*(2), 54–73.
Branson, T. S., & Sanchez, J. C. (2021). Programmatic approaches to antiracist writing program policy. *WPA: Writing Program Administration, 44*(3), 71–76.
Brewer, S. A., & Yucedag-Ozcan, A. (2013). Educational persistence: Self-efficacy and topics in a college orientation course. *Journal of College Student Retention: Research, Theory & Practice, 14*(4), 451–465.
Coleman, T. J., DeLong, R., DeVore, K. S., Gibney, S., & Kuhne, M. C. (2016). The risky business of engaging racial equity in writing instruction: A tragedy in five acts. *Teaching English in the Two-Year College, 43*(4), 347–370.
Community College Research Center. (2021). *Community College FAQs.* https://ccrc.tc.columbia.edu/Community-College-FAQs.html
Craig, S. (2021). Your contract grading ain't it. *WPA: Writing Program Administration, 44*(3), 145–146.
Del Col, L., Fowler, A., Mohamed, S., Onuoha, A., Raphael, S. R., Tamkin, E., Tolan, C., Ulsa, C., & Wade, S. (2021). Do something!: Forging constellations of curricular, co-curricular, and community opportunities for anti-racist writing pedagogies at Bates College in Lewiston, Maine. *WPA: Writing Program Administration, 44*(3), 106–113.
Delpit, L. (2006). Lessons from teachers. *Journal of Teacher Education, 57*(3), 220–231.
Del Principe, A. (2020). Cultivating a sustainable TYC writing program: Collaboration, disciplinarity, and faculty governance. *WPA: Writing Program Administration, 43*(3), 54–72.
Di Tommaso, K. (2011). The connection between lack of support service use and background experience in developmental students. Research and Teaching in Developmental Education, 27(2), 5–21. http://www.jstor.org/stable/42802366
Di Tommaso, K. (2016). Evaluating the effectiveness of a non-cognitive assessment instrument. Research and Teaching in Developmental Education, 32(2), 4–22. http://www.jstor.org/stable/44290294
Felix, E. R., & Castro, M. F. (2018). Planning as strategy for improving Black and Latinx student equity: Lessons from nine California community colleges. *Education Policy Analysis Archives, 26*(56). http://dx.doi.org/10.14507/epaa.26.3223

Holmsten, V. (2002). This site under construction: Negotiating space for WPA work in the community college. In S. C. Brown & T. J. Enos (Eds.), *The Writing Program Administrator's Resource* (pp. 449–458). Routledge.

Inoue, A. (2021). *Above the well: An antiracist argument from a boy of color.* Utah State University Press.

Jaggars, S. S., Edgecombe, N., & Stacey, G. W. (2014). What we know about accelerated developmental education. *Community College Research Center.* https://ccrc.tc.columbia.edu/media/k2/attachments/accelerated-developmental-education_1.pdf

Jaggars, S. S., & Stacey, G. W. (2014). What we know about developmental education outcomes. *Community College Research Center.* https://ccrc.tc.columbia.edu/media/k2/attachments/what-we-know-about-developmental-education-outcomes.pdf

Jones, E. (2007). Predicting performance in first-semester college basic writers: Revisiting the role of self-beliefs. *Contemporary Education Psychology,* 33(2), 209–238.

Klausman, J., Roberts, L., Giordano, J., Griffiths, B., Sullivan, P., Swyt, W., Toth, C., Warnke, A., & Williams, A. L. (2016). TYCA White Paper on Placement Reform. *Two-Year College Association.* https://cdn.ncte.org/nctefiles/groups/tyca/placementreform_revised.pdf

Nastal, J., Poe, M., & Toth, C. (2022). *Writing placement in two-year colleges: The pursuit of equity in post-secondary education.* WAC Clearinghouse.

O'Brien, M., & Pengilly, C. (2021). Telling it like it is: A narrative account of designing a race and ethnicity requirement at a PWI in the middle of Black Lives Matter. *WPA: Writing Program Administration, 44*(3), 128–131.

Pattanayak, A. (2017). There is one correct way of writing and speaking. In C. E. Ball & D. M. Loewe (Eds.), *Bad Ideas about Writing* (pp. 82–87). Open Access Textbooks.

Smith, E. (2019). *A critique of anti-racism in rhetoric and composition: The semblance of empowerment.* Lexington Books.

Stachnik, T. M. (2021). Approaches to grammar instruction in the college composition course. *Michigan Academician, 47*(3), 101.

Suh, E. K., Sullivan, P., McGee, B., & Owens, S. Developmental education and the teacher-scholar-activist: An invitation. *Teaching English in the Two-Year College, 49*(4), 325–352.

Tinoco, L. (2018). *Community college writing program administrators: Implementing change through advocacy* (ISBN: 9780438027954). [Doctoral dissertation, University of Texas El Paso] ProQuest Dissertation Publishing.

Toth, C. (2019). Directed self-placement at two-year colleges: A kairotic moment. *Journal of Writing Assessment, 12*(1), n.p. https://escholarship.org/uc/item/6g81k736

Travis, J., & Bunde, J. (2020). Self-regulation in college: The influence of self-efficacy, need satisfaction, and stress on GPA, persistence, and satisfaction. *Current Psychology* (2020). https://doi-org.myaccess.library.utoronto.ca/10.1007/s12144-020-01091-7

Valentine, J. C., Konstantopoulos, S., & Goldrick-Rab, S. (2017). What happens to students placed into developmental education? A meta-analysis of regression discontinuity studies. *Review of Educational Research, 87*(4), 806–833.

Wang, Zhaozhe. (2020). Toward a rhetorical model of directed self-placement. *WPA: Writing Program Administration, 44*(1), 45–67.

Young, V. A. (2014). *Other people's English: Code-meshing, code-switching, and African American Literacy.* Teachers College Press.

Zajacova, A., Lynch, S. M., & Espenshade, T. J. (2005). Self-efficacy, stress, and academic success in college. *Research in Higher Education, 46*, 677–706.

CHAPTER FIVE

Rethinking WPA Work for Open-Access Contexts: Preparing for Literacy Program Responsibilities

ERIN LEHMAN, IVY TECH COMMUNITY COLLEGE OF INDIANA
JOANNE BAIRD GIORDANO, SALT LAKE COMMUNITY COLLEGE

If you are a graduate student or adjunct instructor, prepare for possible work at a community college. With 935 public community colleges hiring and serving over 5 million students annually, your future career may depend on your ability to teach and engage in effective program work at an open-access institution (Statista, 2021). Open-admissions two-year colleges are sites of complex teaching and writing program work that provide essential pathways toward literacy development and degree attainment for millions of students. Close to one-third of US college students enroll at community colleges each year, and almost half take community college courses at some point in their journeys toward a degree (CCRC, n.d.). Because of their open-access and community-focused missions, two-year colleges and other open-admissions institutions serve the broadest range of learners in college writing programs. The diverse and richly varied cultural, social, linguistic, and educational experiences of community college writers provide faculty with rewarding but challenging opportunities for engaging in equity work. A Writing Studies career at a two-year college creates pathways for faculty to apply disciplinary expertise to equity-focused program development work that makes a meaningful difference in the lives of students who might otherwise be excluded from higher education.

However, Writing Studies as a discipline hasn't paid adequate attention to the needs of professionals who work in and coordinate two-year college writing programs. Two-year college scholars have explored the unique characteristics of community college writing programs and their students (Hassel & Giordano, 2009; Tinberg & Nadeau, 2010; Toth et al., 2013; Del Principe & Ihara, 2017). Existing scholarship highlights how our field provides insufficient attention, evidence-based scholarship, and professional support for faculty who engage in teaching, program administration, and other disciplinary work at open-access two-year colleges (Lovas, 2002; Tinberg, 1997; Calhoon-Dillahunt, 2018; Giordano & Hassel, 2019).

Work of other two-year college scholars and our own experiences with administrative and service work convince us that faculty at community colleges and other types of open-access institutions need to prepare for varied and challenging literacy program development and coordination tasks regardless of whether they will ever have a formal writing program administration (WPA) position. Program coordination work at open-access institutions is often distinctly different from WPA work at a research university. Open-access institutions typically offer more literacy courses that require graduate degrees in English and related fields in comparison to selective institutions–including co-requisite support classes, reading courses, and multi-semester writing program sequences. For that reason, both graduate students and experienced instructors without tenure-line positions can anticipate that they may end up participating in program work at a community college.

In this chapter, we draw from our experiences at two-year colleges to explore the program development and coordination work that English professionals do at open-access institutions. We show why English faculty at two-year colleges need an expanded view of program administration work that includes a range of compensated and uncompensated literacy program development responsibilities. Even faculty who don't have plans for a WPA position should anticipate that they will engage in activities that are traditionally associated with WPA work over the course of a career at a two-year college. We share our advice and describe the types of activities that two-year college faculty engage in to contribute to open-access literacy programs.

TRANSITIONING FROM GRADUATE SCHOOL OR OTHER CONTEXTS TO OPEN-ACCESS TEACHING

As English studies professionals transition from graduate school or other types of institutions to two-year colleges, they must adapt to teaching and program administration contexts that are very different from the research institutions where they received their graduate training (Calhoon-Dillahunt, 2011). For example, the

"TYCA Guidelines for Preparing Teachers of English in the Two-Year College" notes that "most graduate programs either explicitly or implicitly professionalize students for careers at four-year institutions, with little or no attention to community colleges, the contexts where many graduate students are likely to make their careers" (Calhoon-Dillahunt et al., 2017, p. 12). Though TYCA guidelines urge graduate programs to create programs and courses that will effectively prepare students for careers at two-year colleges, the reality is that graduate programs provide little to no preparation for open-access work. This curricular deficit includes the lack of literacy study in graduate English program work.

English faculty and program coordinators at two-year colleges engage in faculty-driven work aimed at closing educational opportunity gaps for students who are excluded from universities with admissions standards. To cultivate more equitable and inclusive literacy programs, two-year college English faculty collaborate across disciplines and with administrators. Del Principe (2020) describes the complicated and pressing need for collaboration at open-access institutions: "The specific material conditions of TYC writing programs—including staffing issues, diversity of disciplinary expertise among the faculty, and ambiguous power dynamics—create a setting in which WPAs must build deep and wide collaborative structures that are both strong and radically inclusive" (p. 56). In other words, collaboration at community colleges is essential for improving educational equity and creating effective work environments. For more on the issue of collaborating and listening to colleagues, see Klausman's chapter in this volume. Two-year college English faculty can't remain theoretical in their approaches to equity and inclusion. They need to participate actively in equity work that improves the literate lives of students who experience structural inequities both inside and outside of school.

Open-access institutions open their doors to the most diverse student populations in higher education. Any learner, regardless of need, situation, or educational background is accommodated by the broad missions of two-year colleges. Open-access faculty and staff make space in higher education for all students—including transfer, first-generation, international, dual credit, beginning English language learners, traditional, and GED students. We teach students who cannot be in other places, due to their personal backgrounds, academic records, location, language barriers, test scores, or income level. Open-access institutions support laid-off workers, local employment needs, and college graduates who need to earn a credential to change careers. This radical accessibility requires open-access instructors to be well-versed in the institutional and community resources available to students and to provide flexibility for individual student needs.

Erin's Advice

As the Faculty Lead (similar to a school dean) for Arts, Sciences, and Education courses within the online department of a large, statewide, community college, I wish my graduate preparation had included experience with open-access institutions as well as guidance on navigating this field for my future career. But I suspect that open access institutions were excluded from my graduate training–or perhaps overlooked as low priority–because they're not seen as desirable employment. If your graduate training excludes open access institutions, you should question why. You should seek out experiences with community colleges to consider a career there.

Before starting my career at a two-year college, I was unaware of open-access institutions. As a child, I once attended an evening class at Coastal Carolina Community College in North Carolina with my mom. Full time secretary and wife to a Marine, the sole parent while her spouse was deployed, maintaining her twelfth home in thirteen years, my mom was taking classes in CCCC's education program. This experience–nontraditional students, many of them working parents, aiming toward a better life by taking evening classes at the local institution–mirrors what I see teaching at a two-year college today. If you're interested in meaningful writing program work with diverse learners, you should seriously consider the many and varied career opportunities at open-access institutions.

Joanne's Advice

My literacy program work for two different institutions has included coordinating and developing curriculum for developmental reading, writing, ESL, corequisite support, and online courses as well as responsibilities for placement, writing centers, and faculty development. Throughout my first decade at two-year colleges in different states, I viewed my time at those institutions as temporary stopping points before moving onto different (but not necessarily better) work. The educational equity missions of those colleges were aligned with my professional interests, but I struggled to figure out how to create a sustainable career for myself at campuses that served students with complex needs.

For many years, I couldn't shake the idea that I was unqualified for the work even though my institutions repeatedly asked me to do increasingly more challenging program coordination tasks. It took me years to realize that practically no early career Writing Studies expert or other literacy educator is adequately prepared to work in open-access programs. Anyone who is fortunate enough to receive full-time work off or on the tenure track at a two-year college should expect intensive on the job learning and ongoing professional development to build the skills required for contributing to literacy programs at their institutions. For example, two-year college faculty often broaden their professional engagement beyond CCCC and CWPA to include reading, conference attendance, and professional activities from organizations focused on student learning (for example, the Two-Year College English Association, the College Reading and Learning Association, and the National Organization for Student Success).

PREPARING FOR PROGRAM DEVELOPMENT RESPONSIBILITIES AT COMMUNITY COLLEGES

Many new two-year college faculty participate in writing program development and change work regardless of whether they have a formal WPA position. Snyder (2020) explains, "Anyone who might be interested in this work should prepare for it as early and as often as possible. Researchers at TYCs can embrace nontraditional career trajectories through TYC WPA positions" (p. 116). Unlike many four-year universities with a limited number of faculty who do program work through WPA positions with oversight for graduate students, most two-year college faculty can expect to participate in varied types of literacy program coordination and development work across their careers.

Coordinating and developing two-year college literacy programs takes many different forms with responsibilities that typically change over time and require faculty to adapt to evolving institutional priorities, student needs, and financial realities. Examples of writing program oversight and coordination responsibilities for two-year college English faculty include tenure-line and non-tenured WPA positions; department and division chair or associate dean positions with writing program responsibilities; program committee members; online course developers; placement coordinators; and writing center directors. Community college English faculty also coordinate other types of literacy programs, including developmental education, reading, ESL, corequisite support, and first-year experience.

Some two-year college faculty are hired specifically to do program administration work. However, most are appointed by administrators, elected by other faculty, required to participate to fulfill service obligations for tenure or promotion, or given an opportunity to volunteer for the work with or without compensation. At universities, faculty often wait to do program development and coordination work until they have time to transition to their institutions or after tenure. However, at two-year colleges, new full-time faculty often do program work immediately as part of contractual service obligations or as an institutional expectation.

Research from the Two-Year College English Association (TYCA) details the types of program work that community college English faculty do as part of their leadership roles and service responsibilities (Suh et al., 2021). In 2019, a TYCA task force conducted a survey that explored workload and working conditions for two-year college English faculty. The 1,062 respondents reported that they engage in varied types of disciplinary service work that is typically associated with writing program administration, including curriculum development, assessment, faculty training, developmental education, writing across the curriculum, and placement. Three out of four participants had a leadership role on their campuses with 20% reporting that they had responsibilities as a coordinator, department chair, or division chair. Other roles included serving as committee chairs and as lead instructors. The results of the survey also illustrate that many two-year college faculty take on the work of leading programs through service rather than dedicated administrative positions. One-third of participants in the survey indicated that they aren't compensated for their leadership roles, while the remaining respondents indicated that they receive stipends, course releases, reassigned time, and/or adjustments to their workload.

Erin's Advice

Though I was an English program chair, responsible for all writing classes at my campus and involved in placement work, I never considered myself a WPA. The only self-identifying WPAs I knew (and still know) taught at four-year institutions. You should understand that the most complex and cutting-edge writing program work is happening at two-year colleges, though those doing the work may not see themselves as WPAs. For example, part of my chair role involved working with online English courses in 2010, which I found exciting and challenging. It wasn't until years later that I saw my experience with online courses as a viable and desirable career path. You can prepare for a compensated writing program position now by paying attention to the trends and gaps in writing classes and programs where you teach. Writing program work at a two-year college requires problem-solving skills from everyone in the program. As needs arise, you can expect and should prepare to step into developing administrative responsibilities.

Joanne's Advice

When I started my career, I couldn't imagine the diverse types of work that I would do to contribute to two-year college English programs. I had to change my thinking about writing programs and my own work as an instructor to encompass a much more expansive view of how literacy courses and programs support students' development as college readers and writers.

What surprised me most about working for a two-year college was how quickly I was asked to take on program development responsibilities even as a contingent faculty member. I co-created a new intercultural communication curriculum in my initial semester at my first two-year institution. In my first semester at the next institution, I was asked to develop a reading program. Within the next few years, I created an ESOL (English for Speakers of Other Languages) program, co-developed a placement process, collaborated with Student Affairs on campus retention, and served as an assessment coordinator. None of these experiences were technically WPA work, but all of them required me to build on my disciplinary expertise and do program administration tasks. I've also had to continue preparing myself for new types of work across my entire career.

My work responsibilities for the past year as a tenured faculty member include chairing the integrated reading and writing program committee, coordinating placement, facilitating an inclusive teaching program, and leading a team in designing a new corequisite writing studio program and related open educational resource. I do that work through a combination of reassigned time (i.e., teaching fewer courses), overload stipends, and uncompensated committee service that I can count toward my annual faculty evaluation.

DOING PROGRAM COORDINATION WORK AS A SERVICE RESPONSIBILITY

Service (especially for literacy programs) is usually an expectation of full-time English employment at two-year colleges. But accountability for that work is often collective rather than individual. Faculty at two-year colleges should anticipate that they will likely do program work some (or even all) of the time in collaboration with colleagues as part of their institutional service.

Two-year college writing programs often lack a dedicated WPA (Charlton & Rose, 2009; Klausman, 2008, 2013). Instead, writing program work happens through committee assignments, which can be given to a single writing program committee or divided among different committees, teams, or individuals. For example, some faculty might have responsibilities for curriculum development while others work on placement. Some departments or programs don't have a compensated administrative position beyond an associate dean, dean, or other administrator who might not have expertise in English or postsecondary literacy. At these institutions, faculty members sometimes use their disciplinary expertise to participate in writing program change work through processes that operate informally outside normal systems for administering a program.

Doing program administrative work outside the support of a dedicated position is a challenging endeavor (Calhoun-Dillahunt, 2011; Spiegel et al., 2020) that requires both disciplinary expertise and training. In the *White Paper on Two-Year College English Faculty Workload*, TYCA advocates for "compensated program coordinator positions with permanent budget lines rather than coordinating programs through service" (Giordano et al., 2021, p. 7). The white paper explains how a dedicated program coordinator position benefits all faculty in a literacy program: "Two-year college English programs can also create more sustainable working conditions for all instructors when one or more individuals within the program have compensated time to mentor instructors, develop resources, work on curricular issues, and coordinate program changes as well as the authority to evaluate and assess the work" (Giordano et al., 2021, p. 7). However, the existing lack of WPA positions at two-year colleges means that graduate students and current two-year college faculty need to become ready to engage in program work and then continue to learn how to adapt their administrative skills over the course of their careers as their institutions continually shift to new equity initiatives and financial realities.

Erin's Advice

You can expect to do program work across the institution doing tasks that graduate school never prepared you for. It's common for English program chairs and faculty at two-year colleges to become the go-to people for academic and non-academic initiatives. Typical English program chairs and faculty perform "extra" tasks for the campus (and anything else their vice-chancellors or deans ask) and teach four or more courses each semester. Though this might seem overwhelming, service work is valuable professional development. For example, I had the opportunity to participate in placement initiatives, the selection of a new Learning Management System (LMS), and explore and implement "project-based learning," and Universal Design for Learning (UDL). These practical and unpaid early service experiences supplemented my graduate training and broadened my professional experience and knowledge, ultimately saving me time later in my career when I had more demands and responsibilities. You should engage in open-access administrative tasks and projects for what they can be–valuable job training.

Joanne's Advice

Expect to do almost all two-year college program responsibilities collaboratively even if you have a dedicated program administration position. For example, all of my current program responsibilities happen through collaborative teamwork. Even though I have program development tasks that I do independently, I share that work for colleague feedback. Most major decisions take place after the entire committee or team has time for discussion and deliberation. When I had a dedicated, compensated program coordinator position, I still worked collaboratively with colleagues both off and on the tenure track who served on relevant committees, used program materials and provided feedback, and voted on program policies and curriculum through shared governance processes. Working with colleagues on program teams taught me how to do collaborative research and writing, which has helped me become a productive teacher-scholar.

REIMAGINING OPEN-ACCESS WPA WORK AS LITERACY COORDINATION

Two-year college faculty often participate in a range of literacy-focused program development and coordination activities that aren't normally part of writing program administration at institutions with more selective admissions standards, including developing or coordinating programs for co-requisite support, developmental education, placement reforms, reading, ESOL, and study strategies (Ostman, 2013). They may also coordinate or have leadership responsibilities for interdisciplinary programs that build on Writing Studies expertise (for example, writing across the curriculum, first-year experience, learning centers, faculty development, distance and online education, dual credit, assessment, and accreditation). All of these activities draw from disciplinary experience while also creating opportunities for English faculty to develop new professional expertise. These responsibilities may fall outside the range of WPA work that graduate students and new faculty anticipate doing across a career, even though they are a routine and ordinary part of how Writing Studies faculty (and English studies professionals more broadly) take on leadership roles and do program work at two-year colleges.

Erin's Advice

As a candidate for two-year college program administrative work, you should understand that the open-access career field is open in a way that the four-year career field typically is not. Despite little formal training in online learning, teaching English at a community college has led me to online teaching and administration as online asynchronous enrollment–now one-third of my institution's enrollment–has created new roles and departments. This online enrollment growth has been a developing trend long before the pandemic changed all of our lives in 2020.

My "WPA and more" work–complicated by issues of placement, technology, student success and information literacy–kept me up-to-date on higher education trends and changes, and prepared me for the future. My work with online courses is far beyond anything I could have imagined in graduate school. If you explore program and literacy coordination work at open-access institutions, your future WPA career has the potential to be challenging, complicated, and exciting in ways you cannot anticipate today.

Joanne's Advice

At a two-year college, anticipate program work that is much more diverse than the scope of a university writing program. In the decades of participating in open-access program development and coordination work, I shifted my thinking entirely away from focusing on writing programs even though much of my work has been connected to writing courses and traditional WPA responsibilities. I now think about two-year college English faculty as literacy educators and view their program-level responsibilities as literacy program coordination regardless of whether they have a compensated administrator job. My thinking has changed because my own open-access English work has gone beyond writing programs to encompass reading, ESOL, learning centers, online education, cultural diversity, faculty development, and retention work. I have had leadership roles in initiatives and programs that don't exist at selective universities. Faculty who aren't able to develop flexible strategies for adapting to diverse literacy coordination tasks beyond a writing program have limited opportunities for professional contributions and growth at open-access institutions.

CONCLUSION AND QUESTIONS FOR REFLECTION AND DISCUSSION

By re-envisioning ourselves in our careers as Writing Studies professionals doing diverse literacy education work at open-access institutions, our careers are broader and more complex than we expected, which has been both challenging and fulfilling. As candidates for open-access work, prepare for program development work now by learning about literacy work early in your career. You may do more varied program work than you expected, and it is unlikely to fall under the umbrella of a compensated and titled WPA position.

With literacy and higher education rapidly changing, and two-year college writing programs dynamically meeting new and shifting student needs, program work at open access institutions is critical, evolving, and cutting-edge. For the future of higher education equity and access, we hope more graduate students and experienced English faculty explore and re-envision their careers at two-year colleges.

As we conclude this chapter, we encourage you to reflect on and discuss the following questions:

- If you have never attended or worked at a community college, what similarities and differences do you notice between our descriptions of two-year college literacy program work and the program coordination activities that take place at your current institution(s)?
- How does the concept of literacy program coordination help you understand the English studies work that takes place at community colleges? What types of experiences might prepare you for literacy program responsibilities that go beyond traditional WPA work?
- How does open-access education reduce social inequities for students who are excluded from higher education at institutions with admissions standards? How might an understanding of the open-admissions function of community colleges prepare you for work at a two-year college?
- If you attended a community college, how did your experiences at that institution shape your thinking about student learning and literacy education? How might you draw from your experiences as a community college student to contribute to professional conversations about educational access and equity within Writing Studies?
- Have you experienced or observed bias against attending or working at community colleges, including within Writing Studies? How does bias against teaching and learning at community colleges reflect hierarchies within higher education that perpetuate inequities? What strategies might Writing Studies professionals use to eliminate bias against community colleges within our discipline?
- To what extent have your graduate courses and teaching experiences prepared you to support learners from diverse educational, linguistic, and cultural backgrounds in open-access contexts? What types of professional experiences and learning do you need to have to prepare yourself for work at a community college?

REFERENCES

Calhoon-Dillahunt, C. (2011). “Writing programs without administrators: Frameworks for successful writing programs in the two-year college.” *WPA: Writing Program Administration, 35*(1), 118–134.

Calhoon-Dillahunt, C. (2018). “Returning to our roots: Creating the capacity and conditions for change.” *College Composition and Communication*, *70*(2), 273–293.

Calhoon-Dillahunt, C., Jensen, D. L., Johnson, S. Z., Tinberg, H., & Toth, C. (2017). “TYCA guidelines for preparing teachers of English in the two-year college.” *Teaching English in the Two-Year College*, *45*(1), 8–19.

Charlton, J., & Rose, S. K. (2009). “Twenty more years in the WPA’s progress.” *WPA: Writing Program Administration*, *33*(1), 114–145.

Community College Research Center. (n.d.). “Community college FAQs.” Retrieved from https://ccrc.tc.columbia.edu/Community-College-FAQs.html.

Del Principe, A, & Ihara, R. (2017). “A long look at reading in the community college: A longitudinal analysis of student reading experiences.” *Teaching English in the Two-Year College*, *25*(2), 83–206.

Del Principe, A. (2020). Cultivating a sustainable TYC writing program: Collaboration, disciplinarity, and faculty governance. *WPA: Writing Program Administration*, *43*(3), 54–72.

Giordano, J. B., & Hassel, H. (2019). “Intersections of privilege and access: Writing programs, disciplinary knowledge, and the shape of a field.” *WPA: Writing Program Administration*. *43*(1), 33–53.

Giordano, J. B., Griffiths, B., Hassel, H., Higgins, K., Klausman, J., Snyder, S., Suh, E., Sullivan, P., Tinoco, L., & Wegner, M. (2021). *White paper on two-year college English faculty workload.* Two-Year College English Association. https://ncte.org/wp-content/uploads/2021/04/TYC_English_Faculty_Workload.pdf

Hassel, H., & Giordano, J. B. (2009). “Transfer institutions, transfer of knowledge: The development of rhetorical adaptability and underprepared writers.” *Teaching English in the Two-Year College, 37*(1), 24–40.

Klausman, J. (2008). “Mapping the terrain: The two-year college writing program administrator.” *Teaching English in the Two-Year College*, *35*(3), 238–251.

Klausman, J. (2013). “Toward a definition of a writing program at a two-year college: You say you want a revolution?” *Teaching English in the Two-Year College*, *40*(3), 257–273.

Lovas, J. C. (2002). “All good writing develops at the edge of risk.” *College Composition and Communication*, *54*(2), 64–88.

Ostman, H. (2013). *Writing Program Administration and the Community College*. Parlor Press.

Snyder, S. (2020). Preparing to become a two-year college writing program administrator. *WPA: Writing Program Administration*, *43*(3), 106–120.

Spiegel, C. L., Jensen, D., & Johnson, S. Z. (2020). “Don’t call it a comeback: Two-year college WPA, tactics, collaboration, flexibility, sustainability.” *Writing Program Administration*, *43*(3), 7–18.

Statista. (2021, November 15). *Community colleges in the United States: Statistics & facts*. https://www.statista.com/topics/3468/community-colleges-in-the-united-states/

Suh, E., Giordano, J. B., Griffiths, B., Hassel, H., & Klausman, J. (2021). “The profession of teaching English in the two-year college: Findings from the 2019 TYCA workload survey.” *Teaching-English in the Two-Year College*, *4*(3), 332–339.

Tinberg, H. B. (1997). *Border talk: Writing and knowing in the two-year college*. National Council of Teachers of English.

Tinberg, H., & Nadeau, J. P. (2010). *The community college writer: Exceeding expectations*. Southern Illinois University Press.

Toth, C., Griffiths, B., & Thirolf, K. (2013). "'Distinct and significant': Professional identities of two-year college English faculty." *College Composition and Communication*, *65*(1), 90–116.

CHAPTER SIX

Ready for a Career and a Family: Experiencing (In)Fertility as an Early Career WPA

KAITLIN CLINNIN, UNIVERSITY OF NEVADA, LAS VEGAS
JENNIFER E. EIDUM, ELON UNIVERSITY
MORGAN HANSON, UNIVERSITY OF SOUTHERN INDIANA
MARIYA TSEPTSURA, UNIVERSITY OF ARIZONA

In graduate school, we asked trusted mentors about having a family while working in academia. Even though we were all fortunate to be part of graduate programs with strong feminist faculty, family planning was still a *verboten* topic. The reality is that academics who choose to have a family often face substantial professional challenges, including: discrimination during a job search, subpar insurance coverage for reproductive health, lack of family leave time (especially for graduate students and contingent faculty), continued professional responsibilities while on leave, inconsistent policies for tenure clock extensions, limited and expensive child care, campuses that prohibit minors, inconsistent teaching and meeting schedules, professional events scheduled outside of business hours, and regular travel for conferences and research.

Despite knowing the challenges of having a family and an academic career, we asked about having families anyway. The advice we received varied from program to program, mentor to mentor. Some advice dealt with timing: planning the ideal time to have a child so as to be as least disruptive as possible to inflexible graduate programs' milestones and funding deadlines (have a child before/after candidacy exams), job searches (definitely do not have a child while searching for a job), tenure timelines (have a child before/after mid-tenure/post-tenure), or the academic calendar (have a child as early in the summer as possible to maximize time off). Some advice dealt with strategies for navigating institutional systems such as learning about family and medical leave policies (if any existed), using these policies, and requesting funding and tenure clock extensions. Much of the advice dealt with balancing careers and families, although the balance was often skewed towards the career ("Every child you have is a book you don't write").

One aspect of the advice remained consistent: it was always assumed that family planning was completely within one's control, that one could choose if and when to become pregnant, and that a pregnancy would result in a child. Unfortunately, the assumed control over our bodies and our family growth has not been our experience, nor is it the experience of many. Our collaborative writing team has experienced infertility, invasive fertility testing and treatments, and recurrent pregnancy losses while in graduate school, on the job market, and in tenure-track positions. We have scheduled work meetings around doctors' appointments, taken ovulation and pregnancy tests in campus bathroom stalls, injected fertility drugs in offices, taken calls from sick beds, and met with students and colleagues while bleeding. We have had emergency surgery for ectopic pregnancies but still graded final papers. We have lost pregnancies while presenting at conferences and while giving job talks.

Our stories are not uncommon. One in eight couples experience infertility, defined as the inability to conceive within a year of trying (CDC, 2021). One in four pregnant people experience a pregnancy loss (Dougas & Slane, 2021). The likelihood of experiencing fertility issues increases with age, which is especially an issue for academics because peak fertility typically coincides with graduate school or early careers. The "best" biological time to have a child is potentially the worst time for professional stability. Academics must try to balance biological and professional clocks if they want both a family and a career (for more on planning families and careers, see Green's chapter in this volume). But (in)fertility throws a wrench into both clocks.

In this chapter, we share our experiences with (in)fertility and pregnancy losses as graduate students and early-career Writing Program Administrators. Our (in)fertility experiences coincided with kairotic professional spaces (Price, 2011) like campus visits and conferences, alongside teaching, research, and service requirements for tenure and promotion. Our experiences heightened our sense of professional and bodily precarity; more support could have helped us navigate the losses we experienced personally (bodily autonomy, pregnancies) and professionally (productivity, credibility). We use a Disability Studies framework to offer mentorship and support to early-career WPAs before and during (in)fertility journeys. We also suggest ways that senior faculty and administrators can create workplaces that accommodate early-career scholars' paths to parenthood.

NAVIGATING KAIROTIC SPACES IN ACADEMIA

As WPAs trying to begin careers and families, we encountered situations where our professional and personal goals conflicted. Our professional responsibilities did not leave much room for our family planning, and our experiences with infertility and loss also threatened our careers. We find Disability and Writing Studies scholar Margaret Price's (2011) conception of kairotic spaces and related *topoi* helpful to frame the interactions and expectations for our work and how these expectations conflicted with our personal needs.

Kairotic spaces are "less formal, often unnoticed, areas of academe where knowledge is produced and power is exchanged" such as classroom discussions, conferences, and job interviews (Price, 2011, p. 61). In these spaces, individuals socialize with others in real-time. The interactions are unscripted yet highly regulated by behavioral and social norms. Price identifies presence, productivity, and collegiality as *topoi* that govern success in academic kairotic spaces. Successful navigation of a kairotic space requires that one is located in the space (presence) and perceived to contribute actively (productivity), and that these contributions are valued (collegiality). Kairotic spaces are challenging for a wide range of people—those with physical and mental health disabilities, as well as those with different cultural, language, and economic backgrounds. Physical access to the space is one major barrier, but the unspoken (racist, sexist, ableist, classist) behavior and social norms also separate insiders and outsiders. The stakes for performing well in these kairotic spaces are high; employment, resources, and careers may be on the line.

WPA work includes additional academic kairotic spaces such as meetings with students, program instructors, campus faculty, and administrators. The resolution to a student grade dispute, an instructor complaint, or an administrator's request requires that WPAs perform according to expectations within that kairotic space. Our effectiveness as WPAs is partially determined based on our presence, productivity, and collegiality in the classroom, the hallway, and the campus board room. And yet, our ability to be present, to be productive, to be collegial is fundamentally changed and challenged by our (in)fertility journeys.

Our experiences with pregnancy, pregnancy loss, and infertility reveal other ways that academic spaces are inaccessible. As rhetorician and disability studies scholar Jay Dolmage (2017) demonstrates, higher education is structurally ableist, or composed of structures that privilege able-bodied individuals and limit access to disabled individuals (pp. 53–54). One manifestation of structural ableism in higher education is the difficulty that disabled academics experience when trying to obtain necessary accommodations for their jobs, such as accessible classrooms, flexible work schedules, or captioning or ASL interpreters at meetings (Kerschbaum et al., 2017). It is difficult enough for those with visible, documented, and publicly acknowledged disabilities to receive the accommodations to which they are legally entitled. Accommodations for (in)fertility are almost non-existent due to structural ableism, the invisible nature of (in)fertility, the new legal uncertainties surrounding reproductive care, and the cultural silence surrounding reproduction.

With an expanded understanding of kairotic spaces that includes administrative spaces occupied by WPAs, we break the silence that typifies (in)fertility with our stories. We use kairotic spaces and the *topoi* of presence, productivity, and collegiality as a theoretical framework to understand our lived experiences and to identify sources of the tension between our personal and professional aspirations, as well as ways to resolve these tensions by reimagining professional expectations.

PRESENCE, PRODUCTIVITY, AND COLLEGIALITY FOR THE (IN)FERTILE WPA

As early career WPAs, we strove to be (and to be perceived as) productive and collegial members of our departments by eagerly engaging in our research, teaching, and service projects. But (in)fertility challenged our ability to do so. In the following sections, we share our stories as WPAs trying to start families and apply Price's framework to examine how professional expectations of presence, productivity, and collegiality caused a conflict between our professional and personal lives.

Some of the most cliched professional advice relates to "showing up" or being present, and academia is no exception. Presence is the external perception that a faculty member is physically, mentally, and emotionally present at work. Presence is about visibility or being seen as an active member of the department, institution, and profession. Presence (or absence) is one way to evaluate job performance and commitment based on the assumption that one's physical presence reflects one's professional commitment. Presence also includes virtual availability, the expectations for which increased during the COVID-19 remote working conditions. Employees demonstrated their virtual presence by attending constant online meetings (and experiencing the accompanying "Zoom fatigue") and quickly responding to greater email volume. As the pandemic public health directives loosen and institutions continue their "return to campus," it remains to be seen how professional expectations shift again to balance physical and virtual presence.

Whether physical or virtual, presence is an unstated expectation for WPAs. WPAs are more often physically present on campus than other non-administrative faculty due to the position responsibilities. Typical WPA tasks like advising, mentoring, scheduling, observing, and meetings combined with typical faculty responsibilities for classes and office hours means that WPAs spend a lot of time on campus (Graziano et al., 2020). Even without formally scheduled meetings, being present on campus allows WPAs to develop the relationships (with students, instructors, campus colleagues, administrators) that are often foundational to a strong writing program. A WPA is also expected to be virtually present, whether by attending online meetings or by quickly, accurately, and empathetically responding to a deluge of emails from students, faculty, and administrators.

However, infertility and pregnancy loss challenge one's ability to be present. Prenatal care requires regular doctor's appointments; fertility treatments require more appointments for testing, monitoring, and medical interventions. And these are only the physical effects. Women who experience infertility and loss often also experience depression and anxiety (Rooney & Domar, 2018), which may make it difficult to focus on work. Morgan describes difficulties with being present during her infertility journey:

> *Whether I'm pregnant or I'm in the middle of infertility treatments or I'm attempting to exist as a "normal" woman, I find that I am constantly distracted. I obsess how each step in each day will affect the outcome of my fertility, pregnancy, or infertility treatment. This obsession with my (in)fertility made participation difficult throughout my graduate WPA and tenure-track WPA years. I have almost always chosen infertility treatments over meetings, research, and networking. I am almost always distracted throughout my workday, wondering if the food I'm eating or the exercise I'm doing or the stress I'm experiencing will cure or further harm my fertility hopes. During infertility treatments, I can't physically attend every meeting, due to the time-sensitive nature of infertility treatments. I don't participate fully in these meetings at the height of my infertility stress, and, to be frank, I have no desire to.*

Morgan's ability to be present in her administrative role is challenged by the amount of time, energy, effort, and mental load that her fertility treatments require. Without disclosing her infertility treatments and the effects on her work, Morgan risks being labeled by her colleagues as not present with the associated connotations about substandard job performance and lacking commitment. However, such a personal disclosure also carries professional risks and may lead to further concerns about her performance and long-term career aspirations.

But to be present is not enough—one must also be productive and collegial, which are standards used to evaluate one's professional contributions. Productivity in an academic context refers to the institutional requirements for tenure and promotion in teaching, research, and service. Productivity for WPAs is especially problematic as expectations are often higher in the service category while maintaining standard expectations for research and teaching. Although the work of writing program administration is intellectual labor (CWPA, 1998), traditionally it is not considered part of research or teaching, rendering it part of the service category that is less valued in performance evaluations. WPAs must be as productive as non-administrative faculty according to the evaluation standards, but they must also demonstrate excellence in their administrative work.

(In)fertility and pregnancy loss challenge academic and WPA productivity. Time that could be spent on professional responsibilities is instead spent in doctors' offices. As Morgan's story shows, the fertility treatment side effects like headaches, nausea, and fatigue may make it difficult to focus or complete job-related tasks. Although popular media presents pregnancy loss as a quick process, many losses last several days or weeks, and while the physical recovery can be lengthy, the mental and emotional healing may take longer. Meanwhile, without accommodations for (in)fertility, the professional evaluation standards remain the same, and programmatic work must continue.

As early career WPAs without secure positions, we felt pressured to maintain our productivity despite infertility and losses. We pushed through physical, mental, and emotional pain lest our productivity be questioned. Jennifer shares her experience prioritizing her service and teaching productivity during an ectopic pregnancy, a life-threatening medical emergency:

> *I was on a department hiring committee, and we had a full day of phone interviews. It was during the end of the fall semester rush, and I had just gotten an exciting positive pregnancy test. Because of previous losses, I was closely monitored. I woke early for blood tests at the clinic an hour away from campus, then raced back to campus to conduct phone interviews. That afternoon, during a short break, I got the call from the clinic: I was pregnant, but the levels were lower than hoped. We were in the zone of uncertainty. I cried from the worry of it all on the couch in the department lounge as colleagues stopped by with concern. I reluctantly shared a bit about what was going on, pulled myself together, and began another interview.*
>
> *More tests revealed that that pregnancy was in the wrong place. Later that week, I was sent from the doctor's office by ambulance to the hospital for a ruptured ectopic pregnancy. I took two weeks to heal over the winter break and then taught our four-week intensive winter term course. Luckily, it was a course I had taught previously and needed little prep (and it was a fun class that distracted me from my feelings).*
>
> *The recognized (yet far too limited) accommodations for childbirth stand in contrast to the lack of accommodations for infertility and pregnancy loss. Any leave taken for infertility or pregnancy loss can count against any future leave for a healthy pregnancy and a living child. In my case, there was no official leave policy for any faculty sick days—you and your department chair figured it out as you go along. I felt tacit pressure to keep my family planning to myself so as not to impact my career aspirations. I took no time from work to heal physically and, perhaps more importantly, grieve my losses. The only accommodation I requested was a delay in turning in my annual review.*

Like Jennifer, Kaitlin also found it impossible to stop her administrative and research work for a pregnancy loss:

I went to campus after a doctor told me that I was going to lose the pregnancy. My husband encouraged me to stay home, but there was an important meeting on campus that day with state and institutional administrators about a major policy change that would directly impact the writing program. I needed to be present to advocate for our program. During the meeting, I talked with deans, vice provosts, and system representatives about the policy and our resource needs while the miscarriage began. I tried my best to appear normal while stepping out of the conference room frequently to attend to physical needs. At the last meeting of the day with a colleague and a supervisee, I began crying and shared that I was having a miscarriage. They were surprised and told me to go home, but I told them we needed to continue because of a coming deadline. We met our deadline.

The following day, I traveled to a conference where I was a workshop leader with several colleagues in a different department. I debated canceling, but the conference felt too important to my career and professional relationships. I worried that showing any sort of sign of illness (including pregnancy) or lack of professionalism would damage my future working relationships. I attended panels, facilitated the workshop, and went to a few social events before giving up on the rest of the conference experience. I was too exhausted and in too much pain. I spent the rest of the conference in my room, grieving the pregnancy loss and worrying about my future family and career.

Jennifer and Kaitlin felt that they must continue their professional obligations and maintain high standards even with serious health complications. Slowing or pausing their productivity would have required disclosing information about their personal lives that they feared would jeopardize their careers and would offer little relief from their professional responsibilities. Our narratives also offer insight into another standard by which WPAs are unofficially measured: collegiality. In contrast to productivity's seemingly more objective standards, collegiality refers to the intangible, personable qualities exhibited during professional encounters. Collegiality measures how an individual conforms to normative expectations such as "personal affection, deferential behavior, or agreement" (Price, 2011, p. 115). These norms often exclude individuals based on race, gender, sexuality, disability, class, or other identity categories. Although the AAUP condemns using collegiality to evaluate performance, collegiality is often an unspoken criterion for evaluation in tenure and promotion cases (AAUP, 2016). And even if it is not a factor in evaluations, collegiality can benefit one's career through partnerships, collaborations, and other career advancements that increase one's academic productivity.

Collegiality routinely influences hiring decisions. When factors such as a candidate's research, teaching, and service potential appear equal, the "intangibles" like collegiality play a decisive role in hiring decisions (Johnson, 2014; see Mecenas's chapter in this collection for more on how gender, race, and sexuality intersect with collegiality). Mariya's narrative exemplifies how presence and collegiality are intertwined in the academic job market experience:

I found out I was pregnant in December 2018, when I was finishing writing my dissertation and interviewing for an academic position. I was invited to a campus visit. Five days before my scheduled visit, my miscarriage started. Two days before my first campus visit for a prospective WPA position, I did my mock job talk, during which a well-meaning faculty member remarked that I needed to "smile more." I did not dispute the validity of the advice, but at the time I found it impossible to follow as I was in the middle of a miscarriage.

My doctor sent me for an emergency ultrasound to confirm that it was not an ectopic pregnancy. The day before leaving for my campus visit, I spent over 6 hours in the ER getting an ultrasound exam. The ER doctor's advice was to stay in bed for the next week and monitor my symptoms. However, rescheduling my campus visit seemed out of the question: I worried that I would risk losing the invitation and that disclosing my health issues would draw unwanted attention to the simple fact that I am a woman who might have children soon. As a non-native English speaker and a recent immigrant, I was already worried about facing prejudice; I did not want to add more reasons for the search committee to consider me a lesser candidate.

I managed the campus visit thanks to high doses of pain killing medications, frequent bathroom visits, and every possible sanitary product I could find at the drugstore. I ended up getting and accepting the job despite the difficulties I had staying present and "smiling more."

Mariya's story points to the inflexibility and unreasonable expectations of the traditional academic job market norms that, as Price puts it, disqualify candidates who are not always able to "operate smoothly" in kairotic spaces.

From our experiences with (in)fertility we offer a fourth *topos*: vulnerability. We existed in personal and professional liminal spaces: the liminal space between infertility and pregnancy in a culture where such topics are not openly shared (Reiheld, 2015), the space between disability and ability, the space between temporary and permanent employment. Our liminal positionality heightened our sense of vulnerability and lack of control. Our bodies and our family plans were not within our control no matter how hard we worked at optimizing our bodies, how many tests or procedures we endured, or how much we hoped for a successful outcome. Professionally, it appeared that our career aspirations were controllable; if we showed up, worked hard, and smiled more, we would be able to achieve that tenure-track job and, eventually, tenure. In reality, academic jobs are nearly as capricious as bodies, and our bodies seemed to jeopardize our careers. We each felt a sense of fear: fear that we could not get or stay pregnant, fear that the treatments would not work, fear that something serious was wrong with our bodies. While privately carrying these bodily fears, we also felt professional fears: fear of being found out and experiencing discrimination, fear that we could not meet expectations, fear that we could not pause our professional trajectories lest they end.

Yet we have found power in our fear and vulnerability. We met online because we individually disclosed our stories; collectively, we felt empowered to share our experiences and hope to encourage others to do the same. By writing about our experiences in professional publications, we blend the professional and personal to meet productivity expectations in our workplaces and perhaps to explain gaps in our presence, productivity, and collegiality. While we recognize that not everyone is in a privileged position to disclose, as a group we found that silence surrounding infertility and pregnancy loss was more personally and professionally harmful than the risk of speaking out. Now that we are not-quite-so-early-career WPAs, we hope to use our positions to change professional expectations so that others do not experience the same challenges that we did.

CONCLUDING THOUGHTS: COMPASSION AND CALL TO ACTIONS

Although our histories of (in)fertility and professional trajectories differ, the commonalities speak to the existence of a collective struggle and a need for broader action. We each struggled with the expectations for early career WPAs while struggling to create our desired families. Since these experiences, we have been fortunate to navigate our professional and (in)fertility journeys in different ways. Thanks to fertility treatments, adoption, and time, each of us has grown our family. We have progressed in our different career paths despite substantial challenges as caregivers.

Our stories are not about overcoming a temporary obstacle. We believe that sharing our stories can help create more "inclusive environments for all WPAs, not only at the time they are hired, but in ways that account for the embodied realities that come with time" (Vidali, 2015, p. 47). We can create writing programs and institutional workplaces that are designed to be more inclusive for those who are experiencing (in)fertility, and such spaces will be more inclusive for all. In this spirit, we offer compassion to those who need it and a call to action to those who can take it.

To our readers who are experiencing (in)fertility, we extend our compassion and welcome you into community. *You are not alone.* What you are experiencing is physically, mentally, and emotionally difficult. We would tell you that you, your family, and your well-being should be the priority and that the job will wait, but we do not want to be hypocrites. We understand the precarity that you feel in your body and your career. We encourage you to take care of yourself and to call on whatever support you have available to make it through this time. Try to find any available resources on campus (a senior colleague, a union, a family task force) to help you navigate your institutional policies. Contact us if you need empathetic listeners or a professional advocate.

Our call to action is directed to colleagues with more institutional power. We call on you to create more accessible spaces for all abilities and disabilities without the need for disclosure. To accomplish this task, we suggest using universal design, a framework that helps ensure that people of all identities and abilities can equally access and use products, spaces, and information (for more information on universal design, see Burgstahler, 2021). Using universal design principles such as flexibility and choice we can create professional spaces and expectations that are more accessible to all. A universal design perspective can also reveal the explicit and implicit standards of presence, productivity, and collegiality inherent in WPA positions and, most importantly, suggest more accessible and inclusive practices. Such practices may look like:

- **Presence:** Establish clear expectations for when and how long WPAs should be on campus; allow for alternative working arrangements (remote work, compressed workweeks); limit mandatory "physical presence" to highest priority tasks or events; practice other types of connecting and check-ins with colleagues, supervisees, and other administrators.
- **Productivity:** Establish clear, reasonable expectations for WPAs and their research, teaching, service, and administrative workload; help early career WPAs to prioritize competing responsibilities; allow for career "pauses" for emergency situations to temporarily reduce or remove research, programmatic, teaching, or professional obligations.
- **Collegiality:** Uncover collegiality expectations in formal and informal evaluations; create supportive workplaces to recognize caretaking responsibilities; offer flexible scheduling; create workplace environments where time off is normalized and does not require explanation or justification.
- **Vulnerability:** Model vulnerability in kairotic spaces (conferences, campus visits, performance evaluations); be an ally and advocate for those who are in more precarious positions.

In this chapter, we shared our stories of tears and blood as early-career professionals. Our (in)fertility experiences illuminate the challenges of navigating the professional expectations of presence, productivity, and collegiality in kairotic academic spaces like job interviews, conferences, and high-stakes teaching and advocacy. Our stories complicate the common trope of the path to parenthood as a direct line. These stories also point out how professional expectations, lack of reasonable accommodations, and cultural silence around reproduction create barriers for people whose embodied realities do not fit within the normative narratives of parenthood. Our chapter offers ideas and strategies for creating more inclusive spaces for WPAs, including an additional *topos*—vulnerability—that can help open up the conversation in our professional spaces to more diverse voices and experiences. Designing WPA positions with accessibility in mind will benefit those experiencing (in)fertility and pregnancy loss as well as a range of other physical and mental experiences. If those in power can provide leadership in clear expectations, flexibility, compassion, and vulnerability, it can begin to create a more equitable workplace for all.

REFERENCES

AAUP. (2016). On collegiality as a criterion for faculty evaluation. https://www.aaup.org/report/collegiality-criterion-faculty-evaluation

Burgstahler, S. (2021). Universal design: Process, principles, and applications. *DO-IT: Disabilities, opportunities, internetworking, and technology.* University of Washington, Seattle. https://www.washington.edu/doit/sites/default/files/atoms/files/Universal_Design_04_12_21.pdf

CDC. (2021). "Infertility FAQs" https://www.cdc.gov/reproductivehealth/infertility/index.htm

CWPA. (1998). Evaluating the intellectual work of writing administration. *CWPA.* https://wpacouncil.org/aws/CWPA/pt/sd/news_article/242849/_PARENT/layout_details/false

Dolmage, J. T. (2017). *Academic ableism: Disability and higher education.* University of Michigan Press.

Dugas, C., & Slane, V. H. (2021) Miscarriage. In *StatPearls [Internet].* StatPearls Publishing. https://www.ncbi.nlm.nih.gov/books/NBK532992/

Graziano, L., Halasek, K., Miller-Cochran, S., Napolitano, F., & Szymanski, N. (2020). A return to Portland: Making work visible through the ecologies of writing program administrators. *WPA: Writing Program Administration, 43*(2), 131–151.

Johnson, J. A. (2014). "The happy hour test." *Inside Higher Ed.* https://www.insidehighered.com/advice/2014/04/25/essay-defending-idea-collegiality-matters-hiring

Mason, M. A., Wolfinger, N. H., & Goulden, M. (2013). *Do babies matter? Gender and family in the ivory tower.* Rutgers University Press.

Price, M. (2011). *Mad at school: Rhetorics of mental disability and academic life.* University of Michigan Press.

Reiheld, A. (2015). "The event that was nothing": Miscarriage as a liminal event. *Journal of Social Philosophy, 46*, 9–26.

Rooney, K. L., & Domar, A. D. (2018). The relationship between stress and infertility. *Dialogues in clinical neuroscience, 20*(1), 41–47.

Vidali, A. (2015). "Disabling writing program administration." *WPA: Writing Program Administration, 38*(2), 32–55.

CHAPTER SEVEN

Unlearning Writing Program Administration

AMY FERDINANDT STOLLEY, GRAND VALLEY STATE UNIVERSITY

It has become a commonplace among WPAs to argue that some preparation is necessary to be an effective writing program administrator, and not without reason (Peterson, 1987; Brown & Enos, 2002; Brown, Lunsford, & White, 2008). WPA work is challenging: it requires us to know composition and rhetorical theory *and* strategies for advocating for, developing, and implementing sound writing pedagogy in the programs we direct. Scholarship that argues the case for WPA preparation positions WPA work as a viable field of study, justifying the need for WPA courses and specializations in graduate programs. These texts also prepare WPAs who are taking on the work by illustrating the various landscapes (and their landmines) in which they may find themselves. It's not an easy task to run a writing program, so turning to the advice of those who have done the work longer has become a standard practice of preparation for those of us whose professional paths lead us to WPA positions.

At the start of my career, I embraced the idea that one could be prepared for WPA work. As a graduate student, I specialized in WPA studies, wrote a WPA-oriented dissertation, and served in two different graduate WPA (gWPA) roles. I have been a WPA at three different institutions over the last fifteen years where I designed and revised curriculum, conducted assessment, and implemented new placement practices. I've had experiences doing all the things my graduate studies prepared me to do.

Yet I have rarely felt prepared for the challenges of WPA work. Often, I have had to unlearn what I thought I knew to best meet the needs of the program I lead, the colleagues with whom I work, and the students I teach. As WPAs, we need to know the history and theory of writing program administration, not to mention practical strategies for assessment, curricular design, faculty development, and navigating complex institutional politics. But I also believe that learning how to be a WPA is an ongoing process that requires on-the-job *unlearning*.

I'd like to offer a brief note to explain my use of the term "unlearning." I used to believe unlearning was simply the act of replacing previously held knowledge or beliefs with new knowledge and understanding. However, I came to a new realization during the summer of 2020 when racial uprisings in support of Black lives illustrated how unlearning racism (or unlearning any previously held idea or belief) is not just reading to learn new information or listening to those whose experiences are different than our own. Rather, unlearning is a process of genuine, often painful, reflection that highlights our own mistakes, vulnerabilities, and prejudices. We don't unlearn for self-improvement; we unlearn because we need to be better allies and accomplices (Kynard, 2019) for our neighbors, our colleagues, and our students.

The concept of unlearning offers a useful frame to think about the arc of our careers as WPAs, and specifically the ideas and arguments that circulate about how best to prepare and sustain those of us who do WPA work. My goal for this chapter is to trouble the notion of WPA readiness using concepts of activity theory to illustrate how WPA knowledge—and WPAs themselves—are in a constant state of mediated, context-specific unlearning. Over the course of my career, I have found that unlearning is central to the work because there is no fixed point of arrival as a WPA. Rather, when we position ourselves as "unready" or "readying" (rather than "ready") WPAs, we allow ourselves to adopt a critical, reflective stance toward our experiences and previously held beliefs, creating space for new knowledge and growth.

LEARNING WRITING PROGRAM ADMINISTRATION

One useful way of considering how unlearning can shape a WPA's professional development comes from Lev Vygotsky's (1978) activity theory, which examines how a person (actor) interacts with the world by doing something (actions) to create something (object/outcome). My graduate education as a WPA focused on what a WPA does and what outcomes we might expect from that labor—the action and objects of the WPA activity network. The central texts and assignments of my WPA seminars focused on scholarship around the activities of WPA work. We read foundational articles in *WPA: Writing Program Administration* and in collections such as *Administrative Problem-Solving for Writing Programs and Writing Centers* (Myers-Breslin, 1999) and *The Writing Program Administrator's Resource* (Brown & Enos, 2002). We also spent a good deal of time discussing the products of WPA labor, such as assessment reports, curriculum documents, and budget proposals. By focusing on the actions taken by the WPA, we could develop a clear description and understanding of the nature of WPA work, and as a byproduct, we'd also learn more about how the work shapes the actor (the WPA) and the object of the actions (the program) as well as other elements of the WPA activity network (e.g., students, other writing curricula in university, the field of WPA Studies).

Through these courses, and my gWPA role as the assistant director of composition, I developed what I thought was a thorough understanding of WPA work. When prospective programs interviewed me for WPA positions at their university, I could say with confidence that I had all of the tools I needed to take on an independent WPA role. I felt ready, and in many ways I was. But I quickly realized that WPA theory and practices are not enough to prepare any of us to do the work; instead, the real work of becoming a WPA comes through an ongoing process of unlearning and creating new tools to help us in our work.

UNLEARNING WRITING PROGRAM ADMINISTRATION

In addition to describing the different nodes of an activity system, Vygotsky also articulated the central role that tools play in any system. Vygotsky defined tools as anything that an actor uses to complete actions and accomplish outcomes—for example, a WPA might use a tool like the WPA Outcomes Statement to argue for a curriculum revision or assessment project. Tools can be both physical or technical (as in the example above), but Vygotsky also identified psychological tools that can, over time and through practice and social conditioning, be internalized by the actor as tools of the mind.

Alexsei Leontiev (1931, 2005) pushed Vygotsky's idea further, theorizing how mental processes and knowledge acquisition rely on tools of the mind differently at various stages of social and psychological development. Leontiev studied preschool, middle-school, and college students to learn how students at different ages used tools (in this case, a set of cards printed with images that students could use as mnemonic devices) to remember a list of words. Younger students relied on the picture cards more heavily than older students, and Leontiev argued this outcome was because older students had internalized, readily-accessible mental images of the words they could use to remember them, whereas younger students did not have those mental images and needed tools (the cards) to complete the task (Kaptelinin & Nardi, 2006, p. 44). A visual representation of his findings has come to be called "Leontiev's parallelogram" (Figure 7.1), which illustrates how tools mediate the performance of a given activity at different stages of cognitive development.

Leontiev used these findings to articulate three stages of cognitive development that are observable in any context: (1) no mediation, when learners have no learning aids or are learning information for the first time, (2) mediated, when learners have some learning aids that help them retain and recall knowledge, and (3) internalized, when learners have integrated knowledge so that it becomes part of their regular thinking processes (Kaptelinin & Nardi, 2006, pp. 44–45). Although the goal is for people to internalize the tools of their activity systems, this does not happen in a vacuum; Lieontiev understood the line between the internal and external world to be fluid, but for learners, the act of "internalization enables external mediation by culturally developed tools to effect internal, mental processes, which become culturally mediated as well" (Kaptelinin & Nardi, 2006, p. 46).

If I look at my career, it's clear that I've spent most of it in stage one or two of Leontiev's model of cognitive development. Early on, I relied on tangible, culturally-mediated tools to help me with my work. If I was stuck, I would go back to the scholarship I read in my WPA seminars or turn to messages and advice of more experienced WPAs shared on the WPA-L listserv, and those tools worked the way notecards did for Leontiev's research participants. Over time I internalized these tools and didn't need to rely on them as I felt more confident in my role. Yet I would still claim that, despite my apparent progression through Leontiev's parallelogram, my work as a WPA has been marked by moments of unlearning when the tools I had developed and internalized simply failed. In

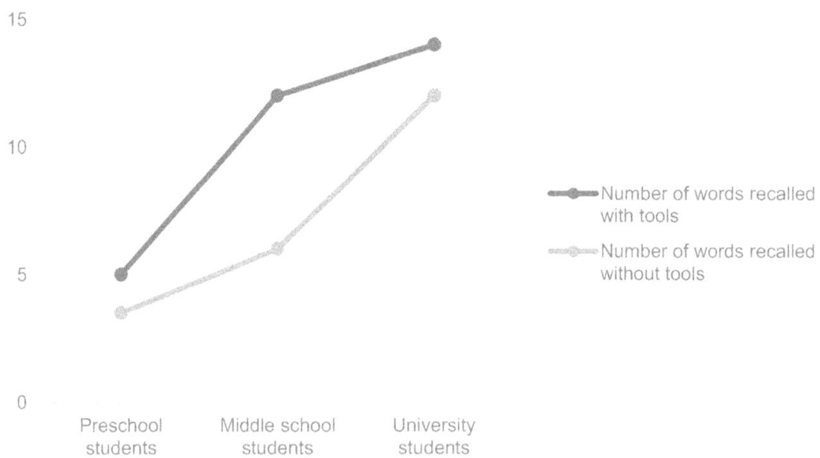

Figure 7.1: Leontiev's Parallelogram (1931)

these moments, I was forced to develop new tools that helped me learn more about the nature of WPA work, but those tools only became usable when I engaged in unlearning that uncovered new understandings about *myself* as a WPA, and what WPA work is when *I* do it. Below, I offer three scenes of unlearning that illustrate that our development as WPAs does not follow a linear, upward trajectory, and it's often the moments when the tools we've internalized break down that teach us the most.

SCENE ONE (OCTOBER 2006)

I wait quietly outside my dissertation director's office for my appointment, trying to figure out what to say. I'm upset because the director of the first-year writing program for which I am a gWPA has made a decision with which I disagree vehemently. I see the decision as a political trade rather than one rooted in the pedagogical principles of our program. The FYW director's choice seems to be diametrically opposed to my training as a WPA—we fight for the things we know to be true; we don't acquiesce. I need help knowing how to fix this, and I need somewhere to put my anger and disappointment.

My advisor opens the door to his office, and I immediately burst into frustrated tears. Warm but reserved, he patiently listens as I unload. It takes a while to get it all out.

He pauses for a beat and then asks me a question: "Why are you the assistant director of composition, Amy?" I pause, a little surprised by the question, and then respond: "I want to support students and instructors here. I want to improve our program. I want to help build a culture of writing at our university."

He smiles and shakes his head. "Nope. You're doing this job to get another job. Your goal here is to finish your dissertation, get experience working in a writing program, and get. another. job."

SCENE TWO (FEBRUARY 2016)

I wait outside my dean's office, mentally reviewing the work I've done in the eight years I've been faculty here: a new first-year writing curriculum, a summer bridge program, annual assessment, and regular faculty development. I said yes to every opportunity I was offered, and I created new projects for myself, too. I was proud of the work I had done.

Her door opens. We sit, exchange pleasantries. I say, "I have another job offer," my eyes welling up. She nods and frowns. "That's what I was afraid you'd say." She says what I already know: "We don't have the money to make you a counteroffer." I'm not surprised by her response, but I'm gouged by grief. I try to imagine leaving, walking away from these students and this university and this program we built. I want to stay, but know leaving is the right thing to do, despite my fear and regret.

We talk about the new job and the opportunities it would offer me—a bigger, better-resourced program in a writing department, new professional development prospects and new challenges. As I move toward the door, she stops me. "This will be good for you, Amy. You've done what you could do here, and you've run out of space to grow. It's time for you to go somewhere you can run."

SCENE THREE (OCTOBER 2020)

I sit at my sewing table, now serving as a make-shift desk, and look at the boxed faces of my first-year writing colleagues on the Zoom screen in front of me. We're midway through our first semester of teaching our new developmental writing course. We're also midway through our first full semester of teaching online during a pandemic. We've been cobbling this curriculum together on the fly for months, planning a few weeks at a time, limping toward the end of the term. I can see and hear my colleagues' stress and exhaustion. I haven't yet learned how to turn off the self-view in Zoom, so I can see the bags under my own eyes, too.

The conversation shifts to next semester and the second course in the Stretch sequence. My heartbeat picks up and my shoulders tighten. An instructor says she's worried the students won't be ready to do the work next semester because this term has been so challenging. My palms start to sweat, and I feel cold as others nod in agreement. Another instructor asks, "Amy, when will we have the syllabus and assignment descriptions for next semester?" I'm having trouble breathing and I want to crawl out of my skin. I softly say, "Soon. Next couple of weeks." A roaring noise drowns fills my ears and my vision blurs. I rush to end the meeting and close my Zoom screen. I push back from my desk and fall to my hands and knees on the floor, struggling to catch my breath. I practice the deep breathing exercises my doctor gave me a few weeks ago to quell the fear and get back to my body.

My breathing slows, and I start to quietly cry. Another panic attack.

DISCOVERING RENEWAL THROUGH UNLEARNING

These moments of unlearning may be familiar to you: I expect you've had moments of frustration with yourself or others, moments when you considered leaving your role for new opportunities (or at least bristled against the limitations of where you were) like what O'Meara explores in this volume, moments when you struggled under the weight of leading a program during a pandemic or other crisis. Although these moments taught me about the work of writing program administration, they taught me more about myself as a WPA because of the self-assessment (see Beavers and Anders, this volume) these experiences required of me. My conversation with my advisor highlighted that I need to see myself as separate from the program I lead and set boundaries to preserve my energy and attention. My conversation with my former dean reminded me that it's okay to change course and pursue new challenges, even though I had expected to stay put for my entire career. The pandemic taught me that best practices are sometimes impossible to pull off in a crisis, and sometimes "good enough" is plenty good. It took me a while to implement Carl Schlacte's (2020) advice to "go against the impulse to rush and to 'return to normal'" during or after a crisis (p. 304); I had to realize that there was no normal to go back to and I needed to slow down for my own sake and to model that practice for my colleagues, too.

These scenes, which functioned as private, "kairotic spaces" (see Clinnin et al., this volume), were specific moments of unlearning for me because the tools of my WPA preparation that I relied on to do my job broke down, and I needed to let them go. I could have trudged along and remained unchanged, carrying on as though the tools still worked. Admittedly, there have been times when I've done that. But by remaining open to—and sometimes seeking out—change, I have been able to find a kind of renewal that has kept me engaged in the work.

My development as a WPA does not map neatly onto Leontiev's parallelogram. Rather, it looks more like a mountain range, marked by upward climbs of personal and programmatic development, avalanches of missteps and failures, big feelings and tears. I've abandoned tools along the way that no longer worked, and repurposed old tools to fit new challenges. In each of the scenes I describe above, I had foundational knowledge about what it takes to be a WPA, but that knowledge wasn't enough to make me ready for the challenges I faced, in part because it didn't incorporate two central elements of the activity system: who I am as a WPA and the specific context in which I work. The tools I had weren't sufficient on their own; rather, I needed to internalize them by re-learning them through the lenses of my institutional knowledge and my growing understanding of myself as a WPA.

STRATEGIES FOR SEEKING UNLEARNING AND UNREADINESS

If we understand WPA readiness as a fixed point, we run the risk of our knowledge becoming ossified, limiting the growth of the programs we direct and our own development as a WPA. We "may be unfitted by being fit in an unfit fitness"

(Burke, 1954, p. 10) if our training keeps us from adapting to our changing contexts. Amy Rupiper Taggart (2018) convincingly argues that WPAs are in a constant state of preparation for WPA work because change, whether it stems from the choices we make or the whims of the universe, is inevitable (p. 154). How many of us felt the urge to hold on to whatever elements of our programmatic structure or curriculum or placement processes or assessment projects during the pandemic because our training taught us that was what mattered? Such a belief brought me to my knees that day in my home office, and I quickly realized that I had to let go of those expectations, those beliefs about what I *should* do, in favor of what I *could* do.

As activity theory scholar and historian Anton Yasnitsky (2020) has noted, a limitation in Leontiev's early work is his assumption that tools used in an activity, which are by nature a product of culture, are universally understood. Although my experiences may be recognizable to you as WPAs and may even be tools you can use in your own work as a WPA, I can't assume that is the case, and it's more reasonable to understand that those experiences happened as they did because of who I am as a person and where I work, not because of some innate element of writing program administration. Were you to experience these moments as I did, they may have had different effects or led you to different decisions or conclusions. I share these then, not to make a universal pronouncement about the nature of WPA work, but rather to highlight the impossibility of trying to do so.

What I can do is offer some suggestions about how you might use critical reflection to seek out or recognize moments of unlearning in your own work as a WPA.

- **Reflect on your preparation as a WPA:** What are areas about which you didn't learn enough? In what areas do you need to do more reading, listening, and learning? As a graduate student in a program that didn't have a course for developmental writers, I didn't know much about developmental education, and I had to get up to speed quickly when I took my first WPA job in a program with a basic writing course. Sometimes these holes in our preparation are obvious once we're on the job, but sometimes, it takes more work to find these gaps (see below).
- **Research gaps in your knowledge:** It can be hard to identify our knowledge gaps; we don't know what we don't know. But you can start by making a list of assumptions you make about WPA work. Read up on new developments in those areas to see how thinking about program administration is shifting. You can catalog the things you think can't or won't change about the program you direct, your colleagues, or your institution, and do some research (journal articles, your network of WPA colleagues, etc.) to see how others have addressed those challenges. You can ask your Institutional

Research office (if you have one) for data sets you don't typically request. Case in point: I recently asked for grade breakdowns based on gender and found that female-identifying students do not do as well in our course as male-identifying students, which highlighted a problem I didn't know we had and created an opportunity for us to learn more about building gender equity into our program.

- **Pay attention to emotion:** When we get angry, hurt, or defensive, it's often a sign of conflict between our interior and exterior worlds, and that conflict can be an indicator that we have things to unlearn. Despite academia's tendency to dismiss feelings in favor of ideas, I've found that moments of emotional friction have something to teach me about my assumptions about WPA work or myself as a WPA. What are the things that make you most angry or hurt as a WPA? Are you responding to a violation of your values? Or are your emotional responses highlighting for you a gap in your own education or experience that you need to learn more about?
- **Keep a WPA journal:** Courtney Adams Wooten (2020) encourages WPAs to keep a journal to track their emotional labor successes and failures (p. 317), but I've also found that simple note taking after meetings, workshops, or hallway discussions can create moments of reflection that lead to opportunities for unlearning. These entries sometimes simply become part of my personal/professional archive, but at other times, such as when a hallway conversation about photo essays with a colleague turned into a pilot for a multimodal curriculum, these moments of reflection can point me to areas that need to be explored with more care and attention.
- **Develop new tools:** Take advantage of opportunities to attend professional development workshops in our field and others. Resources offered by the Council of Writing Program Administrators, such as the summer workshop, institutes, or the CWPA and WPA-GO Mentoring Projects can offer spaces to learn from and with other WPAs even if you're a "veteran" WPA. You might also look outside of our field for new tools. A colleague recently completed a workshop on design thinking, and it has changed how he thinks about the program he directs. Finally, seek out other administrators at your school and talk to them about how they do their work. I recently met a group of administrators at my university through another professional development opportunity, and I've learned much from them about how they're managing budgets, supporting faculty, and spearheading new initiatives, giving me ideas for the program I direct.

These suggestions are just some of many places where you might begin the process of unlearning, and my hope is that if you seek out opportunities to unlearn through critical reflection, you might begin to see that WPA "readiness" is a moving and unreachable target rather than a destination. Vygotsky and Leontiev's analysis of activity systems, actors, and the tools they use offers a useful frame for understanding WPA knowledge and activity, but we can't assume an upward trajectory of our administrative skills similar to what Leontiev's parallelogram illustrates. Relying on one set of tools—administrative skills, practices, and beliefs—without reflection and reconsideration keeps us stuck as individual WPAs and as a field, and it stops us from developing new tools to address our ever-changing contexts. Rather, I encourage us all—no matter where we are in our professional lives—to reflect on and engage with those moments in our professional lives when our tools failed and embrace the messy unreadiness and not knowing of unlearning.

Unlearning frames our previous knowledge as merely a starting point from which we will begin our career-long process of unlearning and relearning how to do WPA work. This is where we begin to understand that the work of learning to be a WPA is fundamentally tied to learning to understand who *we* are as WPAs. When we accept our unreadiness, we create opportunities to learn more about WPA work, our university, our colleagues, and ourselves. Indeed, perhaps our best preparation for WPA work is knowing that we don't yet know what we need to know to do the work, and it's the not knowing that keeps us engaged, seeking, unlearning, and readying.

REFERENCES

Brown, S. C., & Enos, T. (Eds.). (2002). *The writing program administrator's resource: A guide to reflective institutional practice.* Lawrence Erlbaum Associates.

Brown, S. C., Lunsford, A. A., & White, E. M. (2008). Location and the WPA. In T. Enos, & S. Borrowman (Eds.), *The promise and perils of writing program administration* (pp. 126–134). Parlor Press.

Burke, Kenneth. (1954). *Permanence and change.* Hermes Publications.

Enos, T., & Borrowman, S. (Eds.). (2008). *The promise and perils of writing program administration.* Parlor Press.

Kaptelinin, V., & Nardi, B. A. (2006). *Acting with technology: Activity theory and interaction design.* MIT Press.

Kynard, C. (2019). Administering while black: Black women's labor in the academy and the "position of the unthought." In S. M. Perryman-Clark & C. L. Craig (Eds.), *Black perspectives in writing program administration: From the margins to the center* (pp. 28–50). CCCC/NCTE.

Leontiev, A. N. (1931). *Development of memory: Experimental research on higher psychological functions.* Uchpedgiz.

Leontiev, A. N. (2005). Lecture 36. Thinking and Activity (N. Favarov,Trans.) *Journal of Russian and East European Psychology, 43*(5), 41–52. https://doi.org/10.1080/10610405.2005.11059266 (Original work published 1975)

Myers-Breslin, L. (Ed.). (1999). *Administrative problem-solving for writing programs and writing centers: Scenarios in effective program management.* National Council of Teachers of English.

Peterson, L. (1987). The WPA's progress: A survey, story, and commentary on the career patterns of writing program administrators. *WPA: Writing Program Administration, 10*(3), 11–18.

Schlacte, C. (2020). A heuristic for WPAs in disaster response. In C. A. Wooten, J. Babb, K. M. Costello, & K. Navickas (Eds.), *The things we carry: Strategies for recognizing and negotiating emotional labor in writing program administration* (pp. 303–304). Utah State UP.

Taggart, A. R. (2018). Reseeing the WPA skill set: GenAdmins transitioning from WPA to university pedagogical leadership. In C. A. Wooten, J. Babb, & B. Ray (Eds.), *WPAs in transition: Navigating educational leadership positions* (pp. 153–167). Utah State UP.

Vygotsky, L. (1978). *Mind in society: The development of higher mental processes.* Harvard University Press.

Wooten, C. A. (2020). Strategy sheet: How to be a bad WPA. In Wooten, C. A., Babb, J., Costello, K. M., & Navickas, K. (Eds.), *The things we carry: Strategies for recognizing and negotiating emotional labor in writing program administration* (pp. 317–318). Utah State UP.

Yasnitsky, A. (2020). Aleksei N Leontiev's research on memory and its meaning as the Soviet avant-garde science of the future. *Cadernos CEDES, 40,* 123–134. https://doi.org/10.1590/cc224304_in.

PART TWO

RENEWAL

CHAPTER EIGHT

Refusal as Renewal: An Asian/American Woman Saying No while WPA-ing

JOLIVETTE MECENAS, CALIFORNIA LUTHERAN UNIVERSITY

When I was a graduate student, writing program work attracted me immediately as a very pragmatic way to fight the class- and race-based inequities in higher education. My first administrative job was as the staff coordinator of the English Department writing center at a large public university. My current job is as an associate professor of English who also directs first-year writing at a private university. I've been a WPA for about thirteen years now, so that puts me squarely mid-career. This work is not easy. I would not be able to do it without situating my own identity within academia and within our field. WPA readiness requires self-reflection, which fosters the critical thinking necessary for us to do the work with the "intellectual fellowship and radical openness" that bell hooks (1994) celebrated as central to engaged pedagogy in *Teaching to Transgress* (p. 205). Keeping an open mind and heart have been energizing strategies for me. So has resisting and refusing when necessary.

Although resistance and refusal are rhetorical strategies that are valuable for any faculty member with administrative duties, saying no as a WPA who identifies as a queer Filipina woman, and as Asian/American, lands differently. By Asian/American, I mean the collective identity of people working in U.S. higher education who connect their ethnicity or heritage in some way to the many cultures, languages, and nationalities in Asia. Here, I use the slash to denote a relationship between Asian and American identities that contests U.S. nationality as the central identity, the conceptualization of which Morris Young and Terese

Guinsatao Monberg (2018) credit David Palumbo-Liu in their introduction to the *Enculturation* issue on Asian/American rhetoric (par. 7). The collective identity "Asian American" was born in the cross-racial political activism of San Francisco State and UC Berkeley students in 1968. Under this banner, students represented a pan-ethnic coalition of students from East Asian, Southeast Asian, and South Asian ethnicities who resisted the racist legacies of U.S. and European colonialism and imperialism in their education.

How might an oppositional, yet radically open, sensibility shape your role as a writing program administrator? The question stands because WPA work is about institutional compliance. The non-tenure track WPA gets their contract renewed, and the junior faculty WPA achieves tenure after the typical three-to-six years of compliance to their institution's promotion and tenure guidelines. The WPA is hired to ensure that the university gears are greased; we are trained to attune to enrollment and retention patterns, general education learning outcomes, accreditation agencies, disciplinary trends, and union demands/labor laws. The role is not designed for rebels seeking to trouble the waters of academe, but for the middle manager who can steady the ship of institutional life, much like a department chair, but without the *gravitas* and wood-paneled office depicted on television. There is no Netflix miniseries starring Sandra Oh as a WPA.

But there are stories of WPAs of color in our field and listening to their experiences provides another empowering rhetorical strategy for me. These narratives illuminate how WPAs of color build and navigate institutional identity and power. Perryman-Clark and Craig demonstrated how centering intersectional narratives of WPAs of color–specifically of Black WPAs–is critical antiracist work that intervenes in systemic racism in writing programs (Craig & Perryman-Clark, 2011, pp. 39–40; 2019, p. 24). Likewise, minoritized graduate students preparing for WPA work have also documented microaggressions and frustrations they've experienced while asserting their leadership. Al Harahap (2021), who chaired the Council of Writing Program Administrators' graduate organization (WPA-GO), was charged with planning ways to diversify the organization's membership. As a "dark-skinned Asian Islander," Harahap described how his white colleagues challenged his leadership because they perceived him as insufficiently progressive, while failing to understand "the difficult balancing act of presenting radical ideas from the mouth of an intimidating Brown body" (p. 59). In her chapter in this collection, Gabrielle Isabel Kelenyi narrates her turn as chair of WPA-GO, determined to enact anti-racist changes to the WPA-GO bylaws and election process. Kelenyi also describes being in the precarious situation as a woman of color graduate student, sitting in on the CWPA Executive Board meetings, as members deliberated how to respond to accusations that the organization was entrenched in a culture of White supremacy. These important counter-stories challenge the monocultural identity of our profession by illuminating a deeper understanding of how microaggressions impact WPA authority, and how WPAs of color defend their authority and carry out their work. WPA counter-stories also detail how junior WPAs of color–those among us with the most recent training in equity and inclusion in academia–negotiate their lack of authority while marginalized in academia and professional organizations.

Like the scholars of color whom I reference here, and whose work provides me with guidance and community, I write this essay for those whose antiracist and culturally responsive work in writing program administration is intertwined with their scholarship and identities. As I reflect on saying no as a Filipina WPA, I draw from Asian/American rhetorical scholarship to guide my thoughts on an intersectional praxis of WPA work, specifically to think through a tired but persistent line of advice for women in academia to "just say no"–a maxim that, I contend, works within race, gender, and class-based structures of oppression in academia, and thus upholds those same inequities. For those of us who rebel and chip away at institutional inequities, we may rethink resistance and refusal as strategies for creating spaces for belonging, community, and mentorship; for advocating for an ethics of care in WPA work; and for prioritizing our well-being for renewal.

REFUSING THE UNIMAGINED LOCATION OF THE ASIAN/AMERICAN WPA

The summer after my very first year as a college writing instructor, I took some time off to help care for my dying grandmother, Lola Luz. She lived about forty miles east of Los Angeles in the Mojave Desert, an arid landscape populated by commuters seeking affordable housing, and by Joshua trees. I had just spent the year writing lesson plans and teaching composition while slogging through nighttime grad seminars, running the writing center, and writing my MA thesis project. I wanted to share the meaningful work I was doing with my grandmother, a woman who worked throughout her life as a wartime nurse, an International Red Cross nurse, and a turkey farmer. She was also a formidable storyteller.

"The *Filipino* is teaching the *Americans* English? Ha!" Lola Luz quipped, amusement glinting in her eyes. Surprised by her response, I sat in her garden in the cool mid-morning, staring at those spiky trees in the background. I hadn't thought about my nascent academic career through that lens; my parents and grandparents were the immigrants in our family story. I was the first-gen college student, graduate student, and college instructor, a narrative that began when this matriarch, now losing to lymphoma, moved her family across the world to finish out her nursing career in 1960s Los Angeles.

"Actually, Lola..." I was about to clarify that I did not teach the "English" she had in mind, but I stopped myself. I did teach writing and rhetoric in English, to mostly U.S. residents, and to international students, so she wasn't wrong. But her comment still gave me pause. The early summer air was heating up, desert-hot, so we packed up our harvested tomatoes and opo squash and headed inside to make lunch.

Lately, I've been thinking about my late grandmother's amusement. Asian/American rhetorical theory provides me with a critical hindsight into my grandmother's ironic take: her granddaughter, the legacy of colonial subjects, teaching the colonizing language, in the colonizers' universities. Packed into my grandmother's "Ha!" were generations of colonizers and resistors. Luz–descendant of Spanish colonialists *and* of the indigenous Karay, a people who resisted three hundred years of Spanish colonization, and also a guerilla fighter who resisted Japanese occupation of the Philippines–straddled these identities. As Young and Monberg (2018) describe, scholarship in the field has shifted from a focus on representational Asian identities in U.S. media and culture to an examination of "how rhetoric moves across time, space, national boundaries, institutions, languages, and cultures" (par. 11). My grandmother's comment reinserts centuries of colonization back into our family narrative, which includes my professional identity. She passed onto me a way to resist an easy narrative of American assimilation by reminding me that in her lifetime, the U.S. and its language was the dominant political, economic, and cultural power in a one-sided relationship with the Philippines. To my grandmother, I had somehow flipped that script by becoming an English professor to "Americans."

Joseph Eng (2007) describes Asian Americans as "unimagined" in the field, and that "the Asian American WPA remains largely an unknown location" (pp. 153–154). We are still missing more than a decade after Eng's piece: in a qualitative study of college writing programs, writing center directors, and race, the authors coded respondents who self-identified as white/Caucasian, Latino/Puerto Rican/Mexican, black/African American, and Native American (De Mueller & Ruiz, 2017, p. 24). Although this research contributes much to the field, I regret the lack of Asian American participants in a study of race and writing program administration. As Eng proposes, the experience of living as "other" is "*commonly* shared by Asian-Americans teaching college English or administering college writing programs" (p. 154; italics in the original).

Shared experiences of marginalization contradict the prevailing model minority myth that Asian/Americans are easily and eagerly assimilated into white academic culture. In their recent article in *Reflections*, Monberg, Sano-Franchini, and Yoon (2022) historicize how recurring, racialized tropes position Asian/Americans in academia as "a threat that must be harnessed and kept under control." By insisting on political and discursive agency, we rebel against model minority expectations in academia–those patterns of anti-Asian racism in larger U.S. society that divide minoritized peoples within a hierarchy of white supremacy. In the following section, I consider what refusing and being rebellious means for my embodied existence as an Asian/American WPA.

JUST SAY NO

If you are newly on a TT or NTT contract, few maxims are more confusing than this common advice for junior faculty: learn when to say no so that you are not a "doormat," but don't anger senior colleagues who might "nurse a grudge come time to vote on your tenure case" (Perlmutter, 2008). A quick search through the *Chronicle of Higher Education* turns up several columnists dispensing like-minded advice. In "To Find Happiness in Academe, Women Should Just Say No" (Selzer, 2015), women are advised to avoid university service in "time-intensive lower-status positions such as director of undergraduate studies"–or, for that matter, director of first-year writing or the writing center. Women are coached to forgo family visits and to ask others to care for their children in order to focus on research and publication. One columnist proposed more strategies for saying no to increase scholarly productivity (Bernstein, 2017). And the advice for women academics continues: *The No Club* (Babcock et.al., 2022) presents research on gendered expectations for performing "non-promotable work"–i.e., work that supports students and a positive work environment (tasks such as coordinating a retirement gift), but that eats away at the time one has for completing promotable work, such as scholarship. Decades of such "Just Say No" advice illuminated, reinforced, and complied with the capitalist and sexist practices of academic productivity.

In WPA literature, refusing to serve as a WPA is another prevalent theme, influenced by narratives from junior and senior faculty alike, describing WPA work as an imbalance of expectations and institutional power (Micciche, 2002; Dew & Horning, 2007). After completing my Ph.D., I ignored the advice to say no to WPA work, and accepted my first appointment as assistant professor and WPA at a private university. I earnestly believed in my equity-minded program administration, but was unprepared for the power struggle that first exhausting year. As WPA literature points out, the role of the assistant professor WPA can feel like a set-up from the start: the WPA needs the authority to revise curriculum and policies, schedule classes, and persuade colleagues to collaborate, *and* the WPA is an assistant professor (for more on precarious WPA authority, see Green's chapter in this volume). I acutely felt this tension midway through my first year, when I had angered the associate dean of my college. Based on department policy and in agreement with my department chair, I had denied a senior adjunct professor's request to teach an independent study with a student. The associate dean reversed my decision in a long email addressed to the instructor, explaining to her that I didn't know what I was doing. I know this because I was *copied* on the email–excluded from the conversation, but included so that I may know my place. In addition to overriding our department leadership, the associate dean also discredited me with the adjunct professor over email, compromising my leadership role.

Though my experience aligns with the literature on the non-tenured WPA's limited authority, as a Filipina woman, I had to do even more work to establish my authority that first year with my predominantly white tenure-line and adjunct faculty colleagues and senior administrators. Monberg et al. (2022) list common racialized tropes they observed in countless narratives by Asian/American women that monitor and regulate their movement in their disciplinary reputations and in their daily work lives, including a recurring theme that the "Asian body that must know its place and be kept in line." My experience maps onto this theme: my place was to quietly submit to the associate dean's decision. I knew that my well-being, and my ability to do my job, depended on my refusal of this compliant model minority position. Privately, I politely suggested to the associate dean alternative ways we could communicate with each other in the future, other than through email (again, on which I was only copied, to passively witness a conversation *about me*). This suggestion enraged her, prompting a terrible exchange that I immediately reported to my department chair, who then reported it to the dean. As a result, the associate dean was instructed henceforth to communicate with me only through my department chair or the dean himself. I was proud of myself for refusing the demeaning and undermining treatment from the associate dean, and thereby re-establishing my authority and protecting my well-being in the day-to-day. Saying no is not "just" being assertive, as if this action is without greater challenges for minoritized WPAs. The "just" diminishes the oppositional rhetorical power I summoned to push back against microaggressions.

ASIAN/AMERICAN WOMEN SAYING NO IN ACADEMIA

The "Just Say No" advice ignores how microaggressions impact Asian/American WPAs, and particularly the intersectional challenges for women and LGBTQ+-identified people. Despite increasing representation in U.S. higher education, Asian/American women are underrepresented in university leadership positions (Monberg et al., 2022; Roy, 2021, p. 572). The model minority myth exists within a white supremacy model so that Asians are perceived to be more assimilable than other minorities. This myth is used in dominant U.S. culture to drive a wedge between minoritized groups and to negate the existence of structural inequalities, with the generalized success of Asians often cited as evidence that such inequalities are non-existent. Within this model, Asian/Americans are ideal WPAs, as long as they maintain the status quo and are not too ambitious or critical of systemic racism and sexism.

Rebelling against model minority expectations has consequences. While I was still pre-tenure, the English Department chair asked me to schedule faculty from his department to teach first-year writing when their literature classes did not fill up by booting an adjunct instructor from their assignment as needed, just weeks before the start of the semester. Although the writing program was separate from the English department, their chair requested that I put my part-time faculty colleagues in financial hardship so that English faculty had their full contractual load when their scheduled literature courses failed to enroll. I refused to treat my colleagues so unethically because the English department chair mismanaged enrollment in his department. I refused to assign writing sections to literature professors who dismissed teaching writing. Incensed, the English department chair fired off an email to the new dean, copied to the provost, complaining that I was a "power-hungry person." Once again, I was copied on this email as a voiceless, reprimanded, untenured colleague. I volunteered to take the matter to the faculty senate, and didn't hear from the senior colleague again. Nor did I hear from the dean or the provost, who did nothing to censure my senior colleague's attack on my leadership.

I soon understood that my latest deployment of "No" pushed the interlocking button of race and gender with these three male colleagues, two of whom are men of color. Research has established that both immigrant and U.S.-born Asian women face gender-based microaggressions in addition to racial stereotyping, which increases bias against Asian/American women in leadership roles (Roy, 2021, p. 572). Asian American women have provided accounts of how racial microaggressions can work to invalidate them as competent for leadership roles in academia (Monberg et al., 2022; Valverde & Dariotis, 2020). Asians are perceived to be modest and quiet–negatively viewed communication traits in leaders (Roy, p. 569). And yet, Asian/American women who do speak out "are often dismissed and even punished, while the same critique or opinion expressed by a white man or woman or a man of color would be seen as a demonstration of leadership qualities" (Hune, 2020, p. 12). The impossibility I experienced, in addition to being an untenured WPA, was that academic culture expected me to be assertive enough to lead, but because of racist and sexist attitudes prevalent in the same culture, I was also expected to be a compliant, quiet Asian woman. By refusing the English department chair's request to treat my colleagues poorly, I was invalidated as "power-hungry." The dean added his own microaggression when we met soon after, declaring: "You have a *personality*."

Gendered expectations are shaped by Orientalist discourses rooted in 19th century U.S. empire building, particularly with the conquest and colonization of the Philippines, Guam, and Hawaii. Orientalist discourses of power are gendered: "the powerful West was associated with virile masculinity, and the subordinate East with passive femininity" (Yoshihara, 2002, pp. 3–4). Refusing to be passive, I stood my ground as WPA. However, instead of being read as decisive and assertive, I was read as someone with a *personality*, which in this sense meant *agency*. Asian/American women are not supposed to have either, in the Orientalist discourse of subordination. I was met with fury and silence when I offered to involve faculty governance, which makes me think that my male senior colleague and administrators had expected easy submission from my Asian female body–a queer body that has fought since adolescence for the right to exist publicly in the face of violent threats; an Asian body that understands harassment and assault. Saying no to the scheduling requests of male colleagues may be far less threatening, yet their angry response felt very familiar to me. In this instance, saying no as an Asian/American woman in academia is more than "just" saying no; I refused race and gender-based aggressions in higher education, and in the wider U.S. society and cultural imagination.

REFUSAL AS BELONGING: THE SUSTAINING THREADS OF COMMUNITY

My Asian/Asian American caucus colleagues have been generous sources of mentorship, collaboration, and friendly dinner companionship in conference cities over the years. Mentorship negates the narrative that Asian/American WPAs do not exist. *Building a Community, Having a Home*, a history of the NCTE/CCCC Asian/Asian American Caucus, illuminated the little-known history of Asian/Americans in U.S. college rhetoric and composition (Monberg, Yoon, & Sano-Franchini, 2016). The editors describe their feminist rhetorical methodology of listening and engaging in a collective process with Asian/American caucus members, listening for "moments that we might call sustaining threads: the seemingly small, often unseen fibers that critically shape the direction and subsistence of a movement, organization, or collective" (Monberg et al., 2016, p. 4). Narratives by WPAs of color are sustaining threads that continue the conversation, and that help us locate ourselves in relation to others in the shared effort against systemic oppression. For another collection historicizing NCTE, I interviewed the writer and editor Jeffery Paul Chan about his participation in the NCTE Task Force on Racism and Bias in the Teaching of English in 1971, with fellow writer Frank Chin. Jennifer Sano-Franchini located threads of the story in the NCTE archives, and I filled in the details as narrated by Chan, a founding professor of the College of Ethnic Studies at San Francisco State University. Chan's narrative is a sustaining thread of disciplinary presence for Asian American leadership in the field, connecting to a special issue of the *WPA: Writing Program Administration* journal focusing on BLM and antiracist writing program projects, which features contributions by several WPAs who identify as Asian/American, Asian, or Filipina/x.

Building a Community provides an institutional memory of caucus members' leadership in teaching, research, and administration in the field, locating Asian/Americans as having been persistently present in the discipline, a community that remains "committed to a consistent agenda of racial justice in many forms–scholarly, organizational, and activist" (Monberg et al., 2016, p. 3). This history provides the needed stories of how the labor and activism of WPAs of color make saying no a rhetorical act in the larger fight for a sustainable and inclusive academic culture.

REFUSAL AS A PEDAGOGY OF CARE

Pre-tenure, my teaching was renewed by inspiration found in an unlikely space: a faculty assembly meeting. I remember perking up when a colleague shared that he treats his students the way that he hopes his own college-student son is treated by faculty at his university: with care. At the time, I could not imagine talking about parenting during a faculty meeting, even though my own son was at the university preschool nearby. To care for students as I would like my own son to be cared for by his teachers? Suddenly, that perspective made a lot of sense to me. My teaching and administrative work were already guided by a feminist care ethic, in resistance to patriarchal injustices. But I needed to refuse the academic culture I wasn't connecting with by being more vulnerable and engaged.

Self-reflection is necessary for culturally responsive program administration, as is caring for and being cared for by our communities. Though not a WPA, the Asian American and ethnic studies scholar Allyson Tintiangco-Cubales directs a network of mentoring programs embedded within San Francisco's public K-12 schools. Her reflections on her identity as a "community-engaged motherscholar of color" (Tintiangco-Cubales, 2020, p. 352) present a holistic approach to teaching as liberatory praxis in a way that has affirmed my own refusals and resistances as a WPA. Informed by critical pedagogy and Filipina feminism, her pedagogy of care is a praxis that "empower[s] young people to resist racist, sexist, and classist practices" (p. 356). Counter to the advice to junior faculty–and particularly to women–to prioritize productivity over caregiving, Tintiangco-Cubales sustained her scholarship and career by prioritizing caring for her daughter, students, and the Filipino student mentoring project she initiated. When an administrator at her university warned her that she was "fucking up" by spending too much time doing community-engaged work, she persisted in her holistic pedagogy during her stressful tenure bid (p. 358). She refused to accept that caring for her family and community were oppositional to her scholarship, adding that "bridging these spaces has brought me strength, sanity, and balance" (p. 361). I was inspired by Tintiangco-Cubales "motherscholar" pedagogy, as I was inspired by my colleague's declaration of care ethics. I'm not suggesting that parents are more prepared or inclined to practice a pedagogy of care, only holding up my colleague and Tintiangco-Cubales as models for living an academic life guided by a reciprocal nurturance that resists the capitalist logic of individualism, domination, and incessant productivity.

REFUSAL AS RENEWAL

Upon reflecting on saying no during my first WPA appointment, my main intention is not to call out micro (and macro) aggressions that demoralize and wear out faculty of color. Rather, I am theorizing how saying no can be a valuable strategy for renewal–and sometimes that means leaving one's position, even after tenure. Although tenure provided me with professional affirmation, it did little to change an unhappy work environment. So I said my last no and quit. A mid-career change was not easy, but I reached out to my personal and professional communities during this transition, and I am thankful for their care. My new position has re-energized my leadership, while new colleagues have become vital teaching and writing collaborators. By imagining a sustainable and equitable future in academia for myself, I renewed my commitment to inclusive academia for all. Toward this end, I offer some questions for considering refusal as renewal:

- How can we refuse the absence of Asian/Americans and other minoritized scholars in our field, especially in leadership and scholarship? How can we continue the sustaining thread of mentorship and allyship? How can we extend this type of mentorship intergenerationally and across affiliations?
- How can we refuse academic labor practices that value productivity over the kinds of caregiving that is essential to our teaching, mentoring, and administering of programs? That value productivity over less valued appointments such as directing writing or service-learning programs?
- How can Asian/American scholarship in writing and rhetoric, in ethnic studies, and other fields offer guidance to all WPAs to reflect upon and undo systemic oppressions in higher education?

Wherever we are in our careers, renewing our resolve for an intersectional practice of program administration requires taking care of ourselves and of each other. If a global pandemic and related class and racial uprisings have taught us anything, it may be that we rely on one another for our well-being. And that impulse toward grace and community is rebellion in itself against the relentless drumbeat of capitalism, with its colonial legacies of racism and sexism as the air we breathe in academia. Rebel, rebel–tear it down.

REFERENCES

Babcock, L., Peyser, B., Vesterlund, L., & Weingart, L. (2022). *The no club: Putting a stop to women's dead-end work*. Simon & Schuster.

Bernstein, R. (2017). The art of 'no.' *The Chronicle of Higher Education*. https://www.chronicle.com/article/the-art-of-no

Craig, C. L., & Perryman-Clark, S. M. (2011). Troubling the boundaries: (De)constructing WPA identities at the intersections of race and gender. *WPA: Writing Program Administration, 34*(2), 37–58.

De Mueller, G. G., & Ruiz, I. (2017). Race, silence, and writing program administration: A qualitative study of U.S. college writing programs. *WPA: Writing Program Administration, 40*(2),19–39.

Dew, D. F., & Horning, A. (Eds.). (2007). *Untenured faculty as writing program administrators*. Parlor Press.

Eng, J. (2007). Demystifying the Asian-American WPA: Locations in writing, teaching, and program administration. In D. F. Dew & A. Horning (Eds.), *Untenured faculty as writing program administrators: Institutional practices and politics* (pp. 153–171). Parlor Press.

Harahap, A. (2021). The promise and perils of a disciplinary and organizational pipeline. *WPA: Writing Program Administration, 44*(3), 56–62.

hooks, b. (1994). *Teaching to transgress: Education as the practice of freedom*. Routledge.

Hune, S. (2020). Taking action: Asian American faculty against injustices in the academy. In K. L. C. Valverde, & W. M. Dariotis (Eds.), *Fight the tower: Asian American women scholars' resistance and renewal in the academy* (pp. 1–28). Rutgers University Press.

Micciche, L. R. (2002). More than a feeling: Disappointment and WPA work. *College English, 64*(4), 432–458. https://doi.org/10.2307/3250746.

Monberg, T. G., Sano-Franchini, J., & Yoon, H. (2022). Asian/American movements through the pandemic and through the discipline before, during, and after Covid-19. *Reflections: A journal of community-engaged writing and rhetoric, 21*(1). https://reflectionsjournal.net/2022/02/editors-introduction-finding-humanity-and-community-in-pandemic-scholarship-2/

Monberg, T. G., Yoon, H., & Sano-Franchini, J. (2016). Introduction: Re/articulations of history, re/visions of community. In T. G. Monberg, H. Yoon, & J. Sano-Franchini (Eds.), *Building a community, having a home: A history of the CCC Asian/Asian American caucus* (pp. 1–30). New City Community and Parlor Press.

Perlmutter, D. (2008). How to say no (and get away with it). *The Chronicle of Higher Education*. https://www.chronicle.com/article/how-to-say-no-and-get-away-with-it/

Perryman-Clark, S., & Collin C. L. (Eds.). (2019). *Black perspectives in writing program administration.* NCTE.

Roy, S. (2021). Research anthology on challenges for women in leadership roles. In Information Resources Management Association (Eds.), *Challenges for Asian American and immigrant Asian women in the U.S. higher education administration* (pp. 566–585). Information Science Reference.

Seltzer, R. (2015, July 15). To find happiness in academe, women should just say no. *The chronicle of higher education.* https://www.chronicle.com/article/to-find-happiness-in-academe-women-should-just-say-no/

Tintiangco-Cubales, A. (2020). "Mothering is liberation." In K. L. C. Valverde & W. M. Dariotis (Eds.), *Fight the tower: Asian American women scholars' resistance and renewal in the academy* (pp. 350–364). Rutgers University Press.

Valverde, K. L. C., & Dariotis, W. M. (Eds.). (2020). *Fight the tower: Asian American women scholars' resistance and renewal in the academy.* Rutgers University Press.

Yoshihara, M. (2002). *Embracing the East: White women and American Orientalism.* Oxford University Press USA. ProQuest Ebook Central, http://ebookcentral.proquest.com/lib/callutheran/detail.action?docID=241282. Created from callutheran on 2022-01-09 18:30:08.

Young, M., & Monberg, T. G. (2018, December 18). Beyond representation: Spatial, temporal and embodied trans/formations of Asian/Asian American rhetoric. *Enculturation: Asian/American Rhetorical Trans/formations.* Issue 27, http://enculturation.net/27.

CHAPTER NINE

What is Gained in Transition: Lessons from a WPA in Liminal Space

KATHERINE DAILY O'MEARA, ST. NORBERT COLLEGE

> *"We may experience passage to the next stage of life, another place, or a new status among our own, but the crossing of that threshold always holds a great challenge and opportunity for transformation, one built into the fabric of existence itself."* (Carson, *A Liminality Primer*, n.d., para. 25)

It is unlikely that you will serve out your entire career at one institution in a single, unchanging role. A much more probable scenario is that you will decide to change institutions (and, consequently, your role as WPA, your positionality and material conditions, and your day-to-day responsibilities) as you build your WPA career. How do you know when it's time to take stock of what has happened and to re-evaluate what your priorities are? How do you recognize when a transitional experience is happening to you? How can you plan for a change and take care of yourself during it? While the prospect of trading what is known for the liminal unknown can feel daunting, liminality is also an opportunity for *renewal*—for both growth and reinvention. In this chapter, I reflect on the transition from my first WPA role to my second one. In writing from the other side of a liminal space, I am better able to analyze my experience: What precipitated my motivations to make the change, the resources and relationships that were most helpful while in liminal space, and the advice I have for other WPAs who may find themselves in similar situations. I hope this will be helpful to you as you consider your own journeys through liminal space.

LIMINALITY: A WORKING DEFINITION (AND CONNECTIONS WITHIN OUR FIELD)

Before diving into the narrative, let's have a bit of housekeeping on some key terminology. Liminality is a concept popularized by cultural anthropologist Victor Turner (2001), who defines it as the state of being "neither here nor there," and who describes liminal beings as entities who "are betwixt and between the positions assigned and arrayed by law, custom, convention, and ceremonial" (p. 359). In his fieldwork in Zambia, Turner, expanding on the work of ethnographer Arnold van Gennep (1960), described "the 'liminal phase' of *rites de passage*...rites which accompany every change of place, state, social position and age" (p. 359). Turner is also attributed as the original advocate of liminal space as an area of study, "uncovering the potential richness and cultural significance of what all too often is dismissed as a residual category" (Turner, 1979, p. 234).

Liminality scholar and curator of *The Liminality Project* Timothy Carson (n.d.) notes that Turner delineates three distinct phases of liminality: pre-liminal rites, a *separation* or detachment from a previous practice; liminal or transition rites, often a time of *instability*; and finally post-liminal rites, an incorporation or *re-stability* into a new practice or experience. This journey in "tripartite form" (Carson, n.d., para. 3)—separation, instability, re-stability—was a helpful frame for the transition from my first to my second WPA position. Also important to the notion of liminality is what Turner (2001) terms *communitas*, "the special bond between those who share the same liminal passage" at the same time. This bond was a feature that I did *not* experience in my own WPA transition, and it is one for which I now advocate. I'll get to that later.

LIMINALITY IN OUR FIELD(S)

Liminality as a concept has been explored in a number of different spaces within Rhetoric and Composition/Writing Studies scholarship. Tracy Whalen (2004), a rhetorician at the University of Winnipeg, uses *liminality* as a term to explain the positionality of rhetoric as a field and as a metaphor for "understanding rhetoric as practice"(p. 2):

> Liminality entails a position on the margins: on the edges of society, the coast of a continent, the borders of one's body, at the end of one stage of life and the beginning of another, etc. Rhetoric, especially in popular discourse, finds itself quite casually and habitually marginalized.... A bit of a free-floating ion on the margins of the disciplinary schoolyard, rhetoric finds itself attaching to different partners—composition, speech communication, and literary studies, to name a few. (p. 2)

Nordstrom et al. (2019) characterize the writing center as a liminal space on campus, describing the institutional positioning of the writing center as a space "both privileged and illegitimate" (para. 1). The Nordstrom et al. study also contends that more investigation is needed on the liminal experience itself. And recently, Macauley et al. (2021) use liminality as a key concept to discuss the passage "between roles and responsibilities" of composition TAs, who often find themselves as "being neither exclusively students nor fully teachers, and potentially recognizable as neither" (p. 4).

The term is also found in WPA scholarship. Phillips, Shovlin, and Titus (2014) discuss the role of the "liminal WPA," calling for its addition to the collection of categories gWPA, jWPA, and sWPA (and to argue for its fluid positionality within the aforementioned hierarchy). The authors note that the liminal WPA experience "had the authority of graduate students, some of the tasks of sWPAs, and identified most with jWPAs' sense of being caught between [one's] work and the institutional authority needed to achieve it" (p. 43)—in other words, liminal WPAs exist in the space between graduate WPA and WPA work. And Miller-Cochran (2018) recognizes the liminal space that is the *entire* WPA experience, advocating for intentional program administration in her plenary address "How to Lead a Writing Program Without Losing Your Soul" (p. 107). One might label the comprehensive WPA existence *as liminal*—WPAs "answer to multiple groups, and those groups often have conflicting goals" (Miller-Cochran, 2018, p. 108). The diverse array of possible WPA positionalities is all the more reason to give more visibility to the liminal moments and experiences in the life and career of a writing program administrator.

PRE-LIMINALITY: A TIME OF SEPARATION (PHASE I)

After three years in my first tenure-track WPA position, I decided to start looking informally for new WPA opportunities. I had learned that my current position was not sustainable, both in terms of my work/professional life and my personal life. I felt as though I did not have a research future on campus. All of my research was related to instituting a WAC program on campus, and that initiative failed due to financial constraints at the institution. The material conditions of my institution meant there was no money for program development, and therefore no long-term future for my specific research or administrative interests. This realization was a disappointing blow, as it felt as though my good work was being wholly rejected by my institution's upper administration. (For a more thorough discussion on managing rejection, see Green's chapter, this volume.) Stenberg and Minter's (2018) study of the resilience of WPAs reminds us that we must often "navigate the impact of neoliberal pressures that privilege efficiency and austerity" and then decide if the situation is tenable or not (p. 643). I realized that the situation at my institution was not tenable for me professionally, and started to imagine myself somewhere different, at an institution and in a writing program where progress felt more possible and where I could focus more on writing across the curriculum.

The work had also taken a toll. I had questionable-to-downright-appalling work/life balance at first, and the pressures of the job, coupled with my poor time management, were causing a strain on my closest relationships and impacting my health. Deciding to re-enter the liminal space of the job market helped me "acknowledge the inseparability of affective and intellectual work" inherent in WPA labor, a chance to "move out of disappointment" (Stenberg & Minter, 2018, p. 664). In hindsight, the potential of pursuing a new WPA position meant a necessary reevaluation of my priorities. (Both Adams Wooten's (2020) "How to be a Bad WPA" and Hesse's (2013) "What is a Personal Life?" also helped me tremendously with this task.) This experience might also fall under the umbrella of *unlearning* WPA-ing; for a more extended discussion on this, see Stolley's chapter, this volume.

Stenberg and Minter (2018) also note "the necessity of a revisionary review" in resilient WPAs: "rather than remaining bound to one view or solution, they found that as with writing, moving an idea forward requires many attempts and approaches" (p. 656). The authors maintain that "resilience is less about 'bouncing back' and more about 'redirecting' and 'salvaging a difficult situation'" (p. 656). When I couldn't salvage my *institutional* situation, I pivoted to consider what it meant to salvage *my own* situation: My work/life balance, my emotional and physical wellness, my latent desire to move closer to family. I learned in this pre-liminal phase to consider and re-assess my personal and professional priorities in order to inform my decision.

I see this move now as a manifestation of van Gennep's (1960) pre-liminal rites, or the first step toward my move through liminal space. In this first phase, the person typically experiences a separation or *detachment* from previous practices. Not being able to get a WAC program off the ground and the prevailing goal to relocate closer to my partner's and my families gave me the necessary detached perspective to realize that this position was unsustainable for both my work life and personal life. So I applied for a tenure-track WAC director opening, and I was in the fortunate position to be interviewed and to land a campus visit. When, to my tremendous relief, I was offered the position, I would soon learn what liminal space would really be like.

LIMINALITY: A TIME OF INSTABILITY (PHASE II)

Taking the plunge into liminal space was at once exhilarating and disorienting. It was exactly what Turner describes as "an experience of separation from structure without rootedness in community" (as cited in Carson, n.d., para. 11), often accompanied by "feeling a loss of steady and familiar landmarks, the kind of security that accompanied past structure, even as the future has not yet materialized" (Carson, n.d., para. 14). I definitely experienced feelings of isolation and loss, but also relief and exhilaration at the possibilities a new position would bring. Truly, it was a "moment in and out of time" (Turner, 2001, p. 360), as I was feeling "separated from the previous world and ushered into the unknown" (Carson, n.d., para. 2).

During this time, I also spent a lot of time reflecting on the WPA readiness I had experienced thus far in preparation for a renewal. While I knew I would have similar expectations in my new position (e.g., the job had a 2/2 teaching load; my role would be split roughly 50 % administrative and 50 % teaching), there was so much *new* to contend with. I was transitioning from a medium-sized public university to a small, private, religiously-affiliated liberal arts college. Where I worked with mostly grad students in pre-liminal space, in post-liminal space my focus would be almost entirely undergrad. And, of course, I was moving from a composition WPA gig to a WAC WPA gig. Overall it was, admittedly, a chaotic process. However, I am grateful for the messiness and the disorientation, as it helped me realize that "each individual's life experience contains alternating exposure to structure and *communitas*, and to states and transitions" (Turner, 2001, p. 361).

Consider also that change is perennial in all things, including WPAing. At first I was a little apprehensive of the prospect of such a big change, and all the potential confusion and unknowns inherent in the experience. However, I would invite readers to regard liminal space and other big adaptations, rearrangements, and changes to our WPA identities as an opportunity to practice gratitude. Turner (2001) writes, "Liminality implies that the high could not be high unless the low existed, and he who is high must experience what it is like to be low" (p. 360). While not always a high/low binary positionality, a WPA in liminal space certainly has the experiences of before the change and after the change (the pre-liminal and post-liminal times) to contend with. Tangled and messy feelings come with the territory of liminality, and my time in the *inbetween* was necessary to understand who I was as a WPA, to reflect on my past experiences and sort out future aspirations, and to feel (*really* feel) respect and admiration for all I'd learned and for all who had helped me along the way.

POST-LIMINALITY: A TIME OF RE-STABILITY (PHASE III)

As ever, time kept moving forward. Sold a house and bought a house, moved two aggrieved cats across the country, and my new WPA role as WAC Director was underway. I write this chapter at the start of my third year in post-liminal space and can reflect now on the cumulative experience. Thomassen (2009) writes that "liminality is followed by reintegration rituals that re-establish the order of the new personality as a part of the social order that he or she re-enters with a new role, stamped by the formative experience" (p. 22). The biggest impacts on my WPA life can be broken down into (1) the lessons from pre-liminality and liminality that informed the transition to my second administrative position, and (2) the new priorities and opportunities in my current experience of post-liminality that I attribute to those first two steps in the rites of passage.

Lessons from Liminality

Turner (2001) observes that those who transcend liminal space are "endowed with additional powers to enable them to cope with their new station in life" (p. 359). In other words, we come out the other side "stamped by the formative experience" (Thomassen, 2009, p. 22). Certainly I have been able to use my past experiences to inform my new position as WAC director. In deciding to take the plunge into liminal space, you, too, will have the opportunity to assess certain past challenges and affirm new practices.

A personal change I noticed was the idea of "my" ownership over the writing program (Stenberg & Minter, 2018). Where I held *so* tightly to control minor aspects of my first job and do everything solo, I now find myself better able to distribute and delegate responsibility and bring more voices and expertise into the decision-making process. Where I wished I had made more institution-wide connections as comp director, I feel better equipped as WAC director to promote more visibility of the program and pursue more cross-campus projects with faculty colleagues, administrative leadership, and instructional staff. This realization is unsurprising, as WAC work does lend itself to (and may indeed require) cross-campus connections of all kinds to sustain a program; however, I think it took the four years in my first job to gain enough institutional and WPA-related know-how to be confident enough to position myself accordingly.

The time I spent "in the interstices, from the in-between" (Thomassen, 2009, p. 18) had its own collection of takeaways. Turner (2001) maintains that "communitas can be grasped only in some relation to structure" (p. 372), and I now better understand *both* of my WPA positions (past and present) because of my time in liminal space. This is a lesson that can be productive both for graduate students, who may feel apprehension when taking the leap from graduate student (and possible gWPA) into the unknown of their first "real" WPA job, almost always as an untenured faculty member (see Dew & Horning, 2007). This consideration is also relevant for in-service WPAs, who may worry that they are foolish to leave a steady paycheck (and possibly the security of a tenure-track line) to plunge themselves willingly into uncertainty. I advocate for reframing these moments of change and transition (and the time spent in these liminal *inbetweens*) as opportunities to reflect, reprioritize, and reinvigorate as we plan for the new.

WPA Renewal: Post-Liminal Priorities, Opportunities, and Challenges

Those who experience *rites de passage* are said to "return to structure revitalized by their experience of *communitas*" (Turner, 2001, p. 373), and I found this revitalization to be true. I am now more confident reaching outside my discipline and across campus to get work done. These new relationships may give me better positionality and what I hope will turn into enhanced visibility of the WAC program I direct. Because of what I learned from pre-liminal and liminal experience, I feel more informed and able to pursue cross-institutional initiatives that contribute to my college's equity, diversity, inclusion, and belonging (EDIB) efforts. Re-assessing my work/life balance during that liminal time also helped me to feel re-energized to conduct WAC-related research in my new job, and the positive impact this change had on my physical and mental health and other aspects of my life cannot be overstated. In successfully moving through a liminal experience, you will likely notice an opportunity for transformative renewal. These changes (based on my experience) can give WPAs a sense of renewed creativity, feelings of personal accomplishment and satisfaction in their work, and a revitalized attitude toward scholarship.

Of course, the experience was not without its challenges. Though Turner observes that *communitas*, the "community of the inbetween" (Carson, n.d., para. 10), is established by people experiencing liminal space together, for my particular journey I did not feel as though I were in *communitas* with anyone—there was no one within the WPA community with whom I felt I could share my experience. My partner was an incredible support, and I disclosed what was going on with a few close friends outside of academia. However, because so much of the academic job hunt feels secretive and solitary, there was no way for me to create my own community of those who have experienced the *inbetween*.

Mine was a solitary liminality, and that was the exigence for writing this chapter. Stenberg and Minter (2018), citing Micciche, stress the imperative that WPAs "[see] ourselves in connection to others," forging friendships and collegial relationships with people "who can acknowledge and help us investigate the conditions of disappointment [my addition: and change, and transition,] and imagine possibilities outside of them" (p. 664). Conceivably, a chapter like mine (thanks to an edited collection like this one) can help WPAs in transition to create even more opportunities for community at all stages in their careers.

A related critique is of Turner's (2001) claim that all those who experience liminal space are "neophytes"—"a *tabula rasa*, a blank slate, on which is inscribed the knowledge and wisdom of the group" (p. 364). I argue that writing program administrators are rarely blank slates when moving from one position to another. Instead of feeling like a neophyte in liminal space, I brought my experiences from both my graduate coursework and jWPA experiences and the four years on my first WPA job past the first separation/detachment phase and into the transition. In this way, my own story of liminal space offers an alternative experience, critiquing Turner's original conception that seems to ignore the material conditions and knowledge of one's individual situation—and how this distinct positionality determines one's actions and decisions. Luckily, recent scholarship on liminality (e.g., Thomassen, 2009) delineates an updated, more nuanced description of *types* of liminal experiences (pp. 16–17), and it also gestures toward intersectional experience that results in "degrees of liminality" (p. 18). Working to consider all voices, identities, and experiences should therefore be an ongoing goal for our field, whether during liminal circumstances or in general.

CONCLUSION

While this chapter is just one WPA's experience in liminal space, writing it is an opportunity to encourage WPAs at any stage of their administrative lives to share their own stories of transition and change. Furthermore, sharing my individual story is a testament to liminality as a generative and valuable experience, something I think newer WPAs should learn sooner rather than later. Opportunities to experience/transcend liminal spaces are common and can occur at all stages during a WPA's career; Thomassen (2009) asserts that "most (if not all) persons can recognize moments or periods in their lives as liminal" (p. 18). There are important lessons to be learned at each phase, each one imbued with richness and significance (Turner, 1979).

As a fresh, new WPA approaching the pre-liminal phase, I was grateful for scholars who taught me to focus on what's important, including Peters' (1998) advocacy for collaborative administration and initial enculturation, as well as cautionary tales of the perpetual disappointment (Micciche, 2002) and austerity (Welch & Scott, 2016) inherent in our field. Cox, Galin, and Melzer (2018) encourage WPAs to always strive for more sustainable (WAC) administrative processes. Adams Wooten et al.'s (2020) edited collection on emotional labor in

WPA work is an homage to the significance of storytelling and sharing lived experience of our administrative lives.

In processing the arc of my liminal experience, I've been especially appreciative of available liminality scholarship, exciting and transformative, that helps inform more intersectional and comprehensive WPA practices. These include trauma-informed pedagogy; community-driven and -engaged work; inclusive and antiracist classroom, assessment, and administrative practices; and the ways in which embodiment studies and disability studies intersect with WPA studies. As a white, cis-gender, middle class, able-bodied, neurotypical female, my individual intersectional identity and positionality have impacted my experience in liminal space. People with differing positionalities and dispositions are sure to experience things differently. I encourage scholars in these interconnected fields to continue their exploration of the inroads between WPA work and intersectional identities, and how these affect individuals' liminal experience. We can all benefit from listening to one another.

The ubiquity of liminal experience makes it a relevant reality for WPAs, and I encourage others in our field to talk more about our various journeys of being "betwixt and between" (Turner, 1979), as these moments are possible at any moment in the long and winding road of a WPA's career. Thus, I recommend considering the prompts below for further discussion and contemplation:

Questions for Graduate Students:

- How was/is your transition to graduate school? (Or, reflect on any liminal experience you've had.)
  - What lessons did you learn in the transition?
  - What did you only realize after the fact, in hindsight?
  - How might this information help inform your decision-making processes for future events?
- How much should graduate WPA preparation address the precarity, vulnerability, and insecurity that so many WPAs experience?

Questions for WPAs Considering a Job Change:

- Knowing that transition is perennial, what can we as WPAs do to prepare ourselves (and each other) for professional change that is more transparent and supported?
- Brainstorm a list of your priorities, when it comes to the WPA work you do, your work/life balance, and any other important factors. What might be the new priorities and opportunities that deserve recognition in post-liminal space?

Questions for Scholars in the Field:

- How can we amplify diverse voices and value *all stories*, within all three liminal phases, to obtain a fuller, more inclusive picture of liminal experience?
- How might we better acknowledge the ways WPA work impacts our embodied experience, especially when considering the emotional labor that is inherent in (and often inextricable from) our efforts and aspirations?
- What can we do as a field to create sustainable communities and opportunities for sharing, connection, and storytelling—whether we are experiencing "the known and assumed structure of life" (pre-liminality), "the ambiguous transitional period" (liminality), or "the new adjusted and transformed state of being" (post-liminality) (Carson, n.d., para. 3)?

Those who experience liminality are "in a symbolic milieu that represent[s] both a grave and a womb" (Turner, 2001, p. 360). The transition from one WPA job to another, changing contexts and locations and institutions, meant certain practices fell away, while new experiences had the chance to begin. For me, what was gained in transition was the opportunity to be reflective about one's time in liminal space. Also intrinsic is the responsibility of sharing this experience to help others on their own journeys. My liminal experience helped me prioritize what was important to me—it was a chance to slow down for once and reevaluate my goals as a writing program administrator. Ultimately, this experience was, for me, a genuine moment of WPA renewal.

For all of us, liminality can be an opportunity to reposition and reprioritize, to recast or reinvent. We are constantly informed by our own and others' stories, but unless these stories are shared, it can feel like we are going it alone. This edited collection should be acknowledged as a meaningful contribution toward connecting disparate, diverse WPA experiences (whether that difference manifests across time, identity, positionality, material constraint, or administrative lifespan). Bearing witness to experience records a collective history and helps to imagine better futures for each other and for our field.

REFERENCES

Adams Wooten, C. (2020). How to be a bad WPA. In C. Adams Wooten, J. Babb, K. Murray Costello, & K. Navickas (Eds.), *The things we carry: Strategies for recognizing and negotiating emotional labor in writing program administration* (pp. 270–284). Utah State University Press.

Adams Wooten, C., Babb, J., Costello, K. M., & Navickas, K. (2020). *The things we carry: Strategies for recognizing and negotiating emotional labor in writing program administration.* Utah State University Press.

Carson, T. (n.d.). *A liminality primer.* The liminality project. https://www.theliminalityproject.org/the-liminality-primer/

Cox, M., Galin, J. R., & Melzer, D. (2018). *Sustainable WAC: A whole systems approach to launching and developing writing across the curriculum programs.* National Council of Teachers of English.

Dew, D. F., & Horning, A. (2007). *Untenured faculty as writing program administrators: Institutional practices and politics.* Parlor Press.

Hesse, D. (2016). What is a personal life? In R. Malenczyk (Ed.), *A rhetoric for writing program administrators* (pp. 475–482). Parlor Press.

Macauley, W. J., Anglesey, L. R., Edwards, B., Lambrecht, K. M., & Lovas, P. (2021). *Standing at the threshold: Working through liminality in the composition and rhetoric TAship.* University Press of Colorado/Utah State University Press.

Micciche, L. R. (2002). More than a feeling: Disappointment and WPA work. *College English, 64*(4), 32–58.

Miller-Cochran, S. (2018). Innovation through intentional administration: Or, how to lead a writing program without losing your soul [Plenary Address]. *WPA: Writing Program Administration, 42*(1), 107–122.

Nordstrom, G., Wang, I., Iwashita, K., Furtado, N., Kurashige, N., Ito-Fujita, A., Togafau, K., & Gushiken, G. (2019). Affirming our liminality & writing on the walls: How we welcome in our writing center. *The Peer Review, 13*(1) [special issue (Re)Defining Welcome]. https://thepeerreview-iwca.org/issues/redefining-welcome/affirming-our-liminality-writing-on-the-walls-how-we-welcome-in-our-writing-center/#post-775-footnote-1

Peters, B. (1998). Enculturation, not alchemy: Professionalizing novice writing program administrators. *WPA: Writing Program Administration, 21*(2/3), 121–136.

Phillips, T., Shovlin, P., & Titus, M. (2014). Thinking liminally: Exploring the (com)promising positions of the liminal WPA. *WPA: Writing Program Administration, 38*(1), 42–64.

Stenberg, S. J., & Minter, D. (2018). "Always up against": A study of veteran WPAs and social resilience. *College Composition and Communication, 69*(4), 642–668.

Thomassen, B. (2009). The uses and meanings of liminality. *International Political Anthropology, 2*, 5–27.

Turner, V. W. (1979). Betwixt and between: The liminal period in *rites de passage*. In W. A. Lessa & E. Z. Vogt (Eds.), *Reader in comparative religion: An anthropological approach.* Harper & Row.

Turner, V. W. (2001). Liminality and communitas. In M. Lambek (Ed.), *A reader in the anthropology of religion* (pp. 358–374). Wiley-Blackwell. (Original work published 1964)

van Gennep, A. (1960). *The rites of passage.* (M. B. Vizedom & G. L. Caffee, Trans.). Routledge & Kegan Paul.

Welch, N., & Scott, T. (Eds.). (2016). *Composition in the age of austerity.* Utah State University Press.

Whalen, T. (2004). Introduction: Rhetoric as liminal practice. *RHETOR, 1*, 1–11.

CHAPTER TEN

Revolving Doors: Programmatic Renewal and Regeneration through Leadership Reorganization

JACOB BABB, APPALACHIAN STATE UNIVERSITY
SUSAN POPHAM, INDIANA UNIVERSITY SOUTHEAST

The entrances to Knobview Hall, the home of the writing program at Indiana University Southeast (hereafter IU Southeast), used to have cumbersome revolving doors. There were regular doorways on either side, and most students, faculty, and staff favored these doors to avoid the heavy revolving doors. The sheer heft required to push them open enough to allow entry made them nearly inaccessible for most people, especially those carrying armloads of books, papers, lunch boxes, and bags. Without that strength, people needed agility to dash into the brief opening while someone else was doing the revolving push.

In this chapter, we use revolving doors as metaphors to think about how revisiting the structure of WPA positions can lead to programmatic renewal and regeneration. Simultaneously, transitioning into and out of the WPA role offers opportunities for WPAs to experience programmatic renewal. Transitional moments are often difficult for the programs WPAs serve (see Adams Wooten, Babb, & Ray, 2018), but rotating into and out of leadership roles can also be regenerative. While programmatic reorganization can often be stressful, we argue that being open to new visions for program leadership can provide space for programs to be innovative and dynamic.

Writing programs are dynamic structures that ideally outlast their WPAs. There are exceptions, of course, as poignantly chronicled by Heather Bastian (2019) in a contemplative essay on failure in WPA work, but, generally speaking,

WPAs come and go while writing programs continue, creating a history of their own that new WPAs benefit from as they become acquainted with the program's context. In their book *Writing Program Architecture*, Bryna Siegel Finer and Jamie White-Farnham (2017) argue compellingly that we should think of writing programs in terms of architecture, the "constituent parts of a writing program as its foundation, beams, posts," and that thinking in these terms can allow WPAs to "disentangle their role from the program itself" (p. 4). Additionally, the fact that programs outlast their WPAs most of the time might lead WPAs to reflect on their capacity to have long-term impacts on writing programs. One of the most poignant pieces of scholarship on this issue is Laura J. Davies's (2017) "Grief and the New WPA." Davies describes her first two years as WPA as "an exercise in managing the grief of the teachers in my first-year writing program" (p. 41). Her conclusion is similar to our point here, that programs go on: "a writing program, like any human organization, is not a time capsule. It lives, grows, and changes; indeed, the only constant is change" (p. 49). Davies frames her article as an inquiry into the emotional labor of writing program administration, acknowledging the humanity of the WPA who fills an important role in a writing program for a time, whose presence in the program and whose retirement from the leadership role creates room for programmatic growth and change.

The potentially dense history of writing programs most assuredly does not mean that WPAs are incapable of making changes or pushing programs in new directions. WPAs as leaders are often agents of change, striving to keep programs in line with best practices and to make their programs innovative. (For a powerful argument for recognizing WPAs as leaders, a term many of us are somewhat hesitant to accept, see Beavers and Anders in this collection.) However, inevitably WPAs must engage in negotiations with the various stakeholders in writing programs to make such changes. Programs are vibrant things made up of the people involved in them, whether they be teachers, tutors, staff, or other administrators. Tension exists for all WPAs between the program that was and the program that might be. Bradley Smith and Kerri K. Morris (2018) describe the transitions between them as WPAs, highlighting their intentional efforts to collaborate for a smooth transition, but they also note that "our roles have evolved as we have continued to work together on administrative tasks" (p. 268). In other words, even in moments planned for a smooth transfer of leadership, situations and positions continue to evolve and change. To echo Davies, the only constant is change.

To demonstrate the potential for programmatic renewal through restructuring of WPA roles, we share the example of programmatic and leadership changes that we have made at our institution with the intention of establishing our example as a model for other programs and exploring some of the challenges and benefits that can emerge during such reorganizations, both for programs and for WPAs. We describe the tensions and problems of adhering too closely to a traditional model of constant rotation of the roles of co-WPAs, and we describe the changes that we made, along with their attendant challenges and benefits. Finally, we list the lessons we learned from renewing our program's WPA structure in hopes that our lessons might prove useful for those who are also considering structural changes to the WPA role.

We note that there are three distinct yet overlapping ways in which writing programs can plan and experience renewal: changing the program structure by which the WPAs work; planning for a consistent rotation of WPA role; and the personal sense of renewal that the person filling the WPA role feels when stepping away for a while. We focus primarily on the first two kinds of renewal in this chapter while recognizing how vital personal renewal is for WPAs as well. Other programs looking to our experience as a model would be wise to perceive the distinctions among these forms of renewal as they explore possible structures for their own institutions.

RECOGNIZING THE NEED TO REVISE WPA PROGRAMMATIC STRUCTURES

Part of the goal of the co-WPA structure was always to have a more experienced co-WPA in place while the other co-WPA was learning what they needed to know to fulfill their responsibilities. In theory, the system of having two WPAs on offset two-year rotations creates some consistency in program leadership, since at least one of the two held the position the previous year. In practice, this structure created near constant change, but change that was located primarily in the WPA person, rather than dynamic change in the program. In other words, the program remained static because all the programmatic energy was invested in maintaining the co-WPA position rather than studying and revising the program itself.

WPAs and faculty in writing programs should occasionally take stock of how their program leadership structure and hierarchy helps or hinders the work of the program itself. Regardless of what the leadership structure looks like, programs should be willing to engage in periodic reflection to determine if reorganization can be beneficial. In our case, the co-WPA model kept the program running from day to day, but it did not provide sufficient opportunity for long-term planning, implementation, and assessment. We recognized the need to revise how our WPA structure worked to enable us to facilitate the program more effectively.

LINKING LEADERSHIP TO PROGRAMMATIC RENEWAL

Making changes to programmatic leadership can require buy-in from lots of different stakeholders across an institution. Anyone considering redistributing responsibilities or redefining how positions work should consult not only with their program faculty but also with administrators to create pathways to substantive changes. In our case, the dean who would need to sign off on our renovation was supportive, which we knew because we consulted with him as we developed our plan. In 2017, our program adopted a single WPA model, consolidating the responsibilities and compensation from two positions into one.

Beyond restructuring the WPA position itself, we also felt that it was vital to think carefully about how long individuals should serve as WPA. While we felt that shifting to a single WPA was the right choice, we wanted to maintain a relatively short term for the person filling the role. (See Janangelo's chapter for more on the benefits and potential drawbacks of long-term WPAs.) We opted for a three-year term, which was longer than the two-year terms co-WPAs held previously. The three-year rotation was intended to accomplish several things at once. First, by having three years in the position, the WPA would be able to develop and pursue initiatives for a longer period of time, which we hoped would shift the program's energy toward programmatic renewal rather than the constant training of new co-WPAs. Second, any person who took on the role would do so knowing that their term was relatively short, which we hoped would prevent any faculty member who took on the role from experiencing administrative burnout. Third, since several people in the program already had administrative experience and were interested in serving as WPA, the three-year term meant that those interested faculty members would have the opportunity to assume the role at one time or another.

Our purpose in revising the co-WPA model was to create conditions that were conducive to initiatives that would foster programmatic renewal and regeneration. Jacob was the first person to fill the role as solo WPA, and while there were bumps in the road as the program adjusted to the new model, his term as WPA demonstrated that our reasoning for revising the leadership model was sound. During that term, he revitalized the program by introducing significant changes to assessment processes, such as moving toward more standard learning outcomes for our numerous multi-section general education writing courses, and he conducted several semester-long professional development workshops for part-time instructors. By being the first to serve in the newly reimagined role, Jacob established the new ethos of the WPA as a program leader, focusing on a vision for the program and being proactive to enact programmatic change rather than simply reacting to day-to-day crises.

USING WPA ROTATION TO MAKE SPACE FOR INNOVATION

Though the stakes are perhaps not as high, we find that the transition from Jacob to Susan analogous to the peaceful transition of presidential power. Luckily, neither of us is responsible for nuclear codes or anything like that, but we knew that the first transition from one WPA to another in the new model would help us to see if there were any problems with the plan. One issue that became immediately clear is that the identities of the program and the person who led it had started to blur. As Susan transitioned into the role, most adjuncts and other campus administrators did not see Jacob as having stepped out of the position, despite his efforts to make everyone aware of the transition and to present Susan as the next WPA. For several months, part-time instructors emailed Jacob about students or curriculum changes, or administrators copied Jacob on emails sent to Susan.

New WPAs often face such challenges in establishing their credibility and authority. Despite having years of administrative experience, Susan was constantly reminded that Jacob had been the WPA for several years. Because for so long the only changes that were enacted in the program were located primarily in the changing of the people who filled the WPA position, adjuncts and other campus administrators had come to perceive the WPA as synonymous with the program. Jacob and the program had become integrally entwined, a negative effect of our leadership model transition that many programs with solo WPAs must face in moments of transition.

We assert that the difficulties Susan faced offer a powerful argument for program rotation, even as it seems rotation created those difficulties. Such challenges in leadership rotation are inevitable, reminding us of the programmatic grief described by Davies. It took time for instructors to accept Susan as WPA (just as it took them time to accept Jacob as WPA), but it is always necessary for new program leaders to forge the relationships necessary to direct a program. However, despite these complications, Susan assumed the role with enthusiasm and took on the challenge of moving the program forward. The transition of power was a bit rocky, but Susan's term showed that we succeeded in making the WPA position one that facilitated programmatic renewal. One of the main goals, after all, for shifting leadership around is to make space for innovations and improvements that may not flourish under one long-term WPA.

As the current WPA, Susan has made significant progress on aligning learning outcomes for general education courses, and she provided extensive support to full- and part-time instructors who had to shift to new modalities during the pandemic. She has enacted proactive policy changes aimed at making the writing program more accessible for faculty and students. For example, she built a shared file system so that instructors could access sample syllabi, assignments, and standardized course learning objectives. She designed several courses for either online or hybrid delivery modes and shared them as a resource for instructors struggling with virtual delivery. She opted for virtual faculty meetings and tried to incorporate more transparency on curriculum development and assessment processes. If there is a key goal to Susan's work as WPA, it is to emphasize accessibility–that is, that every teacher, student, and campus administrator would be able to access the resources of the writing program and would see the WPA as a helpful resource for the work of the campus community.

The writing program will soon pass the baton to a third solo WPA, who will then be afforded the opportunity to set the agenda for the writing program and to pursue goals intended to foster programmatic renewal. For our institution, our new leadership model works well. We found the right balance between sustained leadership that fostered programmatic renewal and an equitable, humane term of leadership that encourages professional, programmatic, and personal renewal as well. As WPAs, we both had time to set and pursue the agenda for the program over a sustained period. However, we also see this transitional moment as an opportunity to revisit the questions that drove our leadership reorganization, because by periodically reevaluating our model, we create the opportunity to make changes that benefit the program and those of us who lead it.

ADDRESSING CHALLENGES TO PROGRAMMATIC CHANGE

The brevity of our narratives about our terms as WPAs perhaps paints a rosy picture. However, challenges and problems always arise when programs make changes. As program leaders who deal with such routine tasks as hiring and staffing, assessing and revising curriculum, evaluating faculty, and addressing student grievances, WPAs build a lot of experience as problem solvers. That experience is also relevant to addressing the kinds of challenges that arise when a program revises its WPA model. For example, when we first proposed the shift to a solo WPA position, some full-time faculty expressed concern that such an individual would wield too much power and authority. We acknowledged then and now that this concern is valid, since we expressly moved away from a collaborative leadership model toward a model that invested more executive power in the WPA. We had to address faculty concerns by making our actions as WPAs as transparent as possible and seeking input on important programmatic decisions.

Leadership reorganization will inevitably make some people, even those involved in proposing the reorganization, feel shut out. As we have asserted throughout, as WPAs we should always aim for transparency and collaboration, in no small part to prevent individuals from feeling excluded. We should want all our teachers to feel that they have a stake and a voice in our programs. As WPAs, we both actively sought out ways to include program faculty in decision making and in conversations about revising and assessing courses. This collaborative work remains an ongoing challenge: because collaboration is not built into our WPA structure, each WPA who rotates into or out of the WPA position must maintain a constant commitment to this collaborative enterprise. When working as WPAs, we are never finished with the work of collaboration and transparency. Our writing program maintains a deeply collaborative approach, with faculty continuing to participate regularly in conducting and revising assessment, in revising existing and developing new curricula, and in engaging with the broader writing instruction needs of the university.

Programs that adopt a rotating structure also need to be mindful of how they manage transitions between WPAs. The most successful transitions will occur when the incoming and outgoing WPAs make time to consult with one another, so that the incoming WPA will know as much as possible about ongoing initiatives and about problems that still need to be addressed. We do not want readers to think that the only way to re-imagine and renew one's program means kicking out the current program administrator. Instead, we invite readers to see the revolving term as something more like a passing of the baton among the members of a relay team. We are all moving in the same direction–that of the continual improvement of the writing program for the benefit of the students–but just one WPA at a time. There will inevitably be short bursts of speed and energy among the relay team as the members each get a chance to recuperate and renew their strength, but in no way does that suggest that the program falls into a state of stagnation or decomposition (pun intended) during the term of a solo WPA. Transparency and ongoing collaboration with the department faculty and institution leadership can help to pre-empt a sense of relief when one WPA steps away, and incoming WPAs can start fostering this teamwork and these conversations from the very beginning.

A few years ago, the revolving doors on Knobview Hall were replaced with double doors designed for greater accessibility and energy efficiency, with an easily pushed button to open, clearly marked for all people to use as an enactment of universal design. As a result, most students, staff, and faculty do use the accessible door; it's easy for everyone, especially those who use assistive mobility devices or whose arms are full of books, art portfolios, or other items. The building is easier to enter and to exit. Our leadership reorganization has had similar effects on the writing program. We have created a sustainable model of leadership rotation that encourages different faculty members to take turns leading the program and collaborating with program faculty to revitalize the program.

PROGRAM RENEWAL: KEY TAKEAWAYS

While we have used our transformation of the WPA position as the chief example in this chapter, what we have learned over the past several years is broadly applicable to other writing programs that are considering leadership reorganization. We close with a brief listing of lessons that we learned in our work to restructure and renew our program. We offer these lessons as suggestions for any writing programs that may be considering reorganizing their leadership structure or that transition from one WPA to another:

- **Be transparent:** No matter the leadership model, we as WPAs should aim to make our work as transparent as possible. Transparency ultimately means giving instructors opportunities to offer feedback on new initiatives and priorities, which will only make the program stronger as instructors buy into new directions. Also, WPAs who are transparent build trust with all programmatic stakeholders, and that trust is vital for WPAs to do their best work.
- **Collaborate:** We see collaboration closely tied to transparency. We urge WPAs to invite other faculty members in their programs to contribute to determining the direction for writing programs, for providing input on assessment, and for helping to develop and revise curricula. WPAs can be excellent facilitators for this work, but we should never aim to do this work alone; such labor is unsustainable for the WPA and often unproductive for the program.
- **Understand labor and advocate for instructors:** While being transparent and striving to collaborate with everyone in the program is vital, so is an awareness of the amount of labor we ask instructors to invest in programmatic issues. WPAs are typically compensated for their programmatic work–although the extent of that compensation varies widely from one institution to another–while instructors in the program usually are not, and we find it crucial to find a balance between collaboration and labor. We encourage WPAs to be advocates for their instructors and to seek ways to find compensation for programmatic work.
- **Expect challenges during the transition:** All of us have been new WPAs at one time or another and have experienced some kind of doubt or distrust, whether voiced explicitly or not, in our capacity to lead the program. It takes time for any program to accept the leadership of a new WPA. We urge WPAs, both incoming and outgoing, to be patient with faculty and administrators who may struggle to accept changes in leadership. The outgoing WPA should try to be a helpful resource, but they should also strive to give the incoming WPA the space necessary to assume the role

successfully. Former WPAs, even when they are trying to be helpful, can become obstacles to a smooth transition if they cannot step back and give the incoming WPA room to lead.

- **Be open to revision:** We urge WPAs and writing programs to be open to revisiting their leadership structures and revising them as needed. We hope we have made it clear that we do not think our current WPA model is perfect or that it fits all programs. It works well for now, but we are open to future revision when necessary. All of the contextual factors of a program should be considered when determining the best leadership structure for programs. However, we encourage WPAs to be open to the possibility that other leadership models may work better for their programs. We do not need to continue using leadership models just because we inherited them.
- **Remain flexible:** Perhaps the only constant in WPA work is that change is constant. As soon as the position and the responsibilities feel comfortable, some institutional or societal, or even viral, policy will force some kind of change. As WPAs, we need to be responsive to the constant change that the position entails, while also maintaining our own values and goals. We can react to the day-to-day emergencies and issues that WPAs must address while also thinking about the long-term goals and visions we have for our programs. Maintaining the flexibility necessary to be both proactive and reactive is critical for WPAs to stay invested in their work.

We conclude by offering an idea that may seem antithetical to leadership: *think about your own needs.* Our list of recommendations for WPAs emphasizes the fact that we are all human beings, and that we must think about our own needs as well as our own professional goals. (See the chapters by Green, Klausman, and Mecenas for more on the tensions and possibilities involved in balancing personal and professional needs/goals.) The rotational model we describe gives WPAs the opportunity to step away from the work on a routine basis, but for those WPAs who may find themselves in more open-ended positions, we encourage you to think about when it is best for you to step away from the role and to renew your energies. Those of us who find WPA work satisfying and exciting will always have opportunities to lead, whether it means returning to the WPA role in a few years or turning to other work. Ultimately, we encourage all WPAs to think about what you need to sustain yourselves as professionals and as people.

REFERENCES

Adams Wooten, C., Babb, J., & Ray, B. (Eds.). (2018). *WPAs in transition: Navigating educational leadership positions.* Utah State University Press.

Bastian, H. (2019). The F-word: Failure in WPA work. *WPA: Writing Program Administration, 43*(1), 94–110.

Davies, Laurie J. (2017). Grief and the new WPA. *WPA: Writing Program Administration 40*(2), 40–51.

Finer, B. S., & White-Farnham, J. (Eds.). (2017). *Writing program architecture: Thirty cases for reference and research.* Utah State University Press.

Lucas, G. (Director). (1999). *Star Wars: Episode I – The Phantom Menace.* [Film]. Lucasfilm Ltd.; 20th Century Fox.

Smith, B., & Morris, K. K. (2018). Fostering ethical transitions: Creating community as writing program administrators. In C. Adams Wooten, J. Babb, & B. Ray (Eds.), *WPAs in transition: Navigating educational leadership positions* (pp. 260–271). Utah State University Press. https://upcolorado.com/utah-state-university-press/item/3220-wpas-in-transition

CHAPTER ELEVEN

Composing Your WPA Career: Pleasure, Responsibility, and Wisdom

JEFFREY KLAUSMAN, WHATCOM COMMUNITY COLLEGE

As I've been thinking about what lies beyond this current career I'm in, looking three years down the road toward "retirement," I've been reading about what Mary Catherine Bateson (2010) calls "Adulthood II." Adulthood II comprises those years after a person's most identifiable career and generally begins in a person's 50s–60s, when they move into new ways of being and doing in the world (pp. 14–15). The subtitle of her book is "The Age of Active Wisdom," which contains her thesis: that along with the extension in lifespan we've experienced since the early 20th century, we've added two to three decades of productive life post-retirement (p. 11). That's the "active" part. As for the "wisdom" part, through her anthropological work, Bateson (2010) recognized that those who aged "successfully" managed to compose a life in a way that allowed them to carry forward much of what they had learned in their professional and personal lives so that they could be of service to others, fulfilling a sense of responsibility, and in a way that brought pleasure to themselves (p. 19). This was wisdom made manifest in purposeful action.

What I'd like to suggest here is that early-career WPAs—everyone from graduate students looking ahead to what they might do in a college writing program, to official or *de facto* tenure-line WPAs trying to muster up interest in a portfolio assessment scheme—would do well to consider how they can compose their career around the pivot points of responsibility and pleasure. This is especially important, I believe, in times of change and turmoil—which they all are, in fact, but now especially so, given the major changes developing in higher education and the unpredictable consequences arising as part of the COVID crisis and restructuring. Having worked at a two-year college for over a quarter century, and before that at major universities in the U.S. and Japan during a period encompassing the digital revolution and the establishment of writing program administration as a profession, I wish I'd had such a frame. If I had, I might have avoided much of the heavy lifting of the emotional labor I undertook and chosen my path with greater care and, judged from my perspective now, wisdom, culminating in a more pleasurable way of being.

I mentioned Bateson's idea of "Adulthood II," those potentially productive and active years following retirement. She draws upon Erik Erikson's life stage development theories—she was a student of Erikson—and presents the psycho-emotional development of each stage, with crisis and core issue to resolve (Bateson, 2010, p. 66). But in looking at my own career and that of many others I've known, I wonder if it wouldn't be more productive to consider adulthood not as comprising two parts—which requires Adulthood I to account for a lot—but rather in three phases, each comprising a period in which a person is developing their sense of self in the public world: who they are, relative to others; what they are good at and like to do; and how well they do it.

Most of us can probably identify an early phase of adulthood when we were just developing ourselves, a period following high school and including undergraduate years, which probably also included some travel, many moves, several relationships, and for us, ultimately, graduate school. This "Phase I" of adulthood can be considered the exploratory and developmental phase, when we explored and then developed a professional mode of being in the world. If it's true that the world really wants us to be good at something, usually one thing, then Phase I is when we figure out what that one thing is and then develop some chops in it.

Then, "Phase II" begins, when we start to build—a career, a family, a social footprint, so to speak. This phase extends in an arc roughly from the completion of formal study and the taking of our first professional position all the way to "retirement," in the traditional sense. The Harvard Study of Adult Development folks call this the "generative years," when we are building, generating value (see Valliant, 2008).

Then, after traditional retirement, we move into "Phase III" of adulthood, marked by years of productive engagement with the world but without the trappings of a job and without the "upward mobility" climb (and the anxiety that accompanies it) that marks our generative years. In Phase III, our kids have likely moved on, our money worries have mostly subsided (for us lucky ones), and we are more secure in our accomplishments and abilities. We no longer need to prove ourselves.

For new or entering WPAs, there's value in thinking of adulthood (and perhaps your career) as having three phases. You can assess where you are on this developmental arc and make some wise choices about what you want that phase to look like. You can, to evoke Bateson (2010) again, "compose" your career rather than follow the option many of your elders followed, whose careers were likely shaped "less by design than by circumstance," as Doug Hesse (2020) says of his (p. 199). (For more on making decisions intentionally, see Beavers and Anders in this collection.)

But "wise" is a tricky term. What is wise for one person is unwise for another; what is wise today may be foolish tomorrow. But there is a sense of what "wise" means that may act as a guide, and for this, we'll have to step out of our academic boots for a moment because this sense of knowing requires a non-empirical measure. Ram Dass (2000), the spiritual guru who first became famous as Richard Alpert, co-director of the Harvard psilocybin experiments with Timothy Leary in the 1950s, says wisdom is a function of "emptying and quieting the mind, the application of the heart, and the alchemy of reason and feeling" (p. 17).

I like that understanding of how wisdom comes to be, heart plus reason once the busy, analytical, worrying mind is quieted and we can listen for feeling. It reminds me of Chicago philosopher Eugene Gendlin's (1981) concept of "felt-sense": "A felt sense is not a mental experience but a physical one…an internal aura that encompasses everything you feel and know about a given subject at a given time—encompasses it and communicates it to you all at once, rather than detail by detail" (pp. 32–33). This felt sense, perhaps obviously, can't be accessed via the analytical mind but can be accessed only by quieting it.

So, we might have some guidance here in invoking whatever wisdom we have available to us: quiet the mind and pay attention to what our heart (body) plus our reason tells us.

Here, I'd like to relate two stories that exemplify wise and unwise actions, which fall into and perhaps exemplify the exploratory and generative phases of adulthood. What I hope the experiences show is that any move toward composing a career means a move toward consciousness. By definition, that means a move out of unconsciousness, and for us in a professional career, unconsciousness likely has numerous facets, each of which might come clear were the crystal tilted to the light slightly differently.

PHASE I: EXPLORATORY YEARS

When I was my college's first WPA and one of the very few in existence at two-year colleges, I set about reading everything I could on the subject of "being" a WPA. (See Stolley in this collection for more on preparing for and unlearning

WPA work.) One of the things I read over and over was that without buy-in from faculty, especially contingent faculty, any programmatic reforms one might wish to facilitate would die in the "murky waters" of institutional hierarchy (Leverenz, 2020, p. 26). So, accepting the "democratic vision" of the institution (Ostman, 2013, p. 168), I sent an email inviting each contingent faculty member, one at a time, to my office. We were about 2/3 contingent so that meant about twenty meetings. These meetings were cordial. I explained what the new position was about, what I hoped it might accomplish, and how the participation of all faculty, but especially contingent faculty, was the key for success.

Contingent faculty came and went, knocked on my office door (though it stood ajar) and sat in the plastic chair across from my desk

I'm guessing at this point, nearly everyone can see what's wrong with this picture.

But I didn't, not then. I was not operating consciously, making a wise decision by combining heart and reason, but rather enacting a script written by others in other situations. A WPA was "supposed to" get buy-in from contingent faculty and that was what I was doing. Wasn't it? Besides, I knew even as WPA, I had "no [real] power" (Ostman, 2013, p. 4). However, contingent faculty, I learned later, didn't know that.

The results, as you might guess, were less than I'd hoped for and worse than I could have expected. Nearly all the contingent faculty were suspicious and some outright hostile. Anthony Warnke et al. (2020) discovered, albeit after the fact, that even the supposition that a program might be needed brought with it the implicit allegation that there was something lacking in the first place: "Even wanting to conceive of a 'writing program' may cause umbrage as it suggests absence or deficiency" (p. 38). So in all my talk of "collegiality" and "program development," I was unwittingly telling my colleagues that what they were doing, and thus who they were as teachers, wasn't really good enough.

But there's a second layer here, and it's a bit more personal. I identify as male, "white" with quotation marks (I'm a quarter Chinese, an eighth Native American), hold a doctorate (at the time, one of only two members of our English faculty to do so), and am tenured. Privilege with a capital "P." From the perspective of contingent faculty, I could not be more other and still be faculty—and not (yet) administration—although there is that "A" for administration in WPA, isn't there (see Warnke et al., 2020, p. 37)? So I was "other," from the contingent faculty perspective, certainly someone to be suspicious of.

But let's add one more layer of (painful) personal unconscious. I grew up in a household with an emotionally abusive father. I learned early on to stand my ground, to be smart, to be quiet when needed, and to hold in my rage. What I was protecting, of course, was a sense of self-respect, which the abuse of a parent, when they are being abusive, is aimed to destroy. So as I came to the WPA position, I unwittingly brought with me the need to be respected, a need that, when stressed, was tethered to a fight-or-flight sense of survival. At times, when I felt I wasn't being respected, the old demons flared up and I became defensive. Defensive for me means a pointed use of reason.

Without diving too deeply into these particular psychoanalytic chambers, I can say that as resistance to my efforts grew, I pushed back and grew angry (though I suppressed it). So I forged ahead with even more carefully constructed arguments and pointed communications: If reason alone wouldn't win the day, perhaps a bit of force might. What followed were several lengthy email chains, with two prominent and senior contingent faculty, analyzing and discussing pedagogical and curricular issues.

Now, email is a notoriously bad way to solve problems—in fact, it usually makes them worse. But I didn't know that at the time (this was around 2006). So the emails continued, got lengthier and more pointed, and eventually, I cracked and said something snarky and personal in one of them. What ensued was silence and then a complaint to the Division Chair, my heartfelt apology (I knew I was acting out of old malice, aimed inappropriately at the contingent faculty member), and then, a week or two later, an eruption from the second contingent faculty member during a department meeting in which he shouted, with frightful force, that "a certain person" had done certain things and was, in the end, "stupid, *stupid, STUPID!*"

This particular faculty member certainly had serious issues of his own, which I won't go into here, but he left everyone in the room shaken, traumatically so. For days after, I walked in a sort of daze. But there are a couple of things to learn from my initial efforts to bring contingent faculty into program development efforts.

Obviously, the first is, "don't be stupid," but that's hardly helpful. We might know stupid going into a situation sometimes but usually we only know it on the way out. A second and more cerebral lesson is that the very existence of a WPA serves as a reminder of the kind of "entrenched inequity" that Peters (2003, p. 136) and so many others talk about, especially labor inequities which instantiate very real inequities of power. But for us, there are even more helpful things to learn.

Pleasure is a term I mentioned above. As Bateson (2010) points out, citing Konrad Lorenz, pleasure is "an innate teaching mechanism" offering "a reward that reinforces behavior, pleasure leading to repetition" (p. 146). As I was having those pointed email exchanges with contingent faculty members, I was not considering pleasure—theirs or mine—as any sort of criterion in making the decision to continue. If there was any pleasure, it was of a perverse kind (the cowering child striking back at the abusive father). If I had stopped and paused and listened to my heart and paid attention to feeling, I would have known, reasonably, that going down that path of heated explaining was not pleasurable in any way that I would wish to repeat.

And yet repeat I did, and so what does that mean?

It means that I was lacking wisdom. I did not quiet the mind and allow the heart to join reason in leading the way. Quite the opposite. I was all "mind," the busy, analytical, worried mind that I had trained up into a 300-pound gorilla in graduate school. And I let that gorilla loose—or nearly—on those two people who taught in my department and who had put up the most resistance to my reasonable (to me) plans. (See Leverenz in this collection for more on our blindness to the limits of our authority.)

PHASE II: GENERATIVE YEARS

One of the primary functions of a WPA at a small or two-year college, where the instructors you work with are not graduate students but fellow faculty, usually untenured and usually without much formal training in composition (see my "Mapping the Terrain"), is to bring the world of comp-rhet to them, which can be a risky venture (see Blaauw-Hara and Spiegel, 2018, p. 247, and Warnke et al., 2020, p. 49). Not the whole world, of course, but those aspects that can make the faculty and thus the program more effective in fulfilling its mission (the kind of "big agency" Micciche talks about [2011, p. 73]). The field of composition and rhetoric, I don't need to tell you, is both a fascinating and fruitful field, one with a forward-thinking research agenda and a growing body of empirically studied methods.

But in light of the context so painfully exposed by the incident I described above, one of suspicion, fear, and masked hostility, how can a WPA do their job (if not the job of others, [see Gillam, 2003, p. 119]) and further the social justice mission most of us accept as truly ours? How can we avoid the mistake of assuming that "our scholarship [is] more significant than their affect" (Warnke et al., 2020, p. 42)? How can we be true to the field and fair to the faculty?

We could evoke Wenger's "communities of practice" here or possibly employ activity systems theory or some other lens to get a sense of how a loosely affiliated group of faculty might be encouraged to move in a certain direction (see my "Toward a Definition"). All I'll say is that several years later, as WPA again, I saw how inert our curriculum and pedagogy had become and knew we had to change.

Years earlier, I had helped our faculty reform the curriculum around an "introduction to academic discourse" model, based on the work of Bartholomae and Petrosky (1986). But that model had become calcified in the intervening years as faculty bore down on their own practices and, in the separate silos of closed classrooms, drifted further and further away from any collaborative and cohesive whole.

What to do?

Like any good academic facing an existential crisis, I decided we should read something.

I got funding from our college's foundation to pay contingent faculty for their time and sent out an open invitation to the department. Pleasantly, I heard from eleven colleagues and we set about reading *Writing across Contexts: Transfer, Composition, and Sites of Writing* by Yancey, Robinson and Taczak (2014). Weekly, we met in a conference room and each person read aloud two sentences they'd underlined in that week's reading and explained why. We practiced generous listening. This took the better part of the hour. The discussion that followed was generative and caring. People enjoyed coming to the meetings. One said that our discussions were something she'd been missing since grad school. I was thanked, many times, for making the space for camaraderie, for shared discovery. I repeated the reading group the next year and had a similar experience. Collectively, we developed a shared understanding of what we wanted our composition classes to do, how, and why. (See my chapter in Patrick Sullivan's *Sixteen Teachers Teaching* [2020] where I describe my take on our "learning for transfer" curriculum.)

Now, reading groups are nothing new. I had tried "brown bag" reading groups at various times, when we'd read a journal article every month and discuss them. And earlier, in that first curricular reform, I'd led a small group in reading basic writing theory which led to piloting a class that eventually became the basis of the entire writing program. But what made this an effective experience is that it made space for pleasure which, as Bateson (2010) says, "builds the groundwork for responsibility" (p. 147). In other words, without pleasure in our activities, it's unlikely we'll fulfill them with a sense of responsibility; rather, we'll be fulfilling an obligation, grudgingly, without care.

We academics, when allowed to be academics, find pleasure in learning, in thinking, in discourse. It's at least partly why we stayed in school so long. Folks in English studies usually don't "survive graduate school" so that they can become English professors, the way lawyers or medical doctors sometimes view their professional training. For us, the study of texts is itself pleasurable. But often, especially at a teaching college where a 5-5 load is the standard (and 8-8 is not that uncommon; see Calhoon-Dillahunt, 2011, p. 121) that's something that is too rare in our jobs. So the reading of the book together in the spirit of shared discovery was itself an exercise of pleasure.

But I'll also venture that the way the discussions were structured, around sharing and generous listening, was a big part in making that pleasure manifest. Warnke et al. (2020), in reflecting on their errors in developing a new writing program administrator position, warn about the need of "navigating the affective terrain" (p. 38), meaning that how program reform suggestions are received affectively by faculty, especially contingent and long-term tenured, is even more important than the reform ideas themselves. Each of us seeks to be seen and heard. By making space for that, the pleasure of text and textual discourse can also foster more primary feelings of well-being. (See Blaauw-Hara in this collection for more on working with caring colleagues at two-year colleges.)

A second aspect of the frame I'm offering is responsibility (see Adler-Kassner & Harrington, 2010). I've not met a single writing teacher who didn't care, deeply, about their students. And what we want for our students is likely what we want for ourselves: self-efficacy, the pleasure of knowing what we're doing has value, the replacement of fear with confidence. And we know that all those factors are intersected by racial, class, and gender biases. So, social justice is a responsibility that can be marked by pleasure. At my college, like nearly all two-year colleges, we serve a large population of first-generation students, and a growing population of Hispanic as well LGBTQ+ students. We are aware of their uncertainty, of their pain. Our learning-for-transfer curriculum gives us a basis to support their growing empowerment, a basis that has some empirical evidence behind it, and one that we can agree makes sense. So it fulfills our sense of responsibility to our students and ourselves as educators.

Did I pause, listen to my heart as I applied reason, in making the decision to seek funding for that reading group?

I'd like to say yes. I take long walks, often with a meditation track in earbuds, and practice mindfulness (see Wenger [2021] on WPA work and mindfulness). When I am mindful, I'm able to experience my colleagues as others seeking love, peace, liberation. I'm able to experience them as "thou," in the Martin Buber (1996) conception. I can't recall the exact moment when I conceived of the idea of offering the Yancey book to the department and to seek funding for contingent faculty. It simply emerged, a kind of "slow agency" Micciche (2011) talks about (p. 74). Most importantly, I know that I found pleasure in making the offer and I found pleasure in the open-hearted responses that followed. And I found pleasure in the way we all came together to fulfill a meaningful responsibility. I think the entire experience was life affirming for everyone involved and, as a result, advanced programmatic goals in real and sustainable ways. It's been six years since we began those reforms and now they are firmly established as standard programmatic practice.

I'd like to think that the majority of my career decisions have been so, but I don't think I can say that. Most of the time, I've simply been a manager of a program—ordering texts, running workshops, ushering along changes to the wording of outcomes—rather than a wise and compassionate leader. (I have begun to think of leadership not so much as a direct act as one of creating an ecosystem in which space for collaboration seems to happen naturally, a shift from system thinking to ecology.)

And, of course, there are times I acted unwisely, to say the least, which perhaps was necessary for the learning to take place at all (Micciche, 2020, p. ix). But had I had that lens early on—pleasure and responsibility through wise listening to the heart plus reason—I might well have created far more opportunities for life-affirming experiences, like the one I describe, honoring our interdependence, and giving and receiving with "grace" (Bateson, 2010, p. 7).

PHASE III: ACTIVE WISDOM

So what can we learn from this now? As I write this, in July 2022, the Covid pandemic churns on, though with less urgency; our social-political world seems in more turmoil since any time in my memory (since the 1970s, anyway); and the very nature and structure of higher education is in question: What will students want to return to as my college again offers mostly in-person teaching? What will faculty want after teaching remotely for over two years? Is any of what I've written still relevant? And if so, how?

Probably not surprisingly, I think the main point still holds: by anchoring our decision making in the ground of active wisdom—pleasure plus responsibility—we can avoid many of the most vexing errors WPAs are prone to and nurture both self and others for the betterment of the program. Here are the key take-aways I'd like you to get from this piece:

- **See your career in terms of phases:** exploratory, generative, and "the age of active wisdom." Investigate opportunities through this lens to determine whether and how to take on new responsibilities.
- **Foreground "wisdom":** Wisdom arises (or the opportunity for it, anyway) when the mind is quieted and the heart-plus-reason are listened to; reassess your current situation or assess potential future opportunities through a lens of wisdom to balance critical, analytical, or career-based thinking.
- **Use the framework of "pleasure and responsibility":** Inform the wisdom of career decisions—large and small—via pleasure as a natural teacher and responsibility as the calling of us as teachers and program administrators.
- **Strengthen your generous listening:** All of us, as individuals and teachers, wish to be respected, seen, and heard, which brings pleasure via connection; let generous listening be a guiding principle of professional development.

REFERENCES

Adler-Kassner, L., & Harrington, S. (2010). Responsibility and composition's future in the twenty-first century: Reframing "accountability." *College Composition and Communication, 62*(1), 73–99.

Bartholomae, D., & Petrosky, A. (1986). *Facts, artifacts, and counterfacts: Theory and method for a reading and writing course.* Heinemann.

Bateson, M. C. (2010). *Composing a further life: The age of active wisdom.* Vintage Books.

Blaauw-Hara, M., & Lemieux-Spiegel, C. (2018). "Connection, community, and identity: Writing programs and WPAs at the community college." In C. A. Wooten, J. Babb, & B. Ray (Eds.), *WPAs in transition: Navigating educational leadership positions* (pp. 245–259). Utah State UP. DOI: https://doi.org/10.2307/j.ctt22zmb7g

Buber, M. (1996). *I-Thou.* Touchstone.

Calhoon-Dillahunt, C. (2011). "Writing programs without administrators: Frameworks for successful writing programs in the two-year college." *WPA: Writing Program Administration, 35*(1), 118–134.

Dass, R. (2000). *Still here: Embracing aging, changing, and dying.* Riverhead Books.

Gendlin, E. T. (1981). *Focusing.* Bantam.

Gillam, A. (2003). "Collaboration, ethics, and the emotional labor of WPAs." In D. Jacobs & L. Micciche (Eds.), *A way to move: Rhetorics of emotion & composition studies* (pp. 113–123). Boynton/Cook.

Hesse, D. (2020). "Aging through the thirty-year rise of professionalized writing administration." In N. Elliot & A. S. Horning (Eds.), *Talking back: Senior scholars and their colleagues deliberate the past, present, and future of writing studies* (pp. 189–203). Utah State UP. DOI: https://doi.org/10.7330/9781607329763

Klausman, J. (2008). "Mapping the terrain: The two-year college writing program administrator." *Teaching English in the Two-Year College, 35*(3), 238–251.

Klausman, J. (2010). "Not just a matter of fairness: Adjunct faculty and writing programs in two-year colleges." *Teaching English in the Two-Year College, 37*(4), 363–371.

Klausman, J. (2013). "Toward a definition of a writing program at a two-year college: You say you want a revolution?" *Teaching English in the Two-Year College, 40*(3), 257–273.

Klausman, J. (2020). "The theory that remains: Toward a theoretically informed writing assignment." In P. Sullivan (Ed.), *Sixteen teachers teaching: Two-year college perspectives* (pp. 85–117). Utah State UP. DOI: https://doi.org/10.7330/9781607329305

Leverenz, C. S. (2020). Don't worry, be happy: How to flourish as a WPA. In C. A. Wooten, J. Babb, K. M. Costello, & K. Navickas (Eds.), *The things we carry: Strategies for recognizing and negotiating emotional labor in writing program administration* (pp. 19-36). Utah State UP. DOI: https://doi.org/10.2307/j.ctt22zmb7g

Micciche, L. (2011). "For slow agency." *WPA: Writing Program Administration, 35*(1), 73–90

----. (2020). "Foreword." In. C. A. Wooten, J. Babb, K. M. Costello, & K. Navickas (Eds.), *The things we carry: Strategies for recognizing and negotiating emotional labor in writing program administration* (pp. ix–xii). Utah State UP. DOI: https://doi.org/10.2307/j.ctt22zmb7g

Ostman, H. (2013). *Writing program administration and the community college.* Parlor Press.

Peters, B. (2003). An anatomy of radical anger in writing program administration. In D. Jacobs & L. Micciche (Eds.), *A way to move: Rhetorics of emotion & composition studies* (pp. 135–146). Boynton/Cook.

Vaillant, G. E. (2008). *Aging well: Surprising guideposts to a happier life from the landmark study of adult development.* Little, Brown, Spark. DOI: https://doi.org/10.1176/appi.ajp.161.1.178

Warnke, A., Higgins, K., Sims, M., & Sherman, I. (2018). "You lost me at 'administrator': Vulnerability and transformation in WPA work at two-year colleges." In C. A. Wooten, J. Babb, & B. Ray (Eds.), *WPAs in transition: Navigating educational leadership positions* (pp. 37–55). Utah State UP. DOI: https://doi.org/10.2307/j.ctt22zmb7g

Wenger, C. I. (2018). "Navigating WPA emotional labor with mindfulness." In C. A. Wooten, J. Babb, & B. Ray (Eds.), *WPAs in transition: Navigating educational leadership positions* (pp. 251–269). Utah State UP. DOI: https://doi.org/10.2307/j.ctt22zmb7g

Yancey, K. B., Robertson, L., & Taczak, K. (2014). *Writing across contexts: Transfer, composition, and sites of writing.* Utah State UP. DOI: https://doi.org/10.2307/j.ctt6wrr95

CHAPTER TWELVE

Renewal through Cartography: Designing Resilience amidst Persistent Ecological Change

COLIN CHARLTON, UNIVERSITY OF TEXAS RIO GRANDE VALLEY
JONIKKA CHARLTON, UNIVERSITY OF TEXAS RIO GRANDE VALLEY

> Writing has nothing to do with signifying. It has to do with surveying, mapping, even realms that are yet to come.
>
> -Gilles Deleuze & Félix Guattari, *A Thousand Plateaus: Capitalism and Schizophrenia* (1987)

For anyone who has been at the same institution for ten, fifteen (or more!) years, it is so easy to lose that spark that once drove you, to become frustrated or even angry sometimes, and to become jaded by all you've seen and experienced. We've all known (or maybe been, on occasion) those faculty members who, weary from initiative fatigue or the never-ending churn of higher education administrators, punch out or—worse yet—actively work against institutional changes. In this chapter, we will share strategies that helped us maintain agency and connection to our institution over the long haul, and offer advice for how you, too, can strengthen your resilience amidst persistent ecological change to ensure you not only survive, but thrive, in your professional life. A certain agility of mind and disposition are essential to how we have flourished at our institution all these years, and we hope this chapter gives you some insight into how you can find similar agency and resilience.

In writing this chapter on renewal for mid-career WPAs, we see that systemic mapping–and remapping–is a key strategy that has kept us going. At its heart, the map of a system identifies the elements of a network or organization, their active relationships, and also the gaps between or boundaries of those elements. Systemic mapping is also a tool for Vico's (1990) idea of ingenium as the capacity to generate novel connections. To borrow an insight from research in design and innovation, "The systemic map is a tool for deliberation. In this design method, prototypes serve as conversational objects forming the basis for open dialogue about desirable futures. They help to reveal the connections between and among those preferences" (de la Rosa et al., 2021, p. 287). Cartography and the maps of our institutional literacy constitute our social resilience (Stenberg & Minter, 2018, pp. 653–654). A concrete map of the players, units, and values that you are working with allows you to see relationships that fade or die, the ones that strengthen, and the ones that are possible. You become someone who can pivot from disappointment to opportunity (McGee, 2005) without letting what is lost overwhelm that which becomes possible.

At the core of this cartography is our interest in scaffolded and sustainable curricula and our investment in invention and rhetorical design. These can be invaluable in personal, departmental, institutional, and other key stakeholder interactions at a change-rich institution. The questioning of the relationships among multiple academic pieces is the play of productive organizational thinking. Systemic mapping also allows you to create a flowchart for emotional, financial, critical, and personnel allocation and action. Used together, questions and mapping can help you stay inventive in your thinking about people, relationships, cross-unit support, learning gaps, outcomes, and the potentials for commonplaces of action and understanding. Creating an evolving set of ecological surveys can also be a critical strategy for WPAs interested in Stolley's (in this volume) idea of *unlearning*: "a process of genuine, often painful, reflection that highlights our own mistakes, vulnerabilities, and prejudices" which helps us become more equity-minded, effective partners. In the following sections, we'll discuss how different cartographic ways of thinking through administrative work can help you simultaneously design and renew your efforts and investment.

First, we'll look at how mapping writing and the definitions and values associated with it that circulate in your contexts can help ground sustainable interventions. Second, we'll explore how thinking as a cartographer helps expose relationships and partnerships that impact both our projects and personal sustainability as WPAs. In our concluding reflection, we'll offer a summary set of questions that help you think about how you can work towards renewal. We hope our advice and examples help you think about the systems where you work and fret, find joy and disappointment, and discover potentials to engage, connect, develop, and leverage. This exploration of terms, values, and partnerships–the ones we seek, the ones that surprise us, the ones that continue to unfold through change, and the ones that fail and test our resilience–represents the cognitive and affective org chart of our lives and our work. It teaches us something new every time we look at it, move all the pieces around, figure out what will stick, what will develop in the wild, and what will keep renewing the drive to wonder *and* wander.

KEYING DEFINITIONS AND SURVEYING TERRITORY

Maps matter. Before WPAs look at a larger landscape, its constituent pieces, and their fluid relationships, it's important to identify stakeholders who have operating definitions of writing. LaFrance and Nicolas' (2012, 2013) work with institutional ethnography and Miley's (2017) example of extending institutional ethnography to her writing center experiences offer a primer in the strategy we endorse—chart terms and values early and cyclically. We approach understanding writing in a pretty consistent fashion whether we're working with secondary teachers, a first-year writing program, a graduate program in social work, or a college trying to nail down a writing intensive definition for courses. Start a spreadsheet, draw some bubbles, or create a concept map. However, you want to visualize definitions that are circulating, we think it's important to capture the definitions of writing, the values connected to those definitions, and the outcomes or demonstrations of "good" writing partners have. If you organize these dimensions of writing in a relational map, do this and you add to your collection of terms, definitions, and values over time, you will eventually have a key you can refer to each time you need to revise, build, or just comment on a writing-related issue on your campus.

Our early attempts to define or redefine writing, even with writing teachers, took more energy than they should have because it was often a clash of expertise-thinking. Even at the program level, you may find yourself in a room of first year writing teachers with backgrounds in creative writing, literature, linguistics, and rhetoric and composition. As a WPA, you can't hope to navigate and steer a variety of conversations about student performance unless you understand (1) how first year teachers with diverse backgrounds define their content and interpret shared student learning outcomes (SLOs), (2) how a dean perceives course caps and effective writing pedagogy, (3) how other general education teachers and areas depend on writing development, and how (4) writing support areas (learning centers, writing centers, student mentors, etc.) interact with all of the above.

When our current university came into being in 2015, it felt like perpetual change was the new normal. A distributed campus, new departments that almost doubled in size overnight, and new leadership made it difficult for the first-year writing program to define itself in light of so many different re-definitions going on. While we both had a clear idea of the ten years of history that preceded our new university, we had to re-establish the expertise needed to teach writing in a Department of Writing & Language Studies that now housed general education writing courses instead of an English Department. One of our strategies was to work with the dean to bring in the Council of Writing Program Administrators' Consultant-Evaluator Service for support with consultation on a self-study. This partnership with outside experts helped us articulate our history and expose the different sets of circulating terms and values. We were able to give a different forum to our instructors, get a fresh outside perspective on a distributed campus, reflect on our student learning outcomes, and re-calibrate our goals for a new department and campus structure.

Institutional changes too often trigger feelings of reactivity rather than inspire innovation. It's also easy to go into auto-pilot mode and take for granted that everyone in your writing program (still) thinks about writing and how it should be taught the same way. When you stay in one place long enough like we have, you can lose your sense of wonder and possibility. Naysayers can argue that nothing ever changes. Slow developments toward desired program changes can leave you disheartened. But, as people are in their job a long time, they naturally look for ways to change things up, to make it more their own, and before you know it, you may find you no longer have a cohesive writing program with shared definitions of "good writing" and "good writing teaching" anymore.

It is very easy to experience this kind of "mission creep" in programs that have been in existence for a long time, especially with a core, stable group of faculty members. As individuals in your program explore new interests, you may find that, while they can be reinvigorating for the individual faculty, they may lead away from the program's established commitment to core values and definitions of good writing teaching that the program has committed to. You may also find, as we did, that disruptive events, such as the pandemic or the BLM movement, fundamentally challenge the ways you and your faculty have always thought about writing and its teaching at your institution. During the pandemic, our program's teachers, some of the best in the country, found that the strategies and approaches that had always worked for them no longer did. We recognized the need—and the opportunity—to reinvigorate the program by beginning again with a conversation about what we value, an equity-conscious analysis of which of our students have been struggling and why, and a renewed commitment to explore what we're doing and how we can change to better meet the evolving needs of all of our students.

One of the most important things you can do is create an ongoing project grounded in a conceptual understanding of how writing lives at your institution (see Janangelo in this volume on the relationship between WPAs and institutional memory). We can't know exactly what method will work best for you to draw this map and design a key to your institutional contexts. It might be a hierarchical organizational chart. It might be a color-coded Venn diagram. You could use different types of lines (dotted, heavy, light) representing the strength of agreement and relationships among people, areas, and missions. Whatever your approach, we do have a few suggestions to help you make useful maps and the keys that help you read (and shape) them. Mapping––and remapping––answers to these questions gives you data over time and the ability to see patterns, relationships, and possibilities you didn't realize existed before.

- Where is writing happening at your institution (in discipline-specific writing classes in a new STEM major, in satellite tutoring centers in the dorms, in continuing education programs)?
- Who are the groups who have an investment in student writing on your campus (upper- level faculty, the Graduate College, the Career Center, faculty and staff engaged in program review and assessment)?
- Who are the people and offices who are invested in student writing (the provost's office, the General Education Committee, Engineering faculty who teach Senior Design courses, faculty mentors of undergraduate research, the Business Writing Center, etc.)?
- Where are there existing connections between your program and other interested groups and initiatives? How can you best represent the stability and strength of those connections on your map? Are there some relationships that are at risk of dissolving while others are thriving or yet to be drawn?

Mapping the institutional writing geography enables crucial reflection on partnerships past, present, and future that affect(ed) the teaching of writing, and it helps you develop a vocabulary of context, giving you the ability to pivot how you talk about teaching and learning with different stakeholders without sounding too disciplinarily immersed to be approachable. You could develop an institutional map by having a writing-focused tour of colleges or departments to discuss perceptions of writing at your institution with follow up informational sessions on writing goals and services that could reframe (when necessary) or support common writing goals. If you leverage opportunities that are built into your institutional infrastructure––like small internal grants, institutional strategic planning processes, and required accreditation projects such as the Quality Enhancement Plans (QEP) for institutions accredited by the Southern Association of Colleges and Schools Commission on Colleges (SACSCOC) institutions––you can find time and money to do surveys and interviews across ranks and areas to find out how writing is perceived, what "weaknesses" have weight across the institution, and where the opportunities to support or lead reform exist with partners-in-waiting.

If you connect with colleagues in writing centers, general education committees, writing across the curriculum initiatives, and assessment offices, you can experiment with simple meetings of writing-interested leaders to determine your gaps and overlaps in defining writing and writing goals for your students. These can become common collaborations, especially since they would relate to college placement for writing students and larger institutional tracking practices (see Green in this volume for her experience with pursuing assessment knowledge in a contingent position). Even at the program level, you can make a discussion of terms part of assessment calibrations for your writing program, which aligns an investigation of important concepts with measures of student success. Though we may become comfortable with definitions of audience, purpose, and form over years, it's important to bring such rhetorical issues to the forefront of conversation so that teachers can reflect on what they mean by good writing and how that aligns with the pedagogies we deploy and the assessments we use to reflect on how our teaching transfers. Whether you use a long-term strategy like these or other ones that suit your context, collecting, comparing, and mapping out terms together can have the triple benefit of comparative analysis, community building, and rejuvenation.

REDRAWING THE LINES OF PARTNERSHIP & ALIGNMENT

If you approach leadership as we suggest by mapping language and values, which will allow you to link projects and identify areas for growth, you will likely create a network of potential partners along the way. Partnerships are a bit like feedback. You need to collect a lot of both to see your strengths, identify habitual dead ends, and map healthy processes/products. To that end, we urge you to add to your cartography experiences with the language and space of the institution to think about how people, units, and their relationships connect to what you've drawn out by investigating your local contexts. We have found it useful to think about the drivers of different partnerships and why they need us or how our knowledge about how writing, learning, and teaching operate in those locations.

Creating partnerships may seem daunting if you think of them as opportunities to always lead work. Even the most dedicated of us will hit a wall when it comes to our energy or time at some point. To that end, know the difference between the partnership projects that you want to lead, the projects you'd like to be connected to, and the projects that you need to keep an eye on because they are close to your work with student success, writing, and design. Keeping a project and people inventory means that you have a network of categorized profiles and opportunities to help you quickly think about (1) how to put a team together, (2) how to locate resources, (3) how to research the context around a given situation or question, and (4) how to set some strategic and practical outcomes (for a variety of stakeholders).

Again, we're coming back to the idea of mapping out partnerships in terms of what we have collected or could collect about an institutional context. These maps don't have to be large or perfect, and they evolve over time with added partners and understandings and data on the workings of units within an institution. They need to be in development, and they need to be discussed with existing and potential partners, if only to explore potential disconnects (like terminology or funding) and overlaps (like educational experiences or personnel areas of expertise). You may be frequently asked for briefs about different projects you are a part of, but the secret is making them regularly for yourself. When you create an organizational chart for a supervisor or a project summary for a potential funding source, it is an opportunity to map what may be the moving, abstract target of your vision onto real people, units, and resources to see more clearly see how it is or isn't leading to better learning experiences, happier faculty, and responsive, equity-conscious policies.

INSTITUTIONAL CHANGE, RE-VISION, AND RENEWAL

Through representation, maps allow us, at a specific place and time, to see and plan and imagine beyond what we can actually experience with our immediate senses. As environmental keys, they foster movement, curate experience, and document ecological values and change. While our mapping behaviors may be trending more towards pin-dropping on virtual images than napkin-drawing, there is still a lot of value in the experience of making maps for a very simple reason. When we have to think about how to represent a space, we quickly find ourselves reflecting on relationships. In higher education, the acts of representing and reflecting on who we are, where we are, and what we do *with people* are even more critical. In "More than a Feeling: Disappointment and WPA Work", Micciche (2002) investigates the emotional and intellectual dimensions of WPA work, calling on us to engage in an expanded dialogue on administration, to study the affective dimensions of WPA work through material practices, and to re-imagine our professional development activities with a deep understanding of both how our immediate institutional systems work and how the potential for disappointments within them can be leveraged for transformation. Becoming institutional and program cartographers helps you creatively and sustainably challenge the "'fixed' stance" of disappointment Micciche warns against, which can harden into "disillusionment, resignation, and passivity in the face of new, ever-changing situations" (p. 446).

The bulk of this piece is about change—how you can develop a comfort with, and find opportunities within, the persistent developments that will affect what you design and foster. You will likely change leadership positions (see Brunk in this volume on developing a student advocacy mindset over time and across multiple leadership roles). Disciplinary relevance will erode in one place and aggregate in another. Strategic plans will evolve and re-shuffle who the stakeholders for writing are and how they can work together. The list goes on, and not all the changes will be warm and fuzzy and embraceable. *The Things We Carry: Strategies for Recognizing and Negotiating Emotional Labor in Writing Program Administration* (Wooten et al., 2020) catalogs challenges with and strategies for preserving work identities, communities, and emotional balance in the face of traumatic changes. To call back to Micciche's (2002) work on disappointment, the real danger of incessant movement isn't fatigue. It's the sneaky loss of memory and strategy, especially when crises and questions of administrative identity collect and aggregate. But when your capacity for change seems fixed, you can renew by developing a habit of reflectively mapping where you work–strategically asking questions, nurturing partnerships, and expanding your "WPA" identities. To that end, we offer a succinct set of questions to help you reflect, re-invent, and renew at any phase of your cartographic thinking.

- What is the map of the pathway of learning-to-write at your institution, from the year before students enter to the post-graduation pathways they follow?
- What definitions and values of writing are circulating, emerging, and fading in your program, department, college, and institution?
- Which resources in terms of people, space, money, time, and strategies stay relatively stable, and which ones fluctuate?
- Which existing or potential writing-related partnerships can you find by surveying the local goals of programs, degrees, grants, and strategic plans?
- Where do your ideas sputter and fail to gain traction? Where do your initiatives thrive, and who is involved?
- What other leadership positions at your institution would benefit from the way you question, problem-solve, map, design, develop, and assess writing programs? Which ones would provide you with an opportunity to be an architect of new connections and afford you the chance to redraw your institutional map in a way that furthers important values and goals?

Our parting advice: Always keep exploring your institutional landscape, even if you think you know it already. Be open to new leadership opportunities beyond where you currently sit–and allow yourself to grieve the loss of the ones you've left behind. Be on the lookout for opportunities to connect something you care about to institutional and leader-specific priorities and take advantage of what's within your sphere of influence. The more you embed your values, language, and priorities in new strategies and institutional contexts, the more likely those things will persist when leaders change.

To build the kind of resilience that enables renewal, we have to tap into that part of us that is always yearning to build, to make new connections, to mentor and be mentored by those who can stretch our thinking and our experiences, to embrace the new and the possibilities that come with each new chance to iterate. In higher education, it's very easy to allow our frustrations and disappointments (and even disgust or outrage) with life in higher ed to "harden into disillusionment," to lose the hope and possibility for flourishing that our much younger selves wrote about with our co-authors in *GenAdmin* (2011). At the same time, it's important to remember that change can be generative and renewing; it does not have to be threatening, even when that change is accompanied by heartbreak and loss.

While there will always be many inflection moments along your institutional timeline that successively contribute to shaping who you are, your use of cartography to stay grounded and resilient will not follow a linear path. The exploration of institutional landscapes and changing administrative identities over the years is cyclical and iterative. Remaining agile and curious, with a positive mindset about change and even uncertainty, will allow you to persist and thrive.

REFERENCES

Charlton, C., Charlton, J., Graban, T. S., Ryan, K. J., & Ferdinandt Stolley, A. (2011). *GenAdmin: Theorizing WPA identities in the twenty-first century.* Parlor Press.

de la Rosa, J., Ruecker, S., & Giraldo Nohora, C. (2021). Systemic mapping and design research: Towards participatory democratic engagement. *she ji: The Journal of Design, Economics, and Innovation, 7*(2), 282–298.

Deleuze, G., & Guattari, F. (1987). *A thousand plateaus: Capitalism and schizophrenia.* U. of Minnesota P.

LaFrance, M., & Nicolas, M. (2012). Institutional ethnography as materialist framework for writing program research and the Faculty-Staff Work Standpoints project. *College Composition and Communication, 64*(1), 130–150.

LaFrance, M., & Nicolas, M. (2013). What's your frequency?: Preliminary results of a survey on faculty and staff perspectives on writing center work. *Writing Lab Newsletter, 37*(5/6), 10–13.

McGee, S. J. (2005). "Overcoming disappointment: Constructing writing program identity through postmodern mapping." In S. J. McGee & Carolyn Handa (Eds.), *Discord and direction: The postmodern writing program administrator* (pp. 59–71). Utah State University Press.

Micciche, L. R. (2002). More than a feeling: Disappointment and WPA work. *College English, 64*(4), 432–458. https://doi.org/10.2307/3250746

Miley, M. (2017). Looking up: Mapping writing center work through institutional ethnography. *The Writing Center Journal, 36*(1), 103–129. http://www.jstor.org/stable/44252639

Stenberg, S. J., & Minter, D. (2018). "'Always up against': A study of veteran WPAs and social resilience." *College Composition and Communication, 69*(4), 642–668.

Vico, G. (1990). On the study methods of our time (E. Gianturco, Trans.). Cornell University Press.

Wooten, C. A., Babb, J., Murray Costello, K., & Navickas, K. (Eds.). (2020). *The things we carry: Strategies for recognizing and negotiating emotional labor in writing program administration*. Utah State University Press.

CHAPTER THIRTEEN

It's All About the Student: Advocating for Students at All Levels of Leadership

BETH BRUNK, UNIVERSITY OF TEXAS AT EL PASO

In memory of Dr. Diana Natalicio, University of Texas at El Paso President Emeritus

Once or twice a year, faculty, staff, and administrators would receive an envelope from the President's Office with photographs from university events. The packet included a handwritten note card from the president with one's name followed by something like "looking good" or "Go Miners!"

Dr. Diana Natalicio retired from the University of Texas at El Paso in 2019, and she passed away in September of 2021. While processing the news of her death, I looked for that treasure trove of envelopes needing to find a picture of us together. I found one and posted it on social media, but the amazing thing was there were so many similar pictures that came pouring out—*everyone* had a picture with her in it, and the most impactful ones were those with students. Students at commencement, students at pep rallies, students who recognized her in the airport and asked for a selfie, and so on. Many of them commented that it was because of her that they achieved their dream to graduate from college—that being first in their family to go to college was a challenge, but because of her leadership and encouragement, it became possible. And, similarly, so many faculty, staff, and administrators said the same: that they loved being a part of an institution intensely focused on serving students. At an open access Hispanic-Serving Institution attaining Carnegie classified R1 (very high research activity) status in 2018, Dr. Natalicio was clear that we must not lose our focus on students and leave our dedication to teaching behind us. As a colleague said, "She demanded of every one of us that we embrace this work holistically and that we believe these ideals go hand in hand." She often said, "Talent is everywhere, but opportunity is not." Access and excellence, her life's work, was, and still is, also ours.

I start with this memory of Dr. Natalicio as an illustration of what I internalized working at the institution where she served as president for more than three decades. This memory overlaps with the mindset I acquired while serving as a writing program administrator and that I integrated into administrative responsibilities throughout the last decade. At the core of my work, I've long believed that it's all about the student.

DEVELOPING THE STUDENT ADVOCACY MINDSET

For most of us, the role of Writing Program Administrator (WPA) is our first foray into academic administration. Perhaps we were fortunate to participate in a writing program administration graduate course or work as a junior WPA before being hired as an assistant professor or instructor of practice, and at some point, we were asked to assume responsibility beyond our own teaching and to oversee all the first-year writing courses offered at our institution. In spite of its narrow scope of responsibility and perspective, serving as a writing program administrator is one of the most complex leadership roles on any campus. Upon accepting the role, we may then find ourselves overwhelmed with the quantity and scope of tasks and responsibilities on the WPA to-do list: schedule classes, locate classrooms, hire instructors, prepare teaching assistants, select textbooks, offer faculty development workshops, plan assessments, observe instructors, attend meetings… the list goes on. (See Anders and Beavers in this volume for more on rhetorical mindfulness and leadership readiness.) With so much required for a smoothly running and effective writing program, it is easy to get caught up in the to-dos and overlook whom the to-dos serve: the student. However, the responsibilities of the WPA role taught me to place students at the center of all decisions, no matter the administrative position. While I left the role of the WPA as I moved onto other leadership positions, I did not leave the mindset, but rather enriched it with each expanded area of influence and responsibility.

Advocating for students happens at all levels and takes various forms. In this chapter, I discuss significant insights gained through the writing program, college, and institutional level leadership positions at an urban, R1, open-access, Hispanic-Serving Institution. (See Daily O'Meara in this volume for more insight on transitioning between leadership positions.) These insights concerning how institutional processes, practices, policies, and personalities both help and hinder students propelled me into wanting to learn and do more to open pathways, clear the brush, strengthen the quality of programs, and ensure that students are at the center of all decisions within my purview.

As WPA

As WPAs, we broaden our impact beyond the individual courses we teach to influence the direction of an entire writing program. In this leadership position, administrative work becomes less of an "us vs. them" relationship and more a series of productive challenges and opportunities. Most importantly, the role affords us the responsibility to advocate for students at a programmatic level.

Like many of my academic generation and those before, I didn't intend to be a Writing Program Administrator. (See Ferdinandt Stolley's chapter in this volume for more about learning and unlearning how to be a WPA.) In fact, the first time I was asked to direct the First-Year Composition (FYC) program, I declined it to the chair of the department based on advice from the same chair of the department. I was two years away from applying for tenure, and the current WPA was stepping down. As I was considering the invitation, I attended a workshop by the chair on "saying no" to opportunities that diminish chances of achieving tenure. To her surprise, a few days later, I declined the WPA offer in order to focus on my tenure portfolio. However, a couple years later, in 2008, I submitted my tenure packet and was eager to start WPA work.

When I assumed the WPA position, the FYC program had been awarded a grant for improving the quality of general education in public institutions across Texas. Doing so meant collectively brainstorming, developing, and accepting a new program-wide philosophy about the teaching of writing and its impact on students. Of course, a program philosophy and curriculum are only relevant and effective through their implementation at the classroom, or section, level, which means that WPAs must hire and retain a well-prepared teaching team—and sometimes be strong advocates *for* students *to* the faculty. For example, when faculty express concern that students do not effectively and promptly complete simple tasks, fail to appropriately address their professors, do not understand the importance of reading a syllabus carefully, and so on, WPAs should caution against the assumption that students arrive already enculturated into their institution. Rather, we can establish a program-wide mindset in which FYC provides an opportunity to welcome new students to the institution and provide them with an understanding of what it means to be an engaged, self-regulating college student.

Additionally, professional development opportunities—such as workshops, mentoring, program guides and feedback—should be built upon not only developing a sense of belonging across the faculty, but also a philosophy that students are individuals who embody particular and diverse backgrounds. It is not uncommon to assume a somewhat monolithic profile of FYC students similar to what Joanne Baird Giordano and Holly Hassel (2019) call "the mythical norm of college students" who are 18, white, live on campus, have few extra-academic responsibilities, and have consistent access to food and a warm place to live (p. 35). This description may be generally true on many campuses. However, bilingual students, international students, and adult learners, for example, will also be enrolled in our writing programs. In large part, this approach can be supported through encouraging an asset-based mindset which, rather than recognizing certain characteristics as deficits–such as a learning English later in life, being the first in their family to attend college, or needing to work while enrolled–understands these to be advantages or assets that students can build upon.

As literacy/biliteracy education scholar Erika Mein (2018) states, asset-based pedagogy emphasizes "students' individual and collective strengths, skills, and capacities as the starting point for learning and engagement…and [is] focused on reconfiguring teaching and learning to promote equity at the classroom level" (p. 1). Mein explains that rather than operating as if learning English is a deficit, for example, we should understand that "bilinguals have…a linguistic repertoire across multiple languages," and that "fluid movement across the repertoire is normal and should be encouraged particularly in learning contexts" (p. 2). For example, our program invited students to brainstorm, collaborate, research, and even include some excerpts in Spanish—or any other language—in their compositions if it was rhetorically appropriate to their project. We went a step further and changed the prefix of all rhetoric courses from English—or ENGL—to Rhetoric and Writing Studies–RWS–in an effort to demonstrate not only our disciplinary identity, but also that students were not limited to nor limited by a single language.

Understanding the diversity of our student population and engaging in universal design principles for all learners will strengthen the quality of instruction and increase opportunities for learning in multiple formats. Writing courses are foundational to helping students understand how to be engaged, enculturate themselves into the institution, and develop their agency to ask for what they need to succeed.

As Associate Dean of the College of Liberal Arts

Three years into my tenure as WPA, the dean of the College of Liberal Arts inquired about my interest in serving as an associate dean in the College of Liberal Arts. However, I was not ready to move away from the writing program and decided to hold both positions. The first thing that I learned was that two 50 percent appointments equals more, much more, than one 100 percent appointment. However, the second thing I gained was insight into more aspects of the institution that affect students' experiences inside and outside the first-year composition program by learning more about admissions, registration systems, financial aid, policies, degree plans, and so on.

As an associate dean, a significant responsibility was to advise students who were on academic probation or suspension. Students, sometimes in their first semester of academic probation, sometimes their third or fourth, would have to make an appointment, fill out a form, and then anxiously wait to see one of us. None of this process was pleasant for anyone involved, but I made it a goal to help students genuinely reflect on why they were in this situation, think about a plan for the next semester, and have confidence that they could get back on track. The conversations ranged from quick and simple (I know exactly what I did or didn't do) to difficult (I blame my professors because they were all terrible and didn't understand me) to heart-wrenching stories about ever-present challenges and/or life disruptions that simply got them off track. The responsibility of meeting with students on academic probation promoted a holistic view of students and their academic and life experiences. Now, instead of regarding them as "just" a student in one of my classes, or a student who might have a concern in the first-year writing program, I saw students as they were in the institution: students of all different majors, students with all kinds of challenges, many of which were not of their own doing but of the institutional structures that created roadblocks and unnecessary barriers.

Overcoming and possibly removing these barriers for students is achieved by networking across the institution to understand how processes, policies, and their interpretations impact students' coursework and progress toward their degree, as well as their ability to solve challenges. As an associate dean, I quickly learned that creating relationships across campus supports creative collaboration and may help remedy students being shuffled from office to office as they attempt to resolve an issue. Resolving issues in the present is important, but as we move into these levels of administration, we also have the opportunity to advocate for changes at the systemic level and possibly engage in the messy, complex, and often highly political campus conversations about and around student retention and persistence.

I had the perspective of working in both roles at the same time—associate dean and WPA—which illuminated several important points. First, a writing program's agency in retention and persistence is highly contextual, variable, and dependent upon a number of conditions, including if the program has a WPA who can coordinate the work; if the program has an articulated and agreed upon vision that contributes to the conversation; if the program provides effective communication and professional development opportunities to support instructors; and if the instructors buy into the program's and institution's definition of student success and teach with those goals in mind.

However, as an associate dean, I understood more poignantly writing program administration scholar Pegeen Reichert Powell's (2013) caution against retaining students at their expense and that in many cases "there may be very little we can do to prevent our students from leaving" (p. 28). In fact, on more than one occasion, I found myself in the difficult position of not permitting a student to re-enroll the upcoming semester. Such decisions may seem counterintuitive, but occasionally students find themselves in situations where it's more damaging to their success to stay enrolled. Surprisingly, students would often thank me, even hug me, and follow-up later when they were ready to return.

These instances serve as reminders that we should also consider "what our [writing] courses should look like…when we know many of our students won't come back to our institution next year, and that some may never graduate" (Powell, p. 110) and engage in "kairotic pedagogy" that leans more toward participation and less toward preparation (p. 118) —not to "prepare a student to life the life of an intellectual, worker, and citizen, but rather to invite the student to *participate now* as a reader and writer of the world, to recognize that they are currently intellectuals, workers, citizens" —as a means of better serving all students no matter their academic trajectory (p. 118). This mindset may seem at odds with current practices when institutions are heavily invested and engaged in maintaining enrollments. However, my insight as associate dean illustrated that the students' best interests must always be maintained whether they will complete their degree in four years or six years, whether they will return to the institution after not enrolling for ten years, transfer to another institution, or decide that the college experience is not for them.

As Dean of Extended University

Along with a significant adjustment of perspective, serving at the dean level opens pathways for mitigating students' institutional challenges on a more expansive scale. On the one hand, much of the work becomes detached from engagement with or focus on students at the individual level. Organizational charts have two, three, or maybe four levels between the dean and students. When individual students present challenges or concerns, problem solving is attempted by others, and the dean "gets involved" when matters cannot be resolved or when a potentially unfavorable decision must be made. At the same time, however, this leadership role affords the opportunity to make decisions and changes that impact a far greater number of students in the respective college as well as through collaboration with fellow deans, vice presidents, and the institution's provost. Similar to Jeff Grabill, Sarah Gretter, and Erik Skogsberg's (2022) observation about their work at the Hub at Michigan State University, leadership at this level enables us to move from the "individual to the collective, from the classroom to the institution" (p. 7).

Advocating for students through all levels of leadership is achieved with an understanding of the type of institution, its mission, its strengths, and its challenges. The type of institution, ranging from public to private, regional to Ivy, comprehensive to doctoral, religious to secular, for-profit to technical or community college, residential to commuter, Hispanic Serving to Historically Black, and every intersection between and among these influences, determines the culture of the campus. For those who have been promoted into and through leadership positions at the same institution, they likely understand these nuances implicitly; however, as they reach higher levels of administration, they need to articulate those explicitly and consider how their leadership style and decisions reflect and/or impact the mission. At the "upper administration level," institutional missions and strategic plans become increasingly significant in the decision-making process. As European educational leadership scholars Ciaran Sugre et al. (2019) state, "University leaders orchestrate the creation of strategic plans and allocate resources to strategic priorities, with consequent implications for both structures and cultures of the working and learning environments" (p. 3).

In addition to establishing direction and setting the tone, deans also have the opportunity to engage in productive disruptions, particularly when policies and practices are out of alignment with the institutional mission. Grabill, Gretter, and Skogsberg (2022) point out that "since institutions are fundamentally rhetorical entities, rhetoric can be used to change them" (p. 7); and "if we believe that we can and should design the next iteration of higher education, then we also must believe that we are the authors of our institutions" (p. 9). While productive disruptions in support of students can be done at all levels of leadership, deans have the ability set the tone by encouraging departments and programs to consider antiracist and anti-white supremacist practices, similar to writing programs adopting the "Toward Anti-racist First-Year Composition Goals" statement (Beavers et al., 2021). An antiracist alternative to the WPA Outcomes Statement, the Goals statement offers questions and considerations for constructing "broader, . . . inclusive, generalizable writing goals from local conditions, students, and teachers." The learning goals, curriculum, and assessments of all academic programs should be informed by the respective disciplines but developed within and for the local context with our "diverse students, their languages, and their material circumstances in mind." These considerations speak to writing program administration scholars' Elizabeth Vander Lei and Melody Pugh's (2016) observation that "students experience institutional mission most immediately in the classroom, through curriculum and pedagogy" (p. 148). Therefore, all leadership levels should be in conversation about how the "institution articulates its mission, how it has enacted its mission, and how that [everyone] can build on an institution's mission" (p. 143) to "further foster convergences" between the individual classroom and the institutional mission (p. 151).

These convergences can often be supported by thoughtfully and ethically engaging with data that is not solely based on revenue, enrollment, or research productivity. Data is a dominant language in higher education, and while leaders frequently make distinctions between being data-driven versus data-informed, they must invest time into gathering it, analyzing it, and responding to it. Institutional leaders need to seek contextualized data from multiple sources as well as gain access to the reports produced by the office for institutional research and understand with whom the reports are shared and for what purposes. As Vice President for Diversity, Equity, and Student Success and Executive Director for the TRHT Campus Centers with AAC&U, Tia Brown McNair (2020) notes, advocating for students may sometimes mean using data sets to inform college-level and programmatic directions and "ask[ing] equity-minded questions about how and why current practices are failing to serve students experiencing inequities" (p. 61). For example, institutions often track courses with high failure or drop rates, which is a good start, but leaders need to be honest and proactive to address additional causes of these failure rates. Too many times the responsibility is placed on the students with reasons such as poor attendance, lack of study skills, and inadequate attention to detail. Effective leaders analyzing from an asset-based approach, however, will consider the learning experience more holistically and additionally examine the organization of the course, the quality of the assessments, access to learning materials, and the scaffolding students are provided to enhance their learning, for example. While data can be used to expose potential equity gaps, institutional leaders must encourage the community to improve the learning experience in all areas.

CONCLUSION

To conclude, I provide the following questions that encourage us to consider how institutional leaders can best serve students:

- Locate or map the administrative structure of your institution or an institution of your choice from the President/Chancellor to the WPA. What do the structure and reporting lines tell you about the institution and about the visibility of the WPA? Consider what affordances and/or constraints the positionality allows. What could or would you change to serve students better?
- Locate your institution's strategic plan and/or mission statement. What is your current institution's mission? How might a writing program's

curriculum, policies, and pedagogies reflect that mission? How might decisions made by any campus leader work in concert or in contrast to the mission?

- What institutional offices and services should leaders familiarize themselves with to advocate for students? At what levels of leadership and for what specific purposes? What committees should you join or form? On what initiatives might you collaborate to steward changes to the benefit of students?
- If you are already in a leadership position, map out the administrative structure of your organization. How would you describe the structure (vertical: functional, divisional, matrix; open boundary: hollow, modular, network, learning)? (See "Understanding Organizational Structures," SHRM, 2022) Does the structure reflect the mission? Does it allow for ample communication and sharing of knowledge and resources? If not, what can be done to improve things?
- What challenges do institutions face with hiring instructors and ensuring they are well-prepared to teach? How can institutions support continuous improvement of faculty across all teaching modalities, particularly in terms of serving underrepresented students and faculty? How can faculty be encouraged or incentivized to participate?
- How accessible are institutional leaders to students? What processes are available to the student to elevate their concerns to leadership? Is there an effective feedback loop in place? What improvements do you suggest? What are the benefits and challenges of continuing to teach courses—undergraduate or graduate—while working as an administrator?
- Identify institutional policies, practices, or offices that often unintentionally present unnecessary barriers for students. How can they be revised or replaced to improve student experiences?
- Identify institutional policies, practices, or offices that effectively assist students. What about them makes them successful? How can you incorporate their practices into your work?
- Identify attitudes, policies, practices or language that assumes a deficit approach that focuses on perceived weaknesses of undergraduate students at your institution. What is the basis for these? How might they be perceived as an asset? What can you do to encourage this perception?

Through these leadership experiences, I continue to learn how institutions both help and hinder student success and progress. This encourages me to advocate for students across levels, ranges, and modalities, to identify barriers and open new pathways. Drawing on my experiences and learning as a WPA, associate dean, and dean, I have come to appreciate that advocating for students can be achieved through the professional development of faculty grounded in an asset-based understanding of the diversity of students enrolled in our programs as well as an appreciation of students' best interests when they face challenges at the institution. Advocating for students can also be achieved through decision-making processes that align with institutional mission, encouraging an antiracist approach to all aspects of the educational experiences, and using data to ask equity-interested questions and propose holistic solutions.

No matter the leadership position you are presently in or aspire to reach at your current or a different institution, advocating for students is best done by leaders who are prepared, confident, flexible, and welcome collaboration, who are also balanced, open, and attempt to be fair. Seasoned leaders know they can develop the most beautiful design, the most comprehensive plans, and then everything changes when people are involved. But surprise and disruption should not derail our mission and our progress toward it—it is our responsibility no matter what our position at an institution–to design and plan, to implement and enact, and to adapt and change in the service of our students.

REFERENCES

Beavers, M., Brunk-Chavez, B. L., Greene, N.-A., Inoue, A. B., Ruiz, I., Saenkhum, T., & Young, V. A. (2021). Toward anti-racist first-year composition goals. https://tinyurl.com/FYCGoalsStatement

Giordano, J. B., & Hassel, H. (2019). Intersections of privilege and access: Writing programs, disciplinary knowledge, and the shape of a field. *WPA: Writing Program Administration, 43*(1), 33–53.

Grabill, J., Gretter, S., & Skogsbertg, E. (2022). Design for change in higher education. Johns Hopkins UP.

McNair, T. B., Bensimon, E. M., Malcom-Piqueux, L., & Pasquerella, L. (2020). *From equity talk to equity walk: Expanding practitioner knowledge for racial justice in higher education.* John Wiley and Sons.

Mein, E. (2018). Asset-based teaching and learning with diverse learners in post-secondary settings. *Department Technical Reports (CS), 1271*, 1–4.

Reichert Powell, P. (2013). *Retention and resistance: Writing instruction and students who leave.* Utah State UP.

SHRM. (2022). Understanding organizational structures. https://www.shrm.org/resourcesandtools/tools-and-samples/toolkits/pages/understandingorganizationalstructures.aspx

Sugrue, C., Solbrekke, T. D., Bergh, A., Sutphen, M., & Fossland, T. (2019). University leaders' talk about institutional missions and academic developers' contributions. *European Educational Research Journal, 18*(6), 743–759. https://doi.org/10.1177/1474904119866520

Vander Lei, E., & Pugh, M. (2016). What is institutional mission? In R. Malenczyk (Ed.), *A rhetoric for writing program administrators* (2nd ed., pp. 142–154). Parlor.

CHAPTER FOURTEEN

I'm Still Here, Goddammit: Toward Irreverent Understandings of White Nostalgia, White Irreplaceability, and WPA *In-Situ* Longevity

JOSEPH JANANGELO, LOYOLA UNIVERSITY CHICAGO

With deference to WPA doctoral programs and the CWPA Summer Workshop, I think Martha Stewart would make a spectacular WPA, especially of the full professor, endowed chair ilk. I mean *that* Martha Stewart, entrepreneur and influencer *extraordinaire*. Stewart is adept at career renewal, moving from expert to pariah and back again across contexts and media. Her remarkable longevity is predicated on creativity, industriousness, and resilience. Stewart also has that galvanic ingredient, pluck, that helps her rebound from potentially decimating criticism. Case in point: when teased about her signature phrase "it's a good thing," Stewart owned the accusation–and the accuser–by responding, "I invented 'It's a good thing' before you were even born" (Stewart, 2022). Snap. My aspirational WPA creates delectable tortes and retorts. Savoring the crumbs, I will discuss a perceived "good thing" about WPA renewal: the idea that WPAs serving for over six years *in-situ* as their programs' directors benefits all concerned. I hope to offer nuanced understandings of the vexed "good things" about directing a given writing program for a long time. I am not discussing chronological age or career longevity, but the idea of leading the same writing program for 6+ years. Discussing white narcissism and greed, I will focus on two race-imbricated activities. One is nostalgia and programmatic storytelling. Another involves stories seasoned WPAs tell themselves and their, often white, peers about their unique and enduring programmatic value. I begin by exploring some important reasoning and scholarship.

GOOD REASONS WHY WPAS STAY "ON"

Let's understand why WPAs might construe *in-situ* longevity as a good, integrity-based thing:

A. *You paid quite a price to be a WPA.* You have earned your place as your writing program's WPA. You worked hard for your success and deserve it. Remember the saying "the piper must be paid?" For years, on campus and, thanks to the pandemic, on Zoom, you piped melodiously and harmonically to do good work for students, colleagues, and school–sometimes at singular costs your family and wellbeing.

B. *You are singularly qualified and accomplished at what you do.* Moreover, no one else at your school can do the job. All false and gender-prescribed modesty aside, your teaching, publication, and service record suggests that you are the right person for the job. For proof, one could review the good things you have done for the students and faculty you mentor and serve. Your *curriculum vitae* proves that you made a scholarly name for yourself. It shows that, where others slack, you slay by persuading, outwitting, charming, placating, and sometimes outlasting the programmatic and institutional dragons who interfered with your WPA work.

C. *You are your program's most articulate and trusted advocate for helping students and faculty learn and evolve.* As a humanitarian, you work with integrity to use your expertise and eloquence to serve others. That means forming and using your campus and professional networks to be an ally, advocate, co-conspirator, and mentor in all spheres, especially DEI. As your email archive and service/teaching awards attest, you are an effective campus point person for doing good work quickly and well.

D. *You worry that if you stop serving as WPA, bad things will happen to your program and the talented, vulnerable people who teach in it.* You worry that if you leave the WPA position, your already vulnerable adjunct faculty members will fall prey to exploitative labor practices and reductive, outdated pedagogical mandates. You stay on at significant cost to yourself to protect your colleagues and program, knowing that some of the initiatives you stewarded would dissolve without you to defend them. You also suspect that, if you stopped serving as WPA, your school would not replace you at rank. Even if it did, your successor (should they find one qualified to do the job, much less the work) might not champion labor conditions, students' rights to their own language, and equity-driven assessment to the degree that you do. In this sense, staying on signifies caring because your campus presence and clout stand between respect for, and devaluation of, Writing Studies students and faculty.

E. *Your WPA longevity matters in principle and practice.* You remember first-wave scholarship about your WPA forebears who were exploited, mistreated, harassed, disposed of or destroyed by their uncaring, often sexist institutions. Your job security and career recognition constitute partial redress for the persistent mistreatment of your professional and programmatic forebears.

F. *You have a few more things to accomplish before finishing your WPA work.* There is still important programmatic work to do and key projects in process that need your attention and skillset. You also have a leadership vision to finish, with time-sensitive projects in the works, and, *merci la pandémie,* an ever-exfoliating to-do list. Such unfinished business is a big job, and you need a few more years to complete it. As a campus leader dedicated to the programmatic and pedagogical good, you understand the adage "it is not about you." But if WPA longevity were about you, it might go something like this…

G. *You cannot afford to stop being your program's WPA because of the financial hit stopping would entail.* Due to the demands of building a career, you may have deferred starting a family and still have young children to support. You may be providing elder care for your parents, or divorces(s) may have cut your savings in half. Moreover, the pandemic has adversely affected your retirement savings and you need a few more years to better secure your financial future.

H. *You still excel at being your program's WPA.* You add value and cachet to your program and institution by performing at a high level as a dedicated leader and an active scholar. To critical—likely sexist, ageist, racist, homophobic critics—if you are not always working at peak performance, there is much to admire and nothing to admonish about your contributions. As a seasoned program leader, you have achieved maturity without discernible decline. For the nosey set, your chronological age is only a number and not their business. On your many good days, you project youthful vitality if not youth *per se.* Your signature projects (e.g., the placement system you developed) and institutional memory add value and continuity to your leadership. On email and in online meetings, you are seen at your trenchant best. Haters may desist because your WPA sell-by date, however envisioned, is far off.

I. *You are not done being your program's WPA and are not ready to stop.* Over time, you have become so good at WPA renewal, often self-sponsored and institutionally unrewarded, that you keep finding novelty and nuance in your work. You know that you get to have a professional identity, and that yours is productively enmeshed with being your program's WPA. More importantly, you still love your work, have potential to fill, and are

> unprepared for the loss of daily contact with the many talented, needy people in your writing program, some of whom would miss you if you stopped being their WPA.

Points A-I suggest it would be desirable for you to keep serving as WPA. For one thing, your program and colleagues want and need you front and center. Moreover, your continued performance is both lauded and unsurprising. At school, you serve as a source of valuable institutional memory. Professionally, you keep evolving and are a reassuring presence in an inconstant landscape. For example, your knowledge of online course delivery–a marker of your ability to keep evolving and renewing professionally since it has "been a minute" since you were in graduate school–was tested and successfully displayed by your deft guidance of students, tutors, and teachers through the pandemic. Your colleagues say that you are still here because of your ability and integrity. They see you working hard and effectively as a mentor, ally, and co-conspirator to those who seek guidance and protection and in whom you foster pedagogical and WPA readiness. Your knowledge of best practices and commitment to social justice serves everyone well and has garnered admiration. Hence, your colleagues and administrators may understand your *in-situ* longevity as testament to your meritorious service. All of this bodes well for you staying on as WPA, for at least a few more years. With no discernible downside, your *in-situ* longevity signifies a programmatic good thing.

Yet there are other possible understandings. Here I pivot to ask you to review the A-I list of "good things" from an antiracist perspective. Please entertain the idea that what seems like meritorious service can appear, and even be, meretricious actions taken by typically greedy, entitled white people. I owe this train of thought to a trenchant scholar, Carmen Kynard (2021), who became WPA after a rather spectacular WPA moved into upper administration. I focus on Kynard's essay because her astute exposé of the networked cruelty of white privilege in WPA work merits detailed study.

WHEN WHITE PEOPLE STAY "ON"

In "Administering While Black: Black Women's Labor in the Academy and the 'Position of the Unthought,'" Kynard writes that "because so many WPAs have gone into upper-level administration in deans' and provosts' offices, it might seem that there is greater institutional support for writing programs and WPAs at such colleges." She warns, "This is not always the case, as former WPAs-turned deans-and-provosts (for the sake of this essay, I will call them Super-WPAs) can be found across the country implementing and enculturating racist curriculum and policy." Kynard then explains how "the Super-WPAs can also sometimes add further stress to the whitenized project of WPA work for black women." For example, she argues that "faculty in the writing program will often get coerced into locating the newly risen (often white and/or male) bodies of the Super-WPAs as a new site of authority where, quite literally, financial rewards and professional gain are meted out to them" (p. 41).

Kynard describes the coercion meted out by her former school's Super-WPA who "overdirected [her] program in such a way that tenure in FYW did not require any real interest in or knowledge *about* first-year writing, a culture that I was attempting to shape" (p. 41). The Super-WPA would aggress terribly, actively undermining Kynard's authority with students and colleagues. She only got to ventriloquize leadership. He pulled/owned/made the strings. That control, which included undercutting the WPA's authority and encouraging faculty to misuse Writing Studies-directed funds, became a repeated workplace condition for Kynard. As she writes:

> While the shock-and-awe campaigns of the Super-WPA might seem a bit over the top, they were the norm in my experience as a WPA. Whether it was the shock-and-awe campaign of the Super-WPA or the invisibility to fellow WPAs across the country and other administrators on campus, a full-blown constellation of racialized events act simultaneously to deliberately discredit and mock a black woman's leadership while superexploiting every ounce of her labor. (p. 43)

Kynard defines such abuse as part of a "racialized project" contributing to "the mammification of black women" (p. 43), in the allegedly enlightened, but really white-enshrining, WPA workplace. Blocked from achieving programmatic credibility, much less authority, Kynard says such treatment "renders my body as WPA as wholly exploitable but not as capable of equal participation in the making of knowledge on campus or in the wider field" (p. 45).

Kynard evokes the wider field by moving from describing a "programmatic hot mess" (p. 41) to distilling interlocking lessons about white privilege and WPA work. Those lessons show how Black women get schooled and scotched if they dare to expect workplace equity. One lesson involves the Super-WPA's misappropriation of funds: "Even when I attempted to tell other campus figures what was happening (since obviously their junior faculty were not given such funds), the response was only laughter at what the Super-WPA was able to get away with, almost as if in bro-mantic awe of the power of their white comrade" (p. 42). In my distillation, the admiration of the Super-WPA's Wizardry reflects the habit of powerful white people to show fealty while closing rank. The message is: your frustration is our laughing matter. The adage "Welcome to the club" becomes "Behold, but do not question, the spectacular power of the club." Not surprisingly, Kynard left the institution for pastures hopefully less whitely, if no greener.

Kynard ultimately underscores the omnipresence of white supremacy in academia: "These are not the mean, individual acts of a few morally misguided souls. Higher education strategically contains a diverse pool of faculty such that whiteness stays on top" (p. 43). She also articulates a challenge: "The task then is to argue for the pervasive ordinariness of white supremacy and offer analyses that unwaveringly remind us about that banality, no matter how uncomfortable or apprehensive it will make us" (p. 47). Kynard's ideas ring true. I find much WPA work and graduate preparation rich with, yet unbothered by, what I call "white supremic" practices. Moreover, I see aspects of WPA *in-situ* longevity that enact and celebrate white entitlement, self-flattery, and greed.

My guess is that you do not see your WPA self in the actions of the tyrant Kynard survived. There is no comparison between your service and Super-WPA's skullduggery. You don't swan, cheat, or oppress others in spectacles of white supremacy. Neither abusive nor entitled, you use your renewal and longevity in service of students and colleagues. Striving to blend benevolence with professionalism, you use any influence/power you earned to help people do their best work. Beyond that, your unintentional offenses toward colleagues are so infinitesimal that they would not even pass micro-aggressive muster. Perhaps true enough, yet I offer a twin premise for your consideration: 1) you don't have to be a coercive WPA to be a controlling WPA, and 2) you don't have to degrade people to oppress them. Remember Kynard's ideas about "the pervasive ordinariness" and "banality" of white supremacy? Rather than castigate the spectacular assaults Kynard recounts, I will discuss two banal, subtly shading activities intrinsic to WPA *in-situ* longevity that whisper white supremacy: white nostalgia and programmatic storytelling, and white irreplaceability.

WHITE NOSTALGIA AND PROGRAMMATIC STORYTELLING

Scholars Adalberto Aguirre, Jr. (2000) and A.Y. Martinez (2020) argue that white people tell self-laudatory stories, and WPA world features a surfeit of stories and tellers. While we tell stories to soothe, console, and encourage people, they can emit exclusionary whiteness and ownership. I will highlight problems with programmatic storytelling in two spheres: the stories WPAs tell others and those we tell ourselves.

WPA storytellers can celebrate programmatic Elysian days that were much better for white, cisgender, able-bodied, straight people than for anyone else, including contemporary listeners. Here intention clashes with reception. What is meant as a show of sacrifice and industry may be perceived as a familiar spectacle of white narcissism evoking the "good old days" that were likely much less good for listeners, especially people of color. Such stories celebrate times listeners do not remember or view differently. For example, our former WPA seemed disappointed when I didn't laugh at his list of the three questions for interviewing tenure track candidates: "Is he Irish? Is he Catholic? Does he have a Ph.D.?" That nostalgia celebrated times when hiring was simple and untouched by DEI concerns.

WPA stories and storytellers can be routinely self-starring and self-serving. Such stories often underwrite whiteness by casting the WPA as the lead, sympathetic character. They tend to star you and your past (often white) colleagues as noble victims or victors.

WPA storytellers overserve less-senior colleagues and graduate students with detailed narratives of the past that don't help listeners move forward with their own readiness projects and plans. When, as WPA, you remember publicly and force people to endure your flashback, storytelling becomes a command performance where you talk while "they" listen. For whom is that a good thing? Vainglorious and obstructionist, you freeze their story and its progress because your account of success or mistreatment is more important. What could be more whitely?

Here I contend that programmatic storytelling is race-imbricated. Longevity positions us to have stories; whiteness dispositions us to tell them narcissistically. Your stories likely are edifying for you and you may enjoy sharing them. Consider how listeners can perceive your stories as self-aggrandizing and pontifical. They have already heard such narrations by self-focused white people and may listen for different things. To that end, I offer questions for consideration:

- When you tell stories about the past, whose work do you hope to honor or critique?
- Consider your most oft-told stories. Could they be construed, however erroneously, as humble brags, focus pulls, or whitely power moves to draw attention to yourself?
- Which details do you offer because they help listeners understand something or because you prefer telling the long version?
- When listeners signal their wish for a truncated version, do you edit your story or go long?
- Do you ever reminisce at meetings to maintain visibility and relevance? What keeps your reminiscences from being another "glory days" narrative by yet another entitled, attention-seeking white person?
- Consider curricular nostalgia: when discussing older Writing Studies scholarship in graduate classes, do you teach it in ways that don't just ennoble the past? How does antiracist work fuel those conversations (see chapters by Kelenyi and Leverenz, this volume)?

WHITE IRREPLACEABILITY

It is tempting for white people to imagine themselves as enduringly valuable to their programs and people. It is quite white to see yourself as of capital importance to your workplace. That supports you staying in place because it would suffer without you. In my experience, white people perceive and proffer themselves as interesting and indispensable their entire working lives. That belief colludes with white narcissism to fuel the fantasy that others think so, too.

It is too easy for WPAs to understand themselves as the learned, articulate defender of the good. Implicit in white narcissism is the self-characterization as programmatic protector of theory, pedagogy, and people. It assumes "they" need a guardian and that you are it. Coincidentally, and this action may not escape notice, while guarding, you can keep retaining, some uncharitable wags may say, hoarding professional development opportunities, institutional visibility, and financial perks some colleagues wish were in larger circulation.

While staying on as WPA, you can keep renewing and learning new things, but you can also inadvertently limit your colleagues' program leadership and institutional visibility opportunities, delaying their WPA readiness. Here WPA renewal and longevity become weaponized. While you keep renewing and performing well (a good thing), the WPA position remains taken. Where does that leave colleagues who find their WPA readiness plans deferred and delayed? What if ripeness is not all and timing also matters?

Might one person staying on as WPA create a lock on leadership opportunities, leaving little room for others to excel? Newer talent deserves leadership opportunities. To colleagues, a WPA remaining "still here" can seem like a long reign. An acid truth about windows of opportunity is that they are often closing. Consider the programmatic costs of a WPA staying on for a decade or so. Colleagues deemed talented enough to leave may do so in order to enact their own WPA readiness. Those who stay on may resent your enduring turn at bat, which delays their leadership opportunities. Moreover, graduate students will see only one way of directing a writing program. Unsure that is good for them as developing leaders, I offer questions for cogitation:

- To support programmatic health (see Babb and Popham, this volume), how can you learn about your colleagues' WPA aspirations and calendars to build equitable rotation plans?
- Does a part of you remain WPA to forestall change so no one will undo, or draw attention away from, your programmatic contributions?
- Do you ever feel outpaced or outshined by your less-senior colleagues? We discuss intergenerational understandings, but what about intergenerational jealousies and resentments over whose WPA working life is easier?

- Might staying "still here" have anything to do with insulation from teaching more courses, moving your office, or relinquishing visibility and financial remuneration?
- If you worry that your writing program would not be the same without your leadership, consider what drives that feeling. Do you fear the program might become better for some stakeholders, or in some ways, without you at the helm?
- If someone suggested that you are occupying your program's WPA position in whitely ways, would any of that be true? If not, can you see any logic in that perspective?
- How do you distinguish between commitment to leadership (see Beavers and Anders, as well as Brunk, in this volume) and selfish longevity that hoards opportunities and delays WPA readiness?

AN UNDERSTANDING

I conclude by asking you to understand the damage and hubris of the stories seasoned WPAs tell our colleagues and ourselves about our merit/meritorious service. My first point is don't overestimate your singular value to your program. Your writing program still needs you, but it need not star or glorify you. The program needs your colleagues just as much, and not as supporting players who hear your stories or enact your big designs. Second, if you wonder what people would do without you, you might give them a chance to miss you and enact their readiness. What did you do without your predecessors? Was it a deathblow to your creativity and leadership development? Third, don't wait to mentor others; they deserve a chance to lead sooner not later. Fourth, let's rethink the alleged good things and ends of white longevity. Step one might be to imagine the WPA workplace as a shared professional space, not a star vehicle. I mean no disrespect. You are youthfully august, adept, and accomplished. That is to your enduring credit. Speaking of endurance, your well-earned *in-situ* WPA longevity may be a good thing and could be a better one when understood and enacted more inclusively. The understanding I suggest is that you don't inadvertently weaponize your renewal by using whiteness and its ever-attendant privileges as default ways of making people listen to your glory days stories or stay "still here" center stage into perpetuity. For example, if no one else is qualified, and you have been *in-situ* WPA for 6+ years, you might ask how we got here? Was no one interested, suitable, or teachable? Was the talent pool that shallow? Did you try your best to find a successor or are you a bit glad no one can succeed you?

The idea that WPAs stay on selflessly holds power in Writing Studies. That underscores larger problems. We tacitly learn and teach WPA work as solo projects, something "I" want, earn, endure, and help others do. I-infused logic, like our A-I list, can fuel careers predicated on self-interest: get it all, then complain about the emotional labor of its upkeep. Could we teach WPA career journeys as intertwining and interdependent, not just profitably intersecting in project-based, strange bedfellow ways? That would entail alternate messaging: from achieve and thrive to listen, share, and use your networks more for your program than yourself. My point is twofold. WPA work should put programmatic health above individual success. Programmatic health is less about spotting talent than mentoring it. One thing about WPA *in-situ* longevity is that it can become and remain territorial. Regarding stakeholders and beneficiaries, the wins of longevity should not be yours alone or even mostly yours.

Still, I see the logic at play. White privilege supports telling yourself and "others" that you are serving and advocating for them even if, and especially when, you are acting in self-serving ways. Feeling nostalgic and needed, as well as primary and peerless, comes easily and habitually to white straight people. So does the temptation to hoard perks and call it building and to control / efface people and call it stewarding. As white people, it can be difficult to think beyond ourselves because it is always all about us as we are forever vital and invaluable to our workplace and colleagues. Those default self-perceptions reflect centuries of privilege and have strong internal coherence. Yet coherence is not equity and WPA actions and orations that bespeak privilege and ownership have not escaped notice by scholars who demand we stop it now. Critics are tired of, and infuriated by, hearing yet another white person's nostalgic account of how good or tough they had it and what being WPA cost them and why they must stay on. For example, consider a call to action issued by Al Harahap (2021), one of the first scholars of color to serve on the CWPA Executive Board, "I urge all scholars of colour and marginalized groups to keep account of any language, microaggression, moments that are clearly and explicitly, or at times feel subtly, exclusive" (p. 61).

"Subtly, exclusive" sounds familiar. You can understand Harahap's call in several ways. You could say it signals "open season" on white WPAs. That would let you portray yourself as under assault and claim the injured, inured identity WPAs assume so often and well. I recommend a different choice, involving self-examination. You could try to understand how the ends of white privilege fuel and filtrate WPA preparation, work, identity formation, and longevity. That would mean admitting that, left to its own predatory devices, whiteness would self-jubilate, tweet, retweet, friend, and like itself into perpetuity.

By understanding how our nostalgic, self-glorifying practices emit and further enshrine white privilege, you could stand a better chance of seeing yourself as you are seen by colleagues, including graduate students, who are bored with white people narrating their achievements, hoarding workplace opportunities, and touting their singular value. That critical self-perception could underwrite ends beyond those of oft-practiced white privilege. If WPAs don't feel a need to remain singularly and persistently visible, we might envision WPA work in terms of communal equity, shared opportunity, and programmatic health. Working toward writing programs that don't need you center-stage could help you discard the burdens of doing everything for everyone all the time or staying "still here" longer than you wish. That means understanding writing programs and WPA work as ensemble pieces rather than solo projects. Prioritizing programmatic health over individual achievement means it is always everyone's (yours and their) time to shine and lead. To that end, I hope we keep asking how *in-situ* program leadership supports and undermines DEI in order to keep WPA longevity from becoming its own idol, an unquestioned good thing we promote under the self-rewarding credo "I must stay here to provide program continuity."

You are still here because you are talented and game. I wonder if you can become game enough to enact and teach WPA work in ways that share the limelight with your colleagues and support their readiness desires. Enjoying your longevity while eschewing white selfishness and greed, can you use your renewal to spotlight others' contributions and stories? Would you want to? One very good thing about WPA *in-situ* longevity is that you are still *a la mode.* One vexed good thing about such longevity is that, for such an intellectually stylish group, many WPAs have been wearing whiteness long after Labor Day. Still here, we have been teaching it to and too.

REFERENCES

Aguirre, A., Jr. (2000). Academic storytelling: A critical race theory story of affirmative action. *Sociological Perspectives*, *43*(2), 319–339. https://doi.org/10.2307/1389799

Harahap, A. (2021). The promise and perils of a disciplinary and organizational pipeline. *WPA: Writing Program Administration*, *44*(3), 56–62.

Kynard, C. (2019). Administering while Black: Black women's labor in the academy and the "position of the unthought." In S. M. Perryman-Clark & C. L. Craig (Eds.), *Black perspectives in writing program administration: From the margins to the center* (pp. 28–50). CCCC Studies in Writing & Rhetoric Series.

Martinez, A. Y. (2020). *Counterstory: The rhetoric and writing of critical race theory.* Conference on College Composition and Communication.

Stewart, M. (2022). Brainyquote. https://www.brainyquote.com/quotes/martha_stewart_382545

CHAPTER FIFTEEN

Getting Out of the Way: Antiracism and the Unbearable Whiteness of Being a WPA

CARRIE S. LEVERENZ, TEXAS CHRISTIAN UNIVERSITY

"When you know better, you do better." Maya Angelou *(quoted by Oprah Winfrey, 2011)*

In May of 2021, I notified my department chair that I would be resigning as Director of Composition in December, a year earlier than I had planned. I had had one of those last-straw moments, after being stuck in a seemingly endless loop of emails triggered by a student requesting that the "F" he received in his composition course be turned into an Incomplete because of personal difficulties he experienced during the semester. Several factors complicated his case, not least of which was that he had not done a single major assignment in spite of repeated extensions given by his teacher, an adjunct instructor who would not be teaching for us again in the fall. After consulting with student affairs, who agreed that an Incomplete wasn't warranted when no course work had been done, I had sent the student our program policy for Incompletes (reserved for students in good standing with unanticipated emergencies) and reminded the student he could take the course again and replace the failing grade. I copied my Department Chair and Associate Dean on everything. Still, the pleas continued.

I admit, I expressed exasperation (including the use of ALL CAPS) in a response to the other administrators involved. The next day, my department chair emailed an apology to the other administrators and then sent me a request to be more professional. At that moment, I decided I was done. When I submitted my official resignation letter the next week, I imagine my chair felt relief. I know I felt relief, not because I didn't love my composition program but because for more than a year, more than two years if I'm honest, I had felt increasingly distrusted by my colleagues. The admonition to be more professional seemed like confirmation of my fears. In this essay, I will explore my gradual awakening to the limits of my effectiveness as a WPA, limits created by my whiteness, and recommend steps other white WPAs can take to recognize and address their own limitations.

I spent the next few weeks trying to make sense of what had happened. I acknowledged that I was exhausted by all the extra work COVID had added to the job. I was frustrated by budget cuts, an overflow of incoming students, seemingly daily changes in policy coming from our new Provost, and my chair's relentless efforts to keep the department on track. My mother's death a few months earlier had left me emotionally spent. I was facing a long summer of work for minimal compensation. All justifiable reasons for wanting to give up the WPA role.

But underneath it all was a more painful truth. In recent years, TCU's small but increasing number of BIPOC students had begun to agitate for change. In 2017, the English department had come under fire for insufficient support of graduate students of color. As WPA, I was one of several in administrative positions who had been the subject of a graduate student complaint. These complaints prompted years of tense department meetings, behind-closed-door discussions, institutional investigations, and ultimately, a lawsuit, which has only recently been settled. At the same time, the department prioritized hiring additional faculty of color, a move I supported, which kept white supremacy and the unconscious bias that accompanies it at the top of everyone's mind. While my department's efforts to deal with racism are emblematic of the larger struggle within higher education, it became personal when I learned that the composition program had been critiqued in a graduate course on antiracist pedagogy and when some faculty expressed hope that hiring new composition instructors committed to antiracism could help transform the program. Although I recognized the need for increased attention to diversity, equity, and inclusion in writing instruction and had been making incremental changes, I did not yet see how my long history with a program I felt proud of kept me from radically rethinking where the program needed to go.

While struggles over language standards in composition classes are not new, arguments for adopting antiracist practices in writing programs are newly pressing, given the continued injustices suffered by minoritized people both in and outside the university and the work BIPOC compositionists are doing to keep calls for language justice at the forefront of our professional conversations (Baca, Hinojosa, & Murphy, 2019; Baker-Bell, 2020; CCCC Special Committee, 2020; Inoue, 2016, 2019; Kynard, 2018). Like many white academics, I had spent the last few years reading the work of antiracist theorists and convincing myself that I was doing what needed to be done. In his 2019 CCCC Chair's address, "How Do We Language So People Stop Killing Each Other, or What Do We Do about White Language Supremacy?" Asao Inoue addresses this attitude explicitly, as he says to the white compositionists in his audience: "How does it feel to be the problem? How does it make you feel to be the one in the way of progress, no matter what you have said or what your agendas are, how hard you worked, or how sincere you are?" (p. 356). In spite of Inoue's direct address, I did not see myself in his words. Hadn't I added a DEI statement to the program's syllabus for first-year writing, diversified the course readings, offered pedagogy workshops on teaching for DEI? Inoue anticipated just such a response:

> You thinking you're special is the problem. It always has been, because you, and White people just like you who came before you, have had most of the power, decided most of the things, built the steel cage of White language supremacy that we exist in today, both in and outside of the academy—and likely, many of you didn't know you did it. You just thought you were doing language work, doing teaching, doing good work, judging students and their languages in conscientious and kind ways, helping them, preparing them, giving them what was good for them. (pp. 356–357)

I had, indeed, thought I was doing good work, including being sensitive to the needs of students of color and others who were marginalized by the white supremacist culture of academe in general and my Predominantly White Institution (PWI) in particular. I did not yet see how my good work, in fact, was limited by my whiteness. (See Janangelo, this volume, for further critique of the white WPA.)

Inoue's critique of racism in the profession was not new in 2019. He had called out CWPA for its exclusion of minoritized voices in his Plenary address at the 2015 CWPA conference. Adam Banks, in his 2015 Chair's address had also noted the overwhelming whiteness of CCCC. In their 2011 WPA publication, "Troubling the Boundaries: (De)Constructing WPA Identities at the Intersections of Race and Gender," Collin Lamont Craig and Staci Maree Perryman-Clark, both early career Black WPAs, highlighted the organization's lack of attention to race and to the challenges of being a WPA of color. We can go back even further to Victor Villanueva's 1999 CCCC Chair's address "On the Rhetoric and Precedents of Racism" or to Jacqueline Jones Royster's 1995 Chair's address "When the First Voice You Hear Is Not Your Own." While these critiques of the whiteness of our profession have been widely cited, they have barely put a dent in the structures that keep white faculty, white WPAs, and white supremacist language practices in power.

Nothing makes that clearer than the conflict that arose over the proposed revision of the WPA Outcomes Statement drafted by a Task Force of BIPOC compositionists, a revision that was solicited but then resisted by the predominantly white WPA Executive Board. (See the Task Force's (2021) draft here https://tinyurl.com/FYCGoalsStatement.) In response, Inoue publicly disavowed any ties to CWPA and encouraged others to do so as well. Inoue (2021) reflected on his reasons for cutting himself off from the organization in a blog post titled "Why I Left the CWPA (Council of Writing Program Administrators)": "Everyone agrees on the idea of antiracism, but when actual antiracist change is presented, heels dig in. People now think we must move slower, much slower." Within days, the CWPA (2021) responded with a public apology, admitting that "The majority-White members of the Executive Board dismissed, silenced, and questioned the authority of the BIPOC Task Force members." CWPA also announced a suspension of the regular workings of the organization so it could investigate structures that perpetuate white supremacy.

While I hope that this process will yield a changed CWPA, feminist and queer scholar Sarah Ahmed's research makes clear just how difficult it is to create meaningful change in predominantly white organizations. In *On Being Included*, Ahmed (2012) reports on a multi-institutional study of diversity workers in higher education in England. One of her key findings is that appearing to work on diversity—creating committees, writing policies, publishing statements—often stands in for meaningful change. This is how institutions work. Those in power go through the motions of addressing the need for change while keeping existing (white) power structures in place. In an institution like mine, a private, politically conservative PWI located in a once slave-holding state, white supremacy runs deep. Although my institution has made a number of structural changes (offering a Critical Race and Ethnic Studies major, launching a Race and Reconciliation Initiative, reorganizing the office that hears Title VII and Title IX complaints, creating various awards for work in DEI), they also want to keep majority white students, parents, donors, and Board members happy. As antiracist author Ibram Kendi (2019) argues, when you live in a culture founded on racism, you can't help but absorb racist ideas. In such a culture, if you're not actively working to change the system, then you're supporting racism by default. Writing programs work similarly. WPAs may not intend to disadvantage minoritized students and instructors, but if we do not de-center whiteness, our programs will inevitably do harm.

Important work by feminist writers Minnie Bruce Pratt (1984), Marilyn Frye (1995), and Tema Okun (2021), who have theorized the problem of whiteness within feminism, has helped me see how many of my actions as WPA have supported white supremacy. In this, I am likely not alone. Inoue (2021) observes how the "whitely" dispositions identified by Frye (who draws on Minnie Bruce Pratt)—"Being a judge and peacemaker," "Self-understood benevolence," "being procedurally ethical," and "acting with authority"—could describe what our field thinks of as a good writing teacher. These are characteristics aspired to by many WPAs as well.

And really, what could be so wrong in wanting to be a peacemaker and benevolent and ethical? Tema Okun (2021), in "White Supremacy Culture—Still Here," an update of her 1999 article "White Supremacy Culture" explains:

> The original list of white supremacy characteristics is really a list that defines and expresses white middle and owning class values and norms. White middle- and owning-class power brokers embody these characteristics as a way of defining what is "normal" and even "aspirational" or desired – the way we should all want to be. We know this because of how those who do not belong to the white middle and owning classes are required to adopt these characteristics in order to assimilate into this desired norm (when such assimilation is allowed). (pp. 5–6)

When our actions as WPAs are a result of these dispositions, especially when those actions align with dominant practices in the field, it can be hard to question ourselves. And when I do discover my actions have had unanticipated negative consequences for minoritized teachers or students, it can be hard not to be defensive, harder still to apologize, to backtrack, to make things right, if they ever can be made right.

BEING A JUDGE AND PEACEMAKER

Throughout my 20-plus years at my current institution, our graduate program has been mostly, and in some cohorts, exclusively, white. As the department's efforts to recruit more diverse students began to see some success, tensions among graduate students arose, culminating in several explicit complaints of racism. One BIPOC student asked to have her assigned office desk moved so she would not have to sit between two students who, she reported, had complained about not wanting to enroll in graduate courses where all they do is talk about race. Another minoritized student sent me an email letting me know that his 7:30 a.m. conference with a student had been interrupted by a loud conversation that included profanity coming from two white colleagues on the other side of the cubical divide. He attributed this disrespectful behavior to racism and said he would file an official complaint if it didn't stop. Another point of contention was the large white board where instructors left messages for the group (e.g., "Brownies in the fridge; help yourself."). During Visit Day for prospective graduate students, someone wrote on the board the Angela Davis quote: "In a racist society, it is not enough to be non-racist. We must be anti-racist." The quote was erased before the end of the day, but not by the writer.

Although one instructor complained to me privately that they found the quote to be inflammatory, that instructor wasn't the one who erased it. I heard later that the quote had actually been removed by another activist graduate student who felt it falsely misrepresented to prospective students that the current graduate students were antiracist. My initial response was to try to come up with a policy regarding what could and couldn't be written on the white board (and who could or couldn't erase it). I even considered just taking the white board down. I see now that my commitment to being a judge and a peacemaker led me to focus on eliminating the conflict rather than addressing it.

SELF-UNDERSTOOD BENEVOLENCE

Most WPAs probably believe their actions are motivated by benevolence. As a feminist WPA, I certainly thought I was doing what I could to care, in feminist philosopher Nel Nodding's (2013) terms, for all students and all teachers in my program (see Leverenz, 2010). But how do we act benevolently when caring for one person or group harms another person or group? How do we choose whom to care for? I had not yet recognized that in a PWI, caring for everyone equally results in keeping white privilege in place. For example, in writing an assignment prompt for our required argument course, I was imagining the all-white class I normally teach and used the example of Trump's promise to build a wall between the US and Mexico to illustrate the need to persuade others of the existence of a problem, which Trump had failed to do, before proposing a solution.

After I shared the prompt with new instructors, however, two minoritized teachers objected on the grounds that Trump's wall should not be argued for under any condition since it was unjust. When I wrote the prompt, I was mainly hoping it would lead conservative students to question their assumptions about what constitutes a problem; I was not imagining how discussing Trump's wall could traumatize a student in the class who was undocumented or whose family was undocumented. Or how a Latinx teacher might discuss the example with an all-white class. In response to the voiced objections, the instructors had a vigorous discussion about how to respond to student arguments that we find objectionable, and ultimately, I removed the example from the prompt. Still, there is no question that my initial impulse to engage our majority (white) students could have harmed others.

BEING PROCEDURALLY ETHICAL

In my first year back as WPA after a 10-year hiatus, I received an email from an international graduate student asking why he had not been assigned to teach first-year composition in the fall. He was in his third year in the PhD program and had been told he would (finally) be given a teaching appointment after two years of working in the writing center. I had never met the student, so I asked about his status in a scheduling meeting with other (white) administrative faculty. They explained that, based on their view of his oral performance in graduate classes, they had decided his accent was too strong to allow him to teach composition. Not sure how to proceed, I posted to the discussion list WPA-L asking how other programs determined when an international graduate student could teach and found out most used a TESOL score. Subsequent research led me to a state guideline on required TESOL speaking scores for international graduate instructors. Clearly, our writing program needed a policy, and accepting the state's guideline seemed like a logical procedure.

When I conferred with the Director of Graduate Studies to find out this graduate student's score, I discovered that it was, indeed, below the score required by the state. However, the graduate director made a strong case that she had no problems understanding the graduate student when he spoke and that our students could benefit from more exposure to international instructors. After further discussion, the administrative faculty decided to assign this graduate student to co-teach with an experienced instructor from our Intensive English program who was teaching a section of first-year composition designed for international students. If all went well, I told him, he would teach his own course the following spring. The good news is that the co-teaching arrangement worked out well, principally because, as the graduate student himself said, everyone should have someone they can talk to about their teaching. But this was also a case where I saw this student's difference as a problem, one I went on to "solve" procedurally by seeking out the advice of (white) authorities and creating a policy that could be applied to other such "problems" in the future. (See Brunk in this volume for more on the importance of recognizing student differences when developing a student-centered mindset.)

ACTING WITH AUTHORITY

One of the ways my institution chose to deal with the charges of racism within my department was to hire a consulting firm to conduct voluntary interviews with graduate students and faculty. When I shared with the (white) interviewer many of the incidents I describe above, she asked why I had not sought help from the Diversity Office. I told her I thought the conflicts were interpersonal and that it was my responsibility to take care of them. What I also meant was that I thought I had the authority to take care of them. When reflecting on the events that led up to my resignation as WPA, it is clear that my frustration over the student's insistence on a grade change was in part anger over not having my authority respected. I had a policy for giving an Incomplete, I applied the policy, and now others were questioning that policy. Our belief in our authority can be one of the greatest impediments to doing antiracist work as a white WPA. That seems clear from the CWPA Executive Committee's (2021) initial reaction to the proposed changes in the Outcomes Statement. The demise of the once robust discussion list WPA-L might be attributed to a similar assumption about who had the authority to speak in that forum: those with the longest years of experience, most if not all of whom were white and male (Beare, 2021). When these longtime WPA-L participants were called out for mansplaining, they responded with defensiveness and denial that anyone could be offended by their attempts to give advice.

Being blind to the limits of our authority is one reason racism continues within writing programs. It's not that white WPAs are incapable of being antiracist; it's that because we are in positions of power, we are accustomed to having our expertise respected. But we are not experts on what it's like to be a student or instructor of color in a white supremacist system. We are not experts on what those students and instructors need a writing program to be, and we have too rarely asked. More to the point, because we have benefitted from the racist system that is higher education—because we have been awarded our positions of power by following the rules, rules that reinforce the exclusion of nonstandard language practices and nonstandard people--it is very, very hard to see what's wrong with the system and to imagine it working differently, even if we know that it should. Ultimately, it is arrogant for us to think we know what should be done or to assume that others should trust us to do it.

My consolation, in leaving my WPA role, is that I am getting out of the way of the change that needs to come. I am getting out of the way but not going away. I do not want to give in to what Marilyn Frye (1995) calls, in her analysis of the burden of whiteness, "the great enemies in my heart. . . the despair and resentment that come with being required (by others and by my own integrity) to repair something apparently irreparable, to take responsibility for something apparently beyond my powers to effect" (p. 115). Instead, I will stay on my individual journey to know better so I can do better. I will aim to decenter whiteness in my teaching and in other aspects of my personal and professional life. I will keep a critical eye on myself and welcome critique from others. I also commit to being an ally, described by a WPA of color as "someone who believes a person of color and doesn't try to rationalize away the person's experiences and perceptions of racism" (Wible, 2019, p. 78). I will listen and I will hear. Perhaps more importantly, I want to be an accomplice, "someone who gives something up, who puts something on the line, who is willing to be critiqued, who is willing to lose something" (Wible, 2019, p. 79). To get there, I must first give up my need to be seen as a good WPA.

White WPAs have a special responsibility to recognize and counter the limits of their whiteness. Admittedly, doing so early in one's career can be hard, since establishing authority—with students, writing instructors, faculty, administrators—is an important part of the job. But it may be even harder as a senior WPA whose whitely ways have earned her tenure and promotion and professional status. A writing program cannot be antiracist without de-centering whiteness, and for white WPAs that inevitably means de-centering ourselves. Below are a few suggestions for how to start.

- **Create a change agenda.** Admitting the limits of your white WPA perspective means accepting that your perception of what the program needs will also be limited. Make it a goal, then, to create a program that will always be in the process of change. That means policies, curriculum, assessment, literally everything in the program, must be open to change. It also means being willing to question accepted standards (departmental, university, professional), many of which work to maintain white supremacy. Ask, who do these standards privilege? Who do they exclude? While questioning standards can feel risky, especially as an untenured WPA, we can't counter racism unless we look for it where it hides.
- **Structure in program critique.** To keep a change agenda alive requires actively soliciting the perspectives of diverse constituents. Too often WPAs focus on acculturating new teachers into an existing program instead of inviting those with differing experiences to share ideas for change. The invitation is crucial here, since instructors may be reluctant to share critiques with a WPA who supervises them. One of the best structural changes I made when I began to focus on increasing diversity, equity, and inclusion was to create a position on the Composition Committee for a graduate instructor whose role was to advocate for DEI. In fact, it was the first graduate instructor in that role, herself a minoritized teacher, who pointed out the problem with the prompt that included a reference to Trump's wall. Though I felt defensive when I first heard her critique, I also recognized that the instructor was doing exactly the job I asked her to do—pointing out the limits of my white perspective—and I was grateful for the chance to change my thinking.
- **Seek opportunities for collaboration** with those who do not share your white perspective. Although I have been an advocate of collaboration my entire career, I have not consciously sought to collaborate with those whose positionality differs from mine. Imagine if, when trying to create a policy for international graduate student teachers, I had worked with the former graduate director who had been an international student once herself.

- **Get involved in other antiracist work.** While white WPAs need to find ways to understand the limits of our perspective, we should not expect our colleagues of color to carry the burden of countering our whiteness. Productive collaboration must be reciprocal. We need to give as well as take. Involving ourselves in antiracist work outside of our programs, on our campuses and in our communities, being true allies (and accomplices), is a first step toward developing shared interests and goals. From there, productive and reciprocal collaborations can organically form.

Whether we are new or late in our careers, white WPAs need to recognize the ways in which whiteness limits our ability to enact anti-racism in our programs, no matter how good we are at our jobs by traditional measures. It is the measures themselves, measures grounded in white supremacy, that need to change, and we—in productive and reciprocal collaboration with others—who need to change with them.

REFERENCES

Ahmed, S. (2012). *On being included: Racism and diversity in institutional life*. Duke University Press.

Baca, I., Hinojosa, Y. I., & Murphy, S. W. (Eds.). (2019). *Bordered writers: Latinx identities and literacy practices at Hispanic-serving institutions*. SUNY Press.

Baker-Bell, A. (2020). *Linguistic justice: Black language, literacy, identity, and pedagogy*. Routledge.

Banks, A (2015). Ain't no walls behind the sky, baby! Funk, flight, freedom. *College Composition and Communication, 67*(1), 267–279.

Beare, Z. (2021). Cross postings: Disciplinary knowledge-making and the affective archive of the WPA Listserv. *Composition Studies, 49*(1), 42–59.

Beavers, M., Brunk-Chavez, B. L., Greene, N., Inoue, A. B., Ruiz, I., Saenkhum, T., & Young, V. A. (2021). Toward antiracist first-year composition goals. https://docs.google.com/document/d/1xFhdJOIC8Lh4pZRKFIjPeWiUd2dwoRJ16tfiVxJAIDs/edit

CCCC Special Committee on Composing a CCCC Statement on Anti-Black Racism and Black Linguistic Justice, Or, Why We Cain't Breathe! (2020, July). *This ain't another statement! This is a DEMAND for black linguistic justice!* Conference on College Composition and Communication. https://cccc.ncte.org/cccc/demand-for-black-linguistic-justice

Craig, C. L. & Perryman-Clark, S. M. (2011). "Troubling the boundaries: (De)constructing WPA identities at the intersections of race and gender." *WPA Journal, 34*(2), 37–58.

CWPA Executive Board. (2021, April 23). *CWPA Executive Board Statement in Response to the Recent Call to Boycott the Organization*. Council of Writing Program Administrators. https://www.wpacouncil.org/aws/CWPA/pt/sd/news_article/366395/_PARENT/layout_details/false.

Frye, M. (1995). White woman feminist. In L. A. Bell & D. Blumenfeld (Eds.), *Overcoming racism and sexism* (pp. 113–134). Rowman & Littlefield Publishers.

Inoue, A. B. (2016). "Friday plenary address: Racism in writing programs and the CWPA." *WPA: Writing Program Administration, 40*(1), 134–154.

Inoue, A. B. (2019). How do we language so people stop killing each other, or what do we do about white language supremacy? *College Composition and Communication, 71*(2), 352–369.

Inoue, A. B. (2021). *Why I left the CWPA.* Asao B. Inoue's infrequent words https://asaobinoue.blogspot.com/2021/04/why-i-left-cwpa-council-of-writing.html April 18.

Kendi, Ibram X. (2019). *How to be an antiracist.* One World.

Kynard, C. (2018). Stayin' woke: Race radical literacies in the makings of a higher education. *College Composition and Communication, 69*(3), 519–529.

Leverenz, C. (2010). What's ethics got to do with it? Feminist ethics and administration in rhetoric and composition. In K. Ratcliffe & R. Rickly (Eds.), *Performing feminist administration in rhetoric and composition studies* (pp. 3–18). Hampton Press.

Noddings, Nel. (2013) *Caring: A relational approach to ethics and moral education.* University of California Press.

Okun, T. (2021). *White supremacy culture—Still here.* White Supremacy Culture. http://www.whitesupremacyculture.info/uploads/4/3/5/7/43579015/white_supremacy_culture_-_still_here.pdf May 2021. 1–32.

Pratt, M. B. (1984). Identity: Skin blood heart. In E. Bulkin, M. B. Pratt & B. Smith (Eds.), *Yours in struggle* (pp. 27–77). Long Haul Press.

Wible, S. (2019). Forfeiting privilege for the cause of social justice: Listening to Black WPAs and WPAs of color define the work of white allyship. In S. M. Perryman-Clark & C. L. Craig (Eds.), *Black perspectives in writing program administration* (pp. 74–100). NCTE.

Winfrey, O. (2011). *The powerful lesson Maya Angelou taught Oprah.* Oprah's life class. https://www.oprah.com/oprahs-lifeclass/the-powerful-lesson-maya-angelou-taught-oprah-video

UNDERSTANDINGS

Readiness and Renewal: Not Just a Point in Time, but Processes

SUSAN M. LANG, THE OHIO STATE UNIVERSITY

I come to this collection as a first-gen college student, one who is celebrating 30 years post-PhD in the profession, and one who has worked at six different institutions in various levels of administrative capacities during those 30 years. For a week or so after reading the draft manuscript of this collection in response to Joe and Mark's invitation, I found myself thinking about several "R's." In addition to readiness and renewal, the ideas of resilience, reactivity, responsiveness. And a few "P's": preparation, persistence, and participation. What to do with those terms, as well as others like fragmentation, agility, and complexity…finally, during a morning workout, a tagline emerged: reconceive readiness and realize that renewal is constant.

Understanding that line meant some unpacking was in order. In terms of reconceiving readiness, it's clear that the COVID-19 pandemic forced many of us to reconsider many if not all aspects of our daily lives. It highlighted practices and assumptions that underpinned much of postsecondary education's systems and demanded response in visceral, immediate terms. It underscored something about program administration that we must engage: that much of our daily work is responding—and often responding not even to today's problems, but yesterday's problems. This labor can consume so much of our time over a longer arc, that we instinctively prioritize yesterday's (and today's) problems at the expense of meaningfully and realistically engaging with what lies ahead. Is this simply a reality, or because much of the training aspiring WPAs receive and what many of us model is a seemingly unending string of problems-responses and (hopefully) solutions? If our responses, even ones that take months to devise, are not enough to effect meaningful change, what is?

What if we instead acknowledge in both formal and informal training that the future of writing programs—ten, twenty years forward—has yet to come into focus? Fundamental questions about the location of writing instruction at two-year institutions, four-year institutions, and comprehensive universities require discussion, as does the evolution of writing pedagogies and the nature of what constitutes writing and communication taught in these courses (in context of their comprehensive societal functions). And what will constitute the programs that aspiring WPAs will lead? For many WPAs, the "program" has been a single course or two having a first-year designation with large enrollment, housed in a single department. We should consider how best to prepare next-gen WPAs for the reality that something termed a writing program in five to ten years will likely evolve into one or more fragmented systems with multidisciplinary implications, something more aptly described by one or more variations of systems theory of the types Cox, Galin, and Melzer (2018) discuss in regard to sustainable WAC programs. And we should meaningfully engage with the work needed in writing instruction to make our programs in whatever form they take (to paraphrase McNair, et al.), genuinely "student-ready programs."

And what of renewal for those committing at the outset to WPA positions? Perhaps my own experiences are that of an outlier, but I didn't focus on obtaining a particular type of WPA position at the beginning of my career—and I have several types in the early years represented on my CV. Renewal came early with new institutions, new challenges of new positions. Eighteen years of collaborative and primary WPA work brought waves of difference that kept the work interesting and engaging. And while doing that work, I chose to maintain other connections, other involvement in organizations and activities outside of my "day job." Simply making and keeping that commitment kept the ongoing administrative work (and research into that work) fresh. Renewing daily by engaging in other interests, self-care, and the like provides a level of recharging that isn't unique, but essential. And professionally, engaging in work beyond home program and department leveraged personal growth—and prepared me for the next stage of my career. If we are to understand why some administrators move to "next stages" while others cling to a department or program, we need to understand how those who identify as WPAs view themselves as members of their larger institutions—and those of us in mid or late career might consider what types of development opportunities we could provide through microcredentialing for WPAs ready for different leadership positions—or, for that matter, returning to full faculty positions at institutions where that is an option. Considering renewal in systematic ways requires concerted research into career tracking and choices; while we may not be able to duplicate Michael Apted's *Up* documentary series, checking in with a group every seven years for now nine installments, we can engage in more systematic examination of career arcs—and learn what may be transferable to upcoming WPAs.

In the short term, we can challenge ourselves, and each other, to consider how *we* are redefining our administrative and research activities. Instead of prioritizing yesterday's or today's problems, create opportunities, whether f2f or virtual, for WPAs from various types of programs, institutions, and career stages, to gather to discuss the complex short, mid, and long-term look and feel of a writing program or, as we discuss frequently at Ohio State, a culture of writing that underpins an institution. Why not break from the traditional conference structure to form these visioning groups—to consider a wider range of possibilities along with non-incremental research and implementation strategies to achieve those goals? The contributors to this volume demonstrate a fraction of the diversity of institutions, students, and faculty needs that many WPAs, firmly in their own lanes, don't experience. Hearing the ideas of others in academic environments different than our own can provide opportunities for re-envisioning our own work.

REFERENCES

Cox, M., Galin, J. R., & Melzer, D. (2018). *Sustainable WAC: A whole systems approach to launching and developing writing across the curriculum programs.* National Council of Teachers of English.

McNair, T. B., Albertine, S., McDonald, N., Major Jr. T., & Cooper, M. A. (2022). *Becoming a student-ready college: A new culture of leadership for student success.* John Wiley & Sons.

Understanding WPA Readiness and Renewal as Mindful Improvisation

MARK BLAAUW-HARA, UNIVERSITY OF TORONTO MISSISSAUGA

As I consider the chapters in this collection, I notice that WPA readiness and renewal is a complex and many-faceted phenomenon. Taken together, these chapters demonstrate that there is not a single path for readiness, renewal, or anything in between. However, there are characteristics to the concerns of pre-service, mid-service, and later-service WPAs, and threads that run through the different stages of a WPA career.

For example, many of these chapters delve into issues of marginalization and equity, whether concerning race, gender, socioeconomics, or tenure status. Several chapters also describe tensions between the personal and professional as authors attempt to balance the need to craft a fulfilling career with concerns outside of the job. As a number of authors demonstrate, having a theoretical frame to help understand and intentionally chart career trajectories can be extremely helpful, providing us a way to process and plan. We also see how the WPA role connects to larger institutional contexts, and how writing program administration can help prepare us to transition to other administrative roles if we so choose.

As is to be expected, there is also cross-over between these themes, with several authors touching on multiple ones. If you're reading this after skipping around and want to read by theme—or if you'd just like to see how some of the themes I mentioned above run through several chapters—you might find this list interesting:

- *For discussions of equity, antiracism, and marginalization*, note Kelenyi (Ch. 2); Green (Ch. 3); Blaauw-Hara (Ch. 4); Clinnin, Eidum, Hanson, and Tseptsura (Ch. 6); Mecenas (Ch. 8); Janangelo (Ch. 14); and Leverenz (Ch. 15).
- *For discussions of career planning and crafting a leadership identity*, I recommend Beavers and Anders (Ch. 1); Green (Ch. 3); Lehman and Giordano (Ch. 5); Ferdinandt Stolley (Ch. 7); Daily O'Meara (Ch. 9); Babb and Popham (Ch. 10); Mecenas (Ch. 8); Klausman (Ch. 11); Brunk (Ch. 13); Janangelo (Ch. 14); and Leverenz (Ch. 15).
- *For perspectives on WPA work within the larger institution*, I'd like to highlight Lehman and Giordano (Ch. 5); Babb and Popham (Ch. 10); Charlton and Charlton (Ch. 12); and Brunk (Ch. 13).
- *For connections and tensions between personal lives and professional roles*, I recommend Kelenyi (Ch. 2); Green (Ch. 3); Klinnin, Eidum, Hanson, and Tseptsura (Ch. 6); Ferdinandt Stolley (Ch. 7); Daily O'Meara (Ch. 9); Mecenas (Ch. 8); and Klausman (Ch. 11).
- *For theoretical perspectives to help understand and plan your career*, I point to Beavers and Anders (Ch. 1); Ferdinandt Stolley (Ch. 7); Daily O'Meara (Ch. 9); Klausman (Ch. 11); Charlton and Charlton (Ch. 12); Brunk (Ch. 13); and Janangelo (Ch. 14).

Quite fairly, a reader might wonder what might be drawn from looking at all of these themes and chapters together. What should the WPA actually *do*? One step is for WPAs to look first (and frequently) within ourselves and decide what we truly value, what we will put our energies toward. In a sense, we have to serve as our own lodestones, constantly returning to our personal/professional ethics and our desires for careers that feed us both emotionally and physically, that provide us with stability and intellectual enrichment while we work to serve others through leadership.

These chapters demonstrate how interconnected the WPA is with others: to some extent, crafting a successful and sustaining WPA career trajectory relies on finding a balance between our own intentions and the pressures, frustrations, and priorities of others. At each moment in our careers, a challenge is to listen thoughtfully to these outside voices and decide whether and how to respond.

In my own WPA preparation course, Louise Wetherbee Phelps introduced me to the work of the organizational theorist Karl Weick. One of Weick's pieces that made a strong impression on me at the time and continues to influence how I think of WPA work focuses on the role of improvisation in organizational leadership (Weick, 1998). In it, Weick spends much of the article's first half exploring how jazz musicians improvise during live performance. (I have been a working musician for around three decades, and that probably has something to do with why Weick's article jumped out at me.) He points out that musical improvisation always occurs within a loose structure—in this case, a song—and that while the listener tends to focus on what is happening in the moment, the skillful improviser needs not only to choose what to play based on the constraints of the exact moment of play, but also to listen and respond to the other musicians, considering the song's structure and how to improvise in a way that complements that structure without destroying it. Weick suggests that the best organizations—and the best organizational leaders—employ similar strategies of improvisation. Rather than forcing the organization to hold rigidly to a predetermined plan, these leaders constantly make micro-adjustments and hold organizational reins with light hands, continually returning to the central goals and themes of the organization while leaving space for unexpected and in-the-moment decisions.

As WPAs, we often try to ready ourselves for the role by learning the "right" ways to respond to situations. We think that if we learn enough—whether that's in graduate programs, on the job, or through scholarship—we will be ready for any situation we might encounter. The chapters in this collection demonstrate that there is not a single way to WPA, nor a "right" way to respond to problems we might meet at various stages of our careers. Clearly, there is no way to be universally and completely ready to WPA; nor is there a single path leading to renewal, not one way to decide when it is time to move on. Instead, this collection's authors demonstrate that WPA readiness and renewal is as multifaceted as WPAs (and writing programs) are themselves. We cannot fully plan our career trajectories; there are too many variables to account for, too many people and pressures.

However, variability does not equate to randomness, and we are not left flipping coins to make decisions in our programs or careers. As Weick points out, successful improvisation relies on flexibility and expression within a song-structure. Taken together, the chapters in this volume reflect a career structure. Pre-service WPAs negotiate how they can enter the field and decide on their priorities. No matter the institution, WPAs need not only to administer programs, but also to learn and relearn what they need in order to do the job, and to find space for themselves as whole people. And we need to know when to mentor future leaders and when to step aside. As these chapters point out, there is great utility in thinking deliberately and intentionally as we plan our career trajectories—but rather than holding tightly to the details, it may be better to think of those plans as relatively loose intentions that are guided by our principles and priorities. Those principles and priorities are the structures around which we improvise.

And with whom do we improvise? Mostly with the faculty, administrators, and students in our programs and institutions. Those are the other voices we need to heed and to which we must respond. At each point in our careers, we need to decide what we can or should do, what is authentic, what is helpful, what is generative. As we learn more—as we ourselves grow and change, and as our programs and the higher-education landscape change around us—we build more context to draw from. If we listen well through the years, we learn to hear better, and we see more possibilities for improvisation. We get better at holding the song together while leaving space for it to flex and change.

We might consider this collection in a similar way. As I noted earlier in this Understanding, the chapters here do not represent a unilinear path through a WPA's career, precisely because any WPA's career takes place in the midst of an always changing context. I might suggest that you, the reader, look at this book as a loose structure, more of a collection of voices improvising on a theme. Furthermore, I suggest that you lean into that improvisation, dipping back into the book from time to time to read a chapter or two through the new lenses gained from experience. Don't be bound to the organization we chose for these chapters–I think that you will find ideas for renewal in the readiness section, and vice versa. Look at these chapters as a conversation with many voices, and think of how you can enter that conversation yourself, whether it be through your WPA work or your writing and conference presentations. The song we are crafting has room for many instruments.

As Joe noted in our Introduction, understanding is more of an ongoing action than a time-delimited act—a process rather than an end. Perhaps this should be seen as a gift, an opportunity for regeneration, reflection, and mindful improvisation as we pursue the twin goals of readiness and renewal.

REFERENCE

Weick, K. E. (1998). Improvisation as a mindset for organizational analysis. *Organization Science (Providence, R.I.)*, *9*(5), 543–555.

Readiness and Renewal: What Am I Even?

PATTI POBLETE, SOUTH PUGET SOUND COMMUNITY COLLEGE

The longer I do this, the less ready I feel for doing anything. Or, no, that's a lie. The longer I do this, the more I know I shouldn't feel ready to do anything. Or is that a rebound of imposter syndrome? Being a WPA is seriously emotionally complicated, it turns out.

In the spirit of full confession, when I was invited to read for this collection, I was feeling completely ready. I'd just moved cross-country from a small, public liberal arts institution in the South and was about to begin teaching at a small-ish community college in the Pacific Northwest. I was still going to be teaching composition, though, and while my location was vastly different, the student population profile was actually quite similar: a large proportion of first-generation students, a fair number of non-traditional students, a healthy burst of dual-enrollment students, and a growing diversity overall. Sure, it's a new place and new circumstances, but I've been teaching for years! I've totally got this.

Reader, I was a fool. I'm exhausted. (But also: I kind of love my job? Weird how that works.)

There is, and I hope you'll agree, a lot of comfort in spending several days thinking, "Wow, what am I even doing here?" and then discovering an entire clutch of scholars you respect have written in extremely cogent ways about how they feel the same. This sense of recognizing unpreparedness, of rebalancing on-the-fly, is one of the emergent themes of this collection. There is no separation between personal and professional, but rather a seesaw of energy being spent.

Sometimes you push through and do more work, and sometimes your brain gives you a hard "no" and makes you read an entire book about a vampire solving a series of murders at a werewolf resort. Or, uh, something to that effect.

Time to take a break. Jam out. Drink a glass of water.

I should, I suppose, confess to a level of fraudulence: Despite how I ever identify myself as a practitioner of WPA-ness, at this time, I do not currently occupy any administrative position. You can't just shake off WPA-ocity, though—I am constantly smushing down the impulse to volunteer. I'm unsuccessful, but I take pride that I manage to append most of my I-would-love-to-assist-with-your-program-development conversations with a sheepish, "But I've been instructed I should stop doing extra stuff, so."

That's the second emergent theme of the collection, of course. Being a WPA—or, at least, being someone who nerds out on institutional ecologies; you can't deny it, you interpellated yourself when you opened this book in the first place—means being invested in the architecture of your workplace. Programs are made of constituents and stakeholders, facilities and furniture, SLOs and shared folders. Administrative minutiae is never-ending and I'm sure I'm not the only one who gets a kick out of scrawling out a to-do list like it's a CV in and of itself.

But what happens when we, as WPAs, move one locality to another? When we cycle out of our course releases or get promoted to leading different divisions? When we hop from, say, a rural SLAC to an urban two-year college?

The necessity of shifting, emphasized in several of these chapters, is a generative proposition. As sentient nodes of institutional history, WPAs tend to seem essential to the workings of a program. That can be both gratifying and stultifying—"what always has been" too often becomes "what always must be." It's hard to walk away from something you've spent so much time tending, but the roots put down never belonged to you.

Look out your window. Stretch. Send someone a smiley face.

The third emergent theme of this collection is the toughest one, mostly because we are all tiny humans and white supremacy is really, really big. Our field and our society are in the midst of a reckoning and, by necessity, it's an ugly one. It's specifically tough for WPAs because we're a field literally defined by how underappreciated we are. WPAs do too much work, sacrifice too much time, and it's not fun to hear that hey, also? The structures of higher education in general and English composition in particular are designed to maintain a racist hierarchy that goes back centuries.

There's also an ongoing push for us to slow down with the antiracist stuff—the flip side of mindfulness is the need to be always minding everything—and not try to change things too quickly. (My reply to this, perhaps characteristically, is my trusty GIF of a manatee telling an awed toddler to burn it all down.) And there's some value in focusing on inches over yards, but. Well.

The arc of the universe might bend towards justice, but y'all, the universe is a kajillion years old. We humans do not have that much time. It's the nature of a WPA to think in terms of programs, but incremental progress means sacrificing the individual. We should not be willing to sacrifice individuals, even if—especially if—the work is hard to do. Diversity, equity, and inclusion work is never going to end and, if you're the one doing the work, you're never going to get it right, because there is no "right." You just … have to keep doing it.

Read a poem. Take a deep breath. Snap your fingers.

My response to this collection is two and a half paragraphs of "fire" emojis. I'm pretty sure you'll feel the same.

Author Biographies

Abram Anders is Director of Communication Innovation and Associate Professor of English at Iowa State University. His research interests include academic innovation, creative collaboration, innovation and entrepreneurship, and leadership communication.

Jacob Babb is Associate Professor of English at Appalachian State University. He publishes on composition theory and pedagogy, writing program administration, and rhetoric. He is co-editor of *WPAs in Transition: Navigating Educational Leadership Positions* (Utah State UP, 2018) and *The Things We Carry: Strategies for Recognizing and Negotiating Emotional Labor in Writing Program Administration* (Utah State UP, 2020).

Melvin E. Beavers (he/him) is Assistant Professor of Rhetoric and Writing and the Chancellor's Diversity, Equity, and Inclusion Fellow at the University of Arkansas at Little Rock. His work and research focuses on writing program administration and issues of antiracism in composition studies.

Mark Blaauw-Hara (he/him) is Past President of the Council of Writing Program Administrators and Assistant Professor, Teaching Stream in the Institute for the Study of University Pedagogy at the University of Toronto Mississauga.

Previously, he was the Writing Program Coordinator at North Central Michigan College.

Beth Brunk is Dean of Extended University and Professor of Rhetoric and Writing Studies at the University of Texas at El Paso. She was named to the University of Texas System Academy of Distinguished Teachers 2013.

Colin Charlton is Professor and Chair of the Department of Writing and Language Studies at the University of Texas Rio Grande Valley. Colin focuses on designing innovative and engaging curricula for first year students alongside interdisciplinary professional development workshops for their teachers.

Jonikka Charlton is Associate Provost for Student Success and Dean of the University College at The University of Texas Rio Grande Valley. Her work focuses on defining and advancing equity work at majority minority institutions and studying the role of mid-level leadership in institutional transformation.

Kaitlin Clinnin is Director of Composition and Associate Professor of English at the University of Nevada Las Vegas. Her recent work focuses on developing trauma-informed support for students, educators, and administrators in K-20 educational contexts.

Jennifer E. Eidum is Assistant Professor of English at Elon University in North Carolina. Her research focuses on reflection and metacognition, teaching English as a second language, and pedagogies supporting linguistic diversity.

Joanne Baird Giordano is Associate Professor of English, Linguistics, and Writing Studies at Salt Lake Community College. She previously coordinated developmental writing, reading, ESL, and writing center programs for the University of Wisconsin System's two-year colleges.

Elise A. Green is an Assistant Professor of English and Writing at Longwood University. As a WPA, she serves as the University Coordinator for Writing-Infusion in the *Civitae* Core Curriculum. Her research focuses on writing across the curriculum, writing-related transfer, and faculty professional development.

Morgan Hanson is Assistant Professor of English at the University of Southern Indiana. She researches threshold concepts of writing studies, faculty professional development, and writing program administration.

Joseph Janangelo is Past President of the Council of Writing Program Administrators and Associate Professor of English at Loyola University Chicago. A co-founder of The CWPA Mentoring Project, Joe volunteers for Chicago House which supports individuals and families impacted by HIV.

Gabrielle Isabel Kelenyi is a Past Chair of the Writing Program Administrators-Graduate Organization (WPA-GO) and a PhD Candidate in Composition & Rhetoric at University of Wisconsin-Madison. Her community-engaged research focuses on community literacies and writerly self-efficacy.

Jeffrey Klausman is Senior Professor of English at Whatcom Community College in Bellingham, Washington, where he has served as WPA and WAC coordinator for many years.

Susan M. Lang is Director of the Center for the Study and Teaching of Writing and Professor of English at The Ohio State University. She is editor of the *Journal of Writing Analytics* and focuses much of her research on evidenced-based writing instruction and program administration.

Erin Lehman is Associate Professor of English and Faculty Lead for the online School of Arts, Sciences, & Education at Ivy Tech Community College. She serves as a Faculty Advising Editor for *Young Scholars in Writing* and Executive Board member for CWPA.

Carrie S. Leverenz is Professor of English at Texas Christian University in Fort Worth, Texas, where she served as WPA for 11 years and was founding Director of the New Media Writing Studio (now the Center for Digital Expression). Her work focuses on composition pedagogy, teacher training, and feminist writing program administration.

Jolivette Mecenas is Associate Professor of English and Composition Coordinator at California Lutheran University. Her research focuses on writing programs and equity at minority-serving universities. She also writes about minoritized reading and writing publics, centered on life writing and graphic narratives, as advocacy.

Katherine Daily O'Meara is Director of WAC and Assistant Professor of English at St. Norbert College in Wisconsin. She is co-editor of the *Journal of Response to Writing*, and her recent research focuses on accessible assessment, program administration, and inclusive/antiracist pedagogies in the writing classroom.

Patti Poblete [poh-BLEH-teh] is English faculty at South Puget Sound Community College and part of the editorial team for *WPA: Writing Program Administration*. Previously, she acted as WPA at Henderson State University. Her research includes public and digital rhetorics, writing pedagogy, and cultural criticism.

Susan Popham, Associate Professor, directs the writing program at Indiana University Southeast. Previously, she performed a number of administrative roles, including writing program administrator, while at the University of Memphis. Her work focuses on social justice in technical communication and medical rhetoric.

Amy Ferdinandt Stolley is an Associate Professor of Writing at Grand Valley State University where she directs the first-year writing program. Her research focuses on WPA identity, the affective nature of WPA work, and women's rhetorical strategies.

Mariya Tseptsura is Director of Online Writing Programs at the University of Arizona. Her research focuses on writing program administration, online writing instruction, multilingual writing, and shared curriculum and pre-designed online courses.

Index

STUDIES IN COMPOSITION AND RHETORIC

Edited by ALICE S. HORNING

This series welcomes both individually-authored and collaboratively-authored books and monographs as well as edited collections of essays. We are especially interested in books that might be used in either advanced undergraduate or graduate courses in one or more of the following subjects: cultural or multicultural studies and the teaching of writing; feminist perspectives on composition and rhetoric; postmodernism and the theory and practice of composition; "post-process" pedagogies; values, ethics, and ideologies in the teaching of writing; information technology and composition pedagogy; the assessment of writing; authorship and intellectual property issues; and studies of oppositional discourse in the academy, particularly challenges to exclusionary or hegemonic conventions. We also seek proposals in the following areas: the role of autobiography and of identity issues in both writing and writing pedagogy; the influence of social context on composing; the relationship of composition and rhetoric to various disciplines and schools of thought; collaborative learning and peer tutoring; facilitating and responding to student writing; approaches to empowering marginalized learners; the role or status of composition studies within English studies and the academy at large; and the role or status of student writers within the fields of composition and English studies.

For additional information about this series or for the submission of manuscripts, please contact:

editorial@peterlang.com

To order other books in this series, please contact our Customer Service Department at:

peterlang@presswarehouse.com (within the U.S.)
orders@peterlang.com (outside the U.S.)

or browse online by series at:

WWW.PETERLANG.COM

www.ingramcontent.com/pod-product-compliance
Ingram Content Group UK Ltd.
Pitfield, Milton Keynes, MK11 3LW, UK
UKHW021838100926
8556IPUK00004B/411

9 781433 193163